Welcome to the EVERYTHING® series!

These handy, accessible books give you all you need to tackle a difficult project, gain a new hobby, comprehend a fascinating topic, prepare for an exam, or even brush up on something you learned back in school but have since forgotten.

You can read an *EVERYTHING*® book from cover-to-cover or just pick out the information you want from our four useful boxes: e-facts, e-ssentials, e-alerts, and e-questions. We literally give you everything you need to know on the subject, but throw in a lot of fun stuff along the way, too.

We now have well over 100 *EVERYTHING*® books in print, spanning such wide-ranging topics as weddings, pregnancy, wine, learning guitar, one-pot cooking, managing people, and so much more. When you're done reading them all, you can finally say you know *EVERYTHING*®!

FACTS

Important sound bytes of information

SSENTIALS

Quick handy tips

ALERT

Urgent warnings

QUESTIONS?

Solutions to common problems

Dear Reader,

When I was a teenager growing up in a small town in Pennsylvania, my sister and I would often join my dad at the piano and add our enthusiastic, if imperfect, voices to his perfect playing of old show tunes and standards. Tunes by Rodgers and Hart or Hammerstein, Burton Lane, Lerner and Loewe, the Gershwins, and Harold Arlen filled our living room.

Those evenings around the piano instilled in me a love of language as well as music. Who wouldn't revel in phrases like "the breathless hush of evening" or "our wistful little star"? Through singing, as well as reading and writing, I discovered the fun, the power, and the beauty of words.

I wanted to write this book not only because I've been a writer and an editor for more than twenty years, but, more importantly, because I love the written (and the sung!) word. I wanted to share with you my experience and the enthusiasm for creative writing, and encourage you to explore and expand your own creative spirit.

I hope you will use this book to write a story of your own. I'll be cheering you on—and singing your praises.

Sincerely,

Carol Whiteley

THE EVERYTHING®

CREATIVE WRITING BOOK

All you need to know to write
a novel, short story, screenplay,
poem, or article

Carol Whiteley

Adams Media Corporation
Avon, Massachusetts

EDITORIAL

Publishing Director: Gary M. Krebs

Managing Editor: Kate McBride

Copy Chief: Laura MacLaughlin

Acquisitions Editor: Allison Carpenter Yoder

Development Editors: Michael Paydos,
        Julie Gutin

PRODUCTION

Production Director: Susan Beale

Production Manager: Michelle Roy Kelly

Series Designer: Daria Perreault

Layout and Graphics: Paul Beatrice,
Brooke Camfield, Colleen Cunningham,
Michelle Roy Kelly, Daria Perreault, Frank Rivera

An Everything® Series Book.
Everything® is a registered trademark of Adams Media Corporation.

Published by Adams Media Corporation
57 Littlefield Street, Avon, MA 02322 U.S.A.
www.adamsmedia.com

ISBN: 1-58062-647-5
Printed in the United States of America.

J I H G F E D C B

Library of Congress Cataloging-in-Publication Data
Whiteley, Carol.
The everything creative writing book : all you need to know to write a
novel, short story, screenplay, poem, or article / by Carol Whiteley.
p. cm. – (The everything series)
Includes index.
ISBN 1-58062-647-5
1. English language–Rhetoric. 2. Creative writing. I. Title. II.
Series.
PE1408 .W5806 2002
808'.042–dc21
                                                    2002006267

Illustrations by Barry Littmann.

This book is available at quantity discounts for bulk purchases.
For information, call 1-800-872-5627.

Visit the entire Everything® series at everything.com

Contents

Introduction

So there you are, hanging out at the bookstore. You probably told yourself that it was time to find another can't-put-it-down novel. Or maybe you thought you'd look for that book your friend mentioned, a book of travel essays she was so crazy about that she immediately changed her vacation plans and headed off for the Pacific Crest Trail. Maybe you told yourself that you just wanted to relax a bit with a magazine and a cappuccino.

You love reading. You've done a little bit of writing. And you've often wondered if you could be a writer like the incredibly creative authors you admire, but you are not quite sure where to start.

Well, *The Everything® Creative Writing Book* can help. It will guide you through the entire process, from preparing yourself to write—in your workspace and in your mind—to getting fresh ideas to drafting your copy and editing it. Plus you'll learn all about the different formats of writing, and find hundreds of writing tips, resources, examples, inspirational excerpts, advice, and encouragement via interviews with successful authors, how-to pointers, challenges, and even rescue techniques to help you out of those dreaded strikes of writer's block. If you have the interest and the desire to become a more creative writer—and it's looking like you do—and if you take the time to learn and practice, this book can show you how to improve your writing skills and express yourself imaginatively in a variety of ways.

With dedication, skill building, and time, it's entirely possible that you could become another Barbara Kingsolver, E. B. White, Toni Morrison, Michael Chabon, Alice Munro, or P. D. James. You could develop a style so expressive, so true, and so *yours*, that whenever someone reads something that you wrote, he or she might wish, like Holden Caulfield in *The Catcher in the Rye*, that "when you're all done reading it, you wish the author that wrote it was a terrific friend of yours and you could call him up on the phone whenever you felt like it."

You could succeed as a creative writer beyond your wildest, bestselling-author, cross-country-book-signing dreams. But you could also fail. You could put in the time, you could tell everyone you know that you're working to become a writer, you could write and write and write and not get anywhere. The thought is daunting, to say the least. But there's still another possible drawback. While you're courageously giving this writing thing your all, you could run into resistance instead of reinforcement. Friends, colleagues, parents, children, even your partner or your spouse might try to discourage you by telling you what you already know—that you could fail, that you could be hurt, that you might not have what it takes. Such disheartening counsel, whether spoken to spare you pain or from jealousy disguised as caring, can give an author a terminal case of writer's block.

So why try to do it? Why not just carry on quietly and safely behind the perfectly useful and perfectly ordinary words that many people set down on paper when they must write something—in their business documents, their personal correspondence, perhaps in an occasional journal entry or school paper or speech?

Because you love words. Because you feel you have something to say and you'd like to say it in the best possible, most interesting way. Because you love to communicate and connect with all kinds of people. Because you find joy in the colors, tastes, rhythms, and smells of language. Because you have opinions, experiences, and feelings that you need to share with your readers. Because you want to explore and question and make sense of what you see around you, and help others to do the same. Because you see things in a special way.

By giving your love of language a chance to bloom and grow, and by setting yourself the goal of becoming an accomplished creative writer, you might one day find yourself in a Manhattan bookstore, signing your name on hundreds of copies of your latest biography. Or you might find yourself watching a sold-out performance of a play that you penned. Or the marketing copy you produce might turn out to be so innovative and so memorable that the clients pour in and you get a big raise.

All those things could happen. But what will definitely happen when you make the commitment to write more creatively is that you'll learn new skills, gain new knowledge, and find new ways to express yourself— even if you "fail" and not a word that you write is ever published. Learning and growing will expand your horizons and increase your abilities, give you an amazing feeling of well-being and fulfillment, and enable you to put your special stamp on a bit of the world.

CHAPTER 1
Preparing to Write

What do you need in order to write well? There are, of course, tangible things such as a computer or a pen and paper. But you also need time, inspiration, a positive attitude, and the expectation of success to keep writing at your best.

Find a Comfortable Place to Write

In many authors' experience, surroundings and equipment that suit their personalities and styles make it more likely that the blank page before them will eventually be covered with compelling copy. In fact, the ideal writing place may automatically, just by your being there, set your writing muscles in motion.

What would work for you if you had the luxury of setting up a custom workplace? Think about how you like to read or study, how sound affects you, how easily you're distracted, how disciplined you are, if you need people around you, your general nature. I, for example, am incredibly sensitive to sound. If a clock is tick-tick-tocking nearby, it's suddenly the only thing I hear. If there's music playing while I'm reading, I can't appreciate the story because I'm distracted by the words of the song or by the energy of the beat. (Actually, I just want to get up and dance.) Repetitive sounds, like my otherwise-wonderful dog steadfastly slurping as she cleans her paws, or loud, piercing noise, like the whining roar of tree-felling equipment, send me running from the room. In other words, I need—I simply must have—a quiet room and a quiet time for writing.

SSENTIALS   You need a place where you can write comfortably and where your materials will be safe from prying eyes, jelly-dripping fingers (except your own, of course), and constant interruption.

My son, on the other hand, writes, studies, and lives his life with music. In high school and college his CD player was constantly on, whether he was drafting a report, preparing for an exam, or hanging out with his friends. In the office where he now edits a niche magazine, the entire editorial staff works to the beat of the day's musical selections. To my son and others like him, sound is a welcome companion that enhances surroundings and concentration, instead of detracting from them.

Consider the View

Some authors find workspace with a great view very distracting. Anything that catches their eye can break their concentration or interrupt their thoughts. Looking at a white, windowless wall, bare of ornamentation, is the only way for some to see the words instead of the world.

But for others, pleasant surroundings inspire and encourage the creative process. You may find that a window into your garden or the sight of the sun rising over your city's landscape gives you the calm and the visual nourishment you need to write at your best. If no outdoor scenery is possible, fresh or silk flowers on your bookshelf or photos of your latest travels or family get-together might be the inspirational ticket to that perfect word or to nailing down your crime novel's plot. Even if your work area is just an alcove off the kitchen or a corner of the basement that you use when everyone else is asleep, pinning up a soothing, motivational, or challenging poster or drawing may be just what you need to keep those writing juices flowing.

These days, I live most of the time in uninterrupted solitude in a cottage above a wide bay in the west of Ireland—just me and the dog and the southwest wind coming off the sea. . . . [But] eight hours a day of pampered peace do not make art. Or—they never would for me. I write to be read. The impulse comes out of the turbulence of real life. . . . So when the lonely quiet of the west of Ireland begins to slow me down, I head for the streets of New York, where the brawls and traffic and cries and joys begin the minute I arrive at the taxi stand at J.F.K. And once I'm standing at a counter on Sixth Avenue knocking back a hot dog and a papaya juice, shopping bags at my feet—that's when I know I am a part of Creation, and where I muster my own measure of creativity to throw into the mix.
—Nuala O'Faolian, author of *Are You Somebody?*
(*New York Times Magazine*, April 1, 2001)

Your Personal Space

What if you share your space with others? For example, you and your spouse both use the same desk—you for writing and your partner for paying bills and organizing personal records. Or maybe others have easy access to it—perhaps your workspace is in the corner of the family room, where your children often play or you sometimes entertain friends with popcorn and videos. In any case, you'll want to make certain that you have a lockable drawer or file cabinet where you can store your materials safely. There's nothing worse than discovering that the pages that took you so much time and sweat-producing effort to write were "moved out of the way" to make room for a board game, or that the research notes that ate up days of phoning and legwork are nowhere in sight when you need them. Even if you have to put everything away and set it all up again each time you write, it's worth the effort to ensure that you won't be spending your precious writing time redoing what you've already done.

ESSENTIALS

Custom-fit your workspace with an eye and an ear to what will work for you. Then keep adjusting it until your writing room is the way you need it to be to produce your best work possible. You'll discover whether or not you've established the ultimate writing environment by spending a lot of time in it—writing.

Your writing place should be reasonably close to a telephone so that you can do research over the phone—your local library might turn out to be a great source of information—or get takeout when you didn't make it to the grocery store.

Tools of the Trade

According to novelist Fay Weldon, "all a writer needs is a pencil and a piece of paper and a corner and nobody noticing and the desire to do it; that's all it takes." But there are a few other tools writers might need or could use to help them along in their writing endeavors.

Reference Materials

Depending on the type of writing you will be doing, you will need various kinds of reference books: dictionaries (general, topic-specific, and foreign language), a thesaurus, an encyclopedia, an atlas, fact and trivia books, an almanac, grammar guides, quotation books, style guides (see Appendix B for suggestions). Also include books that you might keep around to use as inspirational examples of the type of writing you are aiming to produce.

To build a personal library inexpensively, try these ideas:

- Start a book group and hold frequent book exchanges; look for genres that fill in the gaps on your shelves.
- Organize a regular neighborhood book exchange.
- Frequent garage and yard sales.
- Buy used references from online sources such as Half.com and Amazon.com.
- Browse through the remaindered and greatly marked-down book sections at bookstores.
- Search the library sale shelves.
- Don't miss the big library sales.
- Visit nearby thrift stores.
- Ask for books or bookstore gift certificates for your birthday and other gift-giving occasions.

Writing Medium

In this day and age, you have three writing options available to you: a computer (don't forget to back up all your files), a typewriter, or paper and pen (pens and pencils of different colors can be useful). Pick what works best for you, but remember that if you are planning to publish your work, your writing will eventually have to be converted to computer files.

FACTS

"At age twenty-five I bought my first Mont Blanc Diplomat fountain pen . . . that pen, to me, was the symbol and the tool of a real writer. . . . I also learned that the pen is mightier than the sword but the sword is easier to clean."
—Rita Mae Brown, author of *Rubyfruit Jungle*

Invest in a filing cabinet to keep your work and notes in, Post-it notes, index cards, and other office materials. Some writers find a tape recorder useful for taking notes.

It is also important to find a sturdy, comfortable chair and position yourself near a good light source.

Luxury Writing Tools

For those of you who can afford them, the following items can certainly make your work more efficient.

- Laptop computer and carrying case
- Electronic organizer
- Internet access
- Laser printer
- Copier
- Headset for the telephone
- Ergonomic chair
- Top-quality pen

You might want to invest in a Space Pen—it lets you write anywhere. You can use the wall as a table, write in extreme heat or cold, and more. Check out *www.spacepen.com*.

Don't Leave Home Without It

Make it a habit to travel with your notepad. Once you start writing, you'll find that ideas and phrases and questions and "eurekas!" mysteriously pop into your mind at all times of the day and night. You'll want to capture them when they do—before they disappear forever. Next time you're at the drugstore or an office-supply store, pick up a few small notepads. Then, station one, along with a mini-pen or pencil, everywhere you can think of—on your bedside table with a tiny flashlight (for 2 A.M. jottings), in your purse or pocket, in your car, in the kitchen, in your gardening-tools tote, tucked into a niche on the porch, in the bathroom (for some reason I get some of my best ideas while groggily brushing my teeth in the morning), and on a closet shelf to toss into your coat pocket as you're heading out the door.

Or, instead of stashing notepads the way squirrels stash acorns, you can do what a number of successful creative writers do—always keep a folded index card in your pocket so that you're ready when that perfect word you've been desperate to think of suddenly leaps to mind—while you're walking the dog, running errands, or taking the subway into work. Your friends and family may think you're a bit crazy, but great ideas and great writing solutions can appear just like that—and disappear just as quickly. As in scouting, the key is to "be prepared"—you never know when creative lightning will strike.

Get into the Spirit of Creative Writing

Once you've got your writing space and writing tools set up, there are no more excuses. It's time to start writing. So how do you turn an idea that's been forever rolling around in your mind into a short story, or set down a memory from your childhood that you'd like your children to learn about? How do you put more life into your business materials, or take up the challenge of a completely new format, maybe poetry or a screenplay? How do you get your writing to be more creative?

SSENTIALS

"If you want to write, you can. Fear stops most people from writing, not lack of talent, whatever that is. Who am I? What right have I to speak? Who will listen to me if I do? You're a unique human being, with a unique story to tell, and you have every right. If you speak with passion, many of us will listen. We need stories to live, all of us. We live by story. Yours enlarges the circle."
                              —Richard Rhodes, author of *How to Write*

Waking Up Your Muse

Like creativity in any field—cooking, painting, gardening, or Web design—creativity in writing involves the making of something new or the reinventing of something old. Being creative means causing something unique to come into being and being original. It's seeing something in a different way and putting your own special stamp on it.

The power of creativity is within each one of us. The challenge is to open yourself up to it—to approach your subject in a new and interesting way. To practice being creative, you might try the following:

- Follow a new path—if you always take the same way home, choose a new route and treat your eyes to new views along the way.
- Really look at something you don't usually notice—the plumpness of a peach and its tender blush of color, the collage of patterns on the bark of a birch tree, the scents and sounds of the early morning.
- Immerse yourself in the arts—take up watercolors, master the art of French cuisine, learn a new language in a class or by listening to audiotapes, plant a flower bed, capture a sunrise with your camera.
- Immerse yourself in the world—listen to how people converse: in restaurants, on the subway, over coffee in the neighborhood café. Observe how people walk and dress; notice sounds and colors; experience silence; get the feel of busy streets, fields and forests, small towns, amusement parks—any variety of places and spaces that are accessible in your area.
- Let your imagination go—daydream, fantasize, play "What if," make up stories about people you see walking down the street.
- Do something new—if you've always wondered what it would be like to play the accordion, take a lesson; if you've sometimes thought you might want to be a lawyer, sit in on a court case; if you like to sketch and doodle, sign up for an art class.
- Read, read, read—novels, the newspaper, magazines, comics, brochures, cookbooks, poems, memoirs, how-to guides, travel essays: anything you can get your hands on.

Ten Keys to Creativity

To sum up, what you need are the ten keys to creativity. Keep each one in mind as you begin to write.

1. Curiosity
2. Passion
3. Determination
4. Awareness
5. Energy
6. Openness
7. Sensitivity
8. Stick-to-it-iveness
9. A listening ear
10. An observant eye

FACTS

"In the afternoons, Gertrude Stein and I used to go antique hunting in the local shops, and I remember once asking her if she thought I should become a writer. In the typically cryptic way we were all so enchanted with, she said, 'No.' I took that to mean yes and sailed for Italy the next day."

—Woody Allen, film director, musician, and author

Keep Writing

But you might still have some nagging doubts. Can I really do this? How will I find the time? Will anyone want to read what I have to say? Won't people judge my work—and me?

Writing creatively isn't easy. It takes nerve and determination. But just about everyone has fears about doing it, from famous, bestselling authors to out-and-out beginners. How do they overcome these fears? They sit down and write.

They write every day. They write when the last thing they feel like doing is writing. They write as well as they can and they keep on going. They acknowledge their fears but they don't let fear stop them. Once they see that they can sit down and write, and live to write another day, their fears generally subside and come to have less of a hold on them.

You can overcome your fears in the same way—by writing. As much and as often as you can. But that answer presents another problem. How in the world are you going to find the time?

You're Going to Make the Time

Make the time to write, carve it out even though you don't think you can, because writing is very important to you and because writing every day is the only way to improve your creative skills. As bestselling education author and screenwriter Murray Suid says, like any activity that you want to excel in, make writing a habit.

Some writers find they can do their best work only at a certain time of day; others learn that they can start their engines whenever a free hour surfaces. Some of these authors establish a certain num-ber of hours each day that they must ply their craft. Others determine that they must write a certain number of words or pages at each session. Through writing you'll settle on your own best schedule and writing output goals. But you have to put in the time to find your answer.

ESSENTIALS

If you have the luxury of choosing any part of the day or night to write, think about your style and your personality. Are you a morning person or a night person? Do you need structure and discipline to move forward with a project, or are you more easygoing—you always get the job done, but you don't follow any rules?

If your life is already filled with career, family, volunteer work, and extracurriculars, you can still find time to write. It may be hard, but you can do it. Consider getting up a bit earlier than you usually do, if you're a morning person. Nightlifers will find it easier to head to the writing table after dinner or after everyone else has gone to bed. Instead of going out to lunch every day, you can brown-bag it, close the office door (or go to the library or a park), and set aside that time to write.

On weekends, try setting aside a bigger block of time to create. Think about enlisting friends or family members who might be able to take over chores for you or who you might be able to trade services with. Baby-sitters, dog walkers, and gardeners are also available; the expense may be high, but the cost to you of not writing may be higher. By sitting down and really studying what you do and when you do it, you'll likely find some daily time that you can dedicate to your craft.

FACTS

Did you know that Fred Terman, known as the Father of Silicon Valley, was also a writer? With his busy schedule as Dean of the School of Engineering at Stanford and involvement in the establishment of the Stanford Research Park, Terman didn't find much time to write. But he told friends that by writing just one page a day, at the end of a year he would write a book.

Prepare in Advance

One of the best ways you can help yourself is to be prepared to write each time you do sit down to do it. That means having your pencils already sharpened or enough ink and paper for the printer or your computer glitch fixed or your children off at the park with a neighbor. On a tight schedule, every minute counts, and you don't want to lose even one of them hunting for the pencil sharpener or being interrupted by someone who needs to know where the hammer is. (Once you determine what your regular writing hours will be, it's a good idea to advise friends and family so they're less likely to call you then or knock on your door—and to keep doing so firmly and consistently. It's also a good idea to write those hours into your daily calendar, just as you write in all your other commitments, so that you don't schedule other activities in those spots.)

You can also be prepared by keeping your current project in the back of your mind at nonwriting times (actually, it will most likely stay there whether you want it to or not). While you're mowing the lawn you can be working out a piece of dialogue or a difficult plot point and have it ready to go when you're next able to pick up your pen.

Flex Your Writing Muscle

Another way that you can keep your hand in shape during nonofficial writing times is to hone your writing skills in other ways. Remember that thing that people used to do before e-mail, called writing letters? Getting in touch with a friend by putting pen to stationery is a great way to practice the art of creative writing. You can describe what you've been up to, relay a funny anecdote, recall the good times you spent together—anything that lets you write in an original way. Many famous authors, including Thomas Mann and Henry James, corresponded often with friends and colleagues, which gave them a chance to keep in touch and exchange ideas while exercising their writing muscles. You can also keep a journal that records thoughts and feelings, and even use it to record ideas you later turn into stories or essays.

In a nutshell, do everything you can possibly do to give yourself the time, space, inner reserves, and positive attitude you need to channel your creativity into a positive stream that will fuel improved skills.

The Jarring "J"—Jealousy and Judgment

Fear of what others will think—and say—is a major force that holds a lot of writers back. But jealousy can be just as big a problem, though often an unexpected one. Some authors, as they start to produce copy, compare their work to others' and find themselves and their own work lacking. This can be not only a terrible blow to the ego, but can encourage feelings of anger toward people who appear to be doing better work or having greater success.

But guess what? It's okay to be angry. It's okay to be jealous. (Even therapists say this is true.) But instead of letting those feelings take over your psyche and stop you from writing, you need to channel them into a positive stream that will serve you as fuel to improve your skills. A positive attitude is one of the writer's greatest tools—jealousy may sidetrack you, but believing in yourself and not comparing your writing to anyone else's will take you a long way. Like the Little Engine That Could, you've got to keep saying, "I think I can, I think I can."

Prepare for Criticism

While most of the time you should be able to control your own green-eyed monster, it will often be impossible to control the judgmental or critical words of others. Having others review what you write can be incredibly useful and supportive, in fact, you'll probably seek out certain people—other writers, teachers, writing group colleagues—to give you feedback and to discuss problems or concepts (see Chapter 20, "Working with Others," for more on this).

If you make the decision to let friends, family members, or colleagues read your work, you have to realize that you are opening yourself to both positive and negative critiques.

Sometimes you'll hear more—or less—than you were hoping for. To prepare yourself for this, try to remember that it's your work—not you—that's being judged. And keep in mind that no matter how forceful the person's words or how absolutely right they may seem when you hear them, *you* are the final judge of what you create. It is *your* work, and while you may choose to listen to all who are willing to comment on what you write, you can accept their ideas if they make sense to you and use them to improve your skills, or you can reject them and carry on as you have been. It's a fact of life that you can never please everyone, but it's critical that in your writing you please yourself. In the end, *you* are your own best judge.

"Many wonderful writers . . . have been plagued by insecurity throughout their professional lives. How could it be otherwise? By its nature, art involves risk. It's not easy, but sometimes one has to invent one's confidence. . . . My own advice to writers is: follow your curiosity and your passion."
—Diane Ackerman, author of *A Natural History of the Senses*

Choose Your Format

Part of preparing yourself to write is figuring out what type of writing you are going to be doing. The dictum here is simple: Write what you know, in a format you're familiar with. Suspense novelist Abigail Padgett says that she became a mystery writer not only because she thinks her brain is "genetically predisposed" to spooky rhythms and sounds, but because she's read countless books by P. D. James, Dorothy Sayers, Amanda Cross, and scores of other female mystery writers. She loved their words and learned from their techniques, and through them developed her own special writing style.

If you grew up in a family whose idea of a great time was to attend a Broadway show (lucky you), you may be familiar with the ins and outs of dramas or musicals and want to try your hand at creating a play. Or you may be an ardent admirer of the short story and have a bookcase filled with gems you read by Margaret Atwood, Tim O'Brien, Akhil Sharma, Alice Adams, and Cynthia Ozick. The short story, then, might be your format of choice.

SSENTIALS

To further develop your feel for formats, try reading several works, perhaps award winners or books that friends or colleagues recommend to you (many examples are provided here as well), written in each area.

If you're pursuing creative writing because you want to punch up your business documents or tell others compellingly about your recent trip to Bali, then the format you'll work with is already set. But even if you're thoroughly familiar with a particular form and think you want to follow its framework, or need to concentrate on a particular type for business or other reasons, you still may want to consider several different formats before you sit down and start to compose. Then, once you do start to write, like Anton Chekhov, Oscar Wilde, and many other successful authors, you may find that one form influences and enriches another, and you work happily in several of them. Remember that writing creatively not only involves being original in your words, but being open to new genres and writing styles.

The Writing Process

Every piece of writing, no matter its style or format—poem, short story, travel article, science fiction novel—takes hard work and time to go from notion to concept to reality. Creativity gets the ball rolling, and then careful crafting enables you to produce a finished work that expresses clearly, dramatically, accurately, and with originality the story you want to tell. The seven steps of the writing process—getting ideas, planning, researching, organizing, drafting, editing, and evaluating—will take you from thinking about writing to producing a satisfying work of art. Keep in mind, though, that writing is usually not an A-B-C process. Most likely you'll find that you zigzag back and forth through the different steps on your way to creating a finished piece.

At every step along the way, and in every line and paragraph you write, you'll be making decisions that will affect the final outcome. These decisions will involve asking yourself a lot of questions: Would my character say this? How can I be sure that this date is correct? This word isn't quite right—what would be a better one? Is this scene really necessary? How can I show that Alice is recalling a conversation with Georgia and Lexy while she's speaking with Nick and Alan?

At first all these decisions may seem overwhelming, but the more you write—and rewrite—the better feel you'll have for how to make them. Plus, reading works of other writers, and reading extensively in the format you've chosen, will help you to understand how a good piece of writing is put together.

You'll also find that it can be difficult to keep going. At times you may have to coax, tease, or drag those thoughts and words from your imagination onto the page. As author Anne Lamott says, writers "will have days at the desk of frantic boredom, of angry hopelessness, of wanting to quit forever, and there will be days when it feels like they have caught and are riding a wave." It can be incredibly frustrating. But the rewards of the writing life are waiting.

CHAPTER 2

The Short Story

Many fiction authors start out writing short stories as their first venture into the world of creative writing. But though this genre seems relatively easy to work with, writing a short story requires great skill. So what exactly is a short story?

It's Not Just a *Short* Story

What defines a short story? Is it simply a short novel? What's the difference between a short story and a novella? Most writers, editors, and publishers categorize a short story as a work of fiction comprised of several thousand words, but generally not more than 5,000. The novella is usually thought of as a longer short story or a short novel and can range from 5,000 to more than 40,000 words.

FACTS

E. B. White's sparsely worded but extraordinary "The Second Tree from the Corner" takes up barely five pages in *The Best American Short Stories of the Century* collection; Ernest Hemingway's magnificent *The Old Man and the Sea* is generally found in book form and classified as a novella.

Marian Gavin, author of "The Sparrow's Mother," calls the short story "bits and pieces of life, the brightest and the darkest. . . . Ideally, a short story is Life in a capsule." The key word to understanding the short story format is "story"—in just a few words the best short stories tell us a tale of sight, sound, thought, and action that helps us to understand and relate to a compelling moment. What we learn from what the characters say and do during that decisive moment gives us insight into the human condition and builds our humanity. (More on characters, plot, dialogue, and setting can be found in Chapter 3, "The Novel," which follows.)

The Short Story Versus the Novel

In their own ways, both short stories and novels help us to understand ourselves and our universe, but they do so in markedly different ways. Of course, the most obvious difference is length, but this is not the only important distinction. Whereas a novel might center on one central story and several side stories that can span an extended period of time, generally the action in a short story revolves around just one incident that happens during a brief period of time. In "The Second Tree from the Corner," most of the story unfolds while the main character, Trexler, talks with his doctor during an office visit. The remainder of the story is told to readers by briefly touching on several of Trexler's later visits to the doctor, with the wonderfully satisfying conclusion coming just five weeks after the story began.

Another difference between the short story and the novel is the number of characters. Typically, a short story will focus on only one or a few characters, whereas a novel may give us half a dozen or more. In "The Second Tree from the Corner," only Trexler and his doctor inhabit the pages. In Isaac Bashevis Singer's "The Key," readers follow the harrowing day of an elderly woman named Bessie, hearing only a few words from a neighbor and an apartment super and feeling the hovering presence of Bessie's dead husband Sam.

Dialogue

Good fiction that contains no dialogue, only pure narration, does exist, but well-written, realistic dialogue can be a great addition to the telling of any story. After all, dialogue is conversation, and what better way to tell a story than by having the characters speak the words? If a plot is peopled with interesting, appealing characters, it is very likely that readers will want to know what they have to say. (Dialogue is particularly important to movie and play scripts; for more on writing for the movies, see Chapter 6, "The Screenplay.")

Dialogue serves two purposes in a short story (and in other fiction formats as well)—to deepen our understanding of the characters and their personalities and to further develop the plot. Through dialogue readers add another important layer to their picture of the author's fictional creations, get a clearer idea of the plot as characters talk about incidents or conflicts and say how they feel about them, and are better able to differentiate among these characters. Dialogue also works to liven up any scene and gives it a greater sense of reality.

When characters speak, they give us an indirect line into their minds and their makeup. In fact, author Rita Mae Brown calls fictional speech a "literary biopsy." It shows if characters are argumentative or easygoing, if they're happy or sad, what they like and don't like, their goals and dreams, how educated they are, where they come from, whether they're eccentric or down-home, their fears and their past. Everything about characters can be revealed in their speech.

You can also use dialogue to illustrate the relationships between characters and show how those relationships change in moments of conflict or enlightenment, and to reveal crucial information about plots or other characters.

A related literary device is the monologue—when a character talks to him- or herself. Interior monologues and dialogues can point out a character's uncertainty, inner turmoil, feelings of self-worth or self-loathing, excitement, and anger—the full range of emotions and thoughts.

Viewpoint

Viewpoint is another area in which short stories and longer fiction often differ. While a novel may have several viewpoints—in Charles Frazier's *Cold Mountain,* both of the lead characters tell us their take on the fascinating story of how they met, separated, and eventually reconnected—the short story generally doesn't have the luxury of space in which to do this. Varying viewpoints can also disrupt the strong, immediate identification that readers need to feel with short-story characters.

Pacing

Still another aspect of the short story that is crucial is pacing. Because there are many fewer sentences, each must move the story forward in some way. If you take pages to describe the main character and set the scene for what will unfold, time will run out before you get to the main elements, and the reader will become impatient to discover how the issues will be resolved. Short-story writers need to jump right into their subject and keep right on going.

Which Brings Us to the End

The best short story endings resolve the conflicts that have been ongoing in a way that shows how the characters, or the situation, have changed. Effective endings satisfy readers and often surprise them. "A Jury of Her Peers," first written by Susan Glaspell in 1916 as a one-act play and then later rewritten by her into short-story format, is about two Midwestern women portrayed as "dutiful wives" to their law-enforcement husbands' way of thinking. In the course of the story, these women learn about a wife accused of murdering her husband. Though they know her only slightly, they come to understand her completely through the state of her home and the evidence only they see there. In the end, they do an extraordinary thing—something they know to be wrong but in the situation completely right. The ending makes you catch your breath and smile at the same time.

In Short

To sum it all up, short stories generally have:

- A simple subject, usually one that lets the story take place within a brief period of time.
- Only a few characters, which are quickly developed.
- Dialogue and action that move the story forward.
- One point of view.
- A fast-paced, reader-grabbing beginning.
- A middle that doesn't ramble but proceeds in a direct route to the end.
- A strong ending that completes the story and provides understanding and satisfaction.
- A plot and characters that give us insight into the human condition.

"A short story must have a single mood and every sentence must build towards it."
　　　　　—Edgar Allan Poe, poet, short-story writer, and literary critic

The short story is an excellent and challenging format in its own right (a personal favorite of mine), but it has also worked as the training ground for many great novelists. Writing a successful short story may eventually lead to your writing longer and more complex pieces.

Short Story Starters

Starting is always a difficult part. The beginning of a piece sets the tone of the story, introduces the characters, and, of course, has to grab the reader's attention. Take a look at the following well-known beginning, from "The Necklace" by Guy de Maupassant:

> She was one of those pretty and charming girls born, as though fate had blundered over her, into a family of artisans. She had no marriage portion, no expectations, no means of getting known, understood, loved, and wedded by a man of wealth and distinction; and she let herself be married off to a clerk in the Ministry of Education.

Choose one of these jumping-off points or create one of your own, then write a 1,000-word story that develops the concept. Who knows, you might end up with a great tale.

- A huge storm is approaching and a family must invite an unwelcome guest to stay.
- Three teenagers who have grown up together set off for a day at the beach.
- While visiting her ailing father, a middle-aged woman has a telling memory.
- Watching a football game with his wife reveals an important truth about their relationship to a young husband.

A Great, Gripping End

Equally important, and a challenge to write, is the short-story ending. Try to effect a sense of closure, without going overboard on the melodrama.

In the story "Charades," by Laurie Moore (published in *Birds of America*), a family game at Christmas reveals the dark, unhappy side of several characters, yet ends with an encouraging truth:

> [Therese] stands up and looks at Ray. It is time to go. She has lost her judicial temperament hours ago. She fears she is going to do another pratfall, only this time she will break something. Already she sees herself carted out on a stretcher, taken toward the airport, and toward home, saying the final words she has to say to her family, has always had to say to her family. Sounds like "could cry."
>
> "Good-bye!"
> "Good-bye!"
> "Good-bye!"
> "Good-bye!"
> "Good-bye!"
> "Good-bye!"
> "Good-bye!"
>
> But first Ray must do his charade, which is Confucius. "Okay, I'm ready," he says, and begins to wander around the living room in a wild-eyed daze, looking as confused as possible, groping at the bookcases, placing his palm to his brow. And in that moment, Therese thinks how good-looking he is and how kind and strong, and how she loves nobody else in the world even half as much.

Did this wonderful ending inspire you to write? For other great endings, check out these outstanding short stories:

- "The Things They Carried" by Tim O'Brien
- "The Gift of the Magi" by O. Henry
- "The Legend of Sleepy Hollow" by Washington Irving
- "Miss Brill" by Katherine Mansfield
- "The Secret Life of Walter Mitty" by James Thurber
- "The Speckled Band" by Arthur Conan Doyle

- "The Tell-Tale Heart" by Edgar Allan Poe
- "The Manchester Marriage" by Elizabeth Gaskell
- "Bright and Morning Star" by Richard Wright
- "The Metamorphosis" by Franz Kafka
- "The Great Good Place" by Henry James
- "If You Sing Like That for Me" by Akhil Sharma
- "The Piano Tuner" by Peter Meinke
- "Meneseteung" by Alice Munro

Interview with Short-Story Writer Susan Fry

Susan Fry lives and works in the San Francisco Bay Area. Her mystery/horror stories appear in the anthologies *The Doom of Camelot, Cemetery Sonata II,* and *The Museum of Horrors.* Susan has also written nonfiction articles for such publications as *The Red Herring, The San Jose Mercury News, Salon,* and *San Francisco Magazine.*

CW: Susan, your stories have elements of several genres: science fiction, mysteries, and horror. Do you categorize your work in a particular way?

SF: I write what's called "speculative fiction," a term that hasn't really caught on in the mainstream market yet. My stories have mystery, fantasy, and horror elements.

Genre definitions are really difficult; I think they're an artificial construct. They're more about how a publisher markets different books. A story is easier to sell if you can pitch it to an agent or a publisher by saying, "This is a thriller," "This is a literary novel," "This is a romance." But I tend to enjoy the books that don't fall within a specific genre. They're more complex. They play with your expectations more, challenge you more. So I think you can cross genre boundaries pretty easily. I try not to pay too much attention to genre.

• • •

CW: Susan, do you have a certain amount of time you try to work every day, or a certain number of words you set as a goal?

SF: Not words. I try to work four hours a day, which is about my maximum. Sometimes that'll include research. Sometimes I'll do extra research. I tape-record most of my ideas because I have trouble with repetitive strain injury, it's a huge problem for writers, very big. I dictate the first draft, and then revise on the computer. It just flows more easily— and I like talking! I don't picture anybody when I talk, it just seems very natural, like telling a story.

• • •

CW: Do you prepare some kind of outline before you start talking?

SF: I do start with an outline. I outline pretty comprehensively, enough so that I know what's in each scene and what has to be revealed in each scene. If I don't outline, it's like drawing without making a preliminary sketch. You can wind up not being able to get the person's leg in the picture because you didn't leave enough space.

I usually write a page of gobbledygook. Then I put it aside and say, okay, so that's the idea for the story: How would it be structured? And I write the structure out, and then I usually name the characters and write very brief sketches of them. Then I usually get the idea for the first paragraph and I have to write it. I never wind up using it, but I still have to get it down. Finding out where a story starts can be really difficult for me, so an outline can help, because you realize, oh, I don't actually need this first section at all.

• • •

CW: So you find that you revise a lot?

SF: Most people write a first draft and expect it to be perfect, and it's never perfect. Usually it goes through a bunch of revisions. One of the major tools that a writer has is revising. Being a reader and a rereader, I think, is really helpful for revising. I really believe that if you can't reread a book, you can't revise your own fiction. When you read something you love for the first time, you think, "Oh, I love this, this is great." You don't know why. The second time you read it, you can analyze it. Same thing with revisions. The first time you write, it's usually on gut. The second time, when you go back, you can analyze much more clearly.

• • •

CW: Do you often base your characters on real-life models?

SF: Yes. One of my favorite ways to get ideas for characters is to sit in cafés and watch people. I get great details from that. I've never based a character on somebody I knew personally, though I probably should start doing that, just because I imagine you get the most well-rounded characters that way. But I like seeing somebody and then imagining what he's about, like, this guy has a limp and he's wearing a business suit—what happened to him? Characters and story ideas can come from that kind of questioning. Like seeing two people having an argument, and thinking, oh, what if they were in high school? What would this imply about their relationship? Inspiration is unpredictable and completely uncontrollable.

Actually, a big source of inspiration for me is museums. That may be a weird thing to say, but exhibits give me really interesting ideas. For example, right now I'm writing a story set in 1312 Venice because of an exhibit that I saw. And one of the stories I published came from an idea I got when I was at an exhibit called "The Impressionists in Winter." That's what I called my story—it's about two French impressionist painters in the countryside.

* * *

CW: When you set something in the 1300s, do you write in a very stylized manner?

SF: I prefer to write in what's called "transparent prose"—you don't really notice the writing. I'm not a stylist. In other words, I don't want people to read my work and say, "What beautiful sentence structure! What a great metaphor!" I want people to say, "What an interesting story! What wonderful characters!" For me the use of archaic language throws me out of the story. I want prose that doesn't call attention to itself. The writing is there for a purpose; it's a vehicle for the story, not the other way around. But there are a lot of authors and readers who would disagree with me.

* * *

CW: Do you find that mystery/horror stories need a different pace than other types of writing—that you need to get into the story more quickly or more slowly?

SF: Horror seems to move a little more slowly and depend more on atmosphere. It tends to build a mood before any significant action occurs. In science fiction, you're usually trying to build a world and you have to clue the reader in pretty quickly. Mysteries need to have conflict up at the front. But with horror it's more like you're looking for a feeling of unease, you're trying to make the reader a little uncomfortable.

• • •

CW: When you have a story that's ready for publication, how do you decide where to send it? Do you work with an agent?

SF: Short fiction authors don't usually need an agent. The best thing to do is to go to the newsstand and read the magazines that are there, and decide which ones are best for your story. But you have to do your homework, you can't just send something off. Most magazines have guidelines that you should follow. For example, if the guidelines say they don't want any stories from the point of view of children, and you send them a story from the point of view of a child, they know you haven't read their magazine and they're not going to respect you very much. You have to be really careful about that. Word of mouth is important too, especially for anthologies. A lot of the anthologies that are put out by the bigger editors don't get advertised, so you have to know somebody who knows somebody.

• • •

CW: It's usually not fun to talk about, but what are your thoughts on having work rejected?

SF: Rejection. Rejection is never easy. It's easy to get your feelings hurt. But you've just got to suck it up. And you have to realize that *you're* not being rejected, the material is. You can't take a rejection personally. When my writers' group picks apart a story that I like, it hurts. But at the same time, I realize, they're not attacking me personally. They're trying to help me. And editors who reject your work are actually helping you, because they're telling you something about the work, they're contributing to making you a better writer. And if you keep getting better, maybe they'll accept your next piece. I know so many stories of authors of bestselling novels who were rejected thirty, forty times. And then somebody says, "Oh, this is good," and boom!

• • •

CW: Susan, do you have any writing tips you'd like to pass on to other writers?

SF: There's a great book on writing by Stephen King, called *On Writing*. I thought it was marvelous. One of the major things that King says that I completely agree with is that you have to have a good grasp of the

English language in order to write well, which a lot of beginning writers don't have. So that's the first thing, to make sure that you can actually write a decent sentence.

Another thing, especially with the short story, is to not start your story six pages in, after a long introduction. The action, the main conflict, needs to be revealed right away. Because with readers, you have maybe ten minutes to get their attention—five seconds for an editor.

It's also a really good idea to get your story down first and not edit it as you write. That's one reason to use a tape recorder—you can't edit. Using a tape recorder forces me to finish a whole story, whereas if I'm at the computer I'll write two pages and then I'll think, oh, that first paragraph wasn't written exactly the way I wanted it. So then I start editing, and I have two perfect pages of an unfinished story after two weeks.

One of the best pieces of advice that I ever got was from Greg Bear, a science fiction writer who wrote *Darwin's Radio* and *Blood Music.* He says, "Write what you love, and write what you fear." And he's right: I mean, what's the point of writing about everything else? So many people write about something that is kind of intellectually interesting to them but it doesn't engage them. You really need to be writing about something you're deeply involved with, that you're conflicted about. Even though it can take a huge emotional toll and put you through a wringer.

CHAPTER 3
The Novel

From *Don Quixote* to *The Great Gatsby*, great novels capture our imagination and take us into a world all their own. Probably the most popular genre of fictional writing, the novel can be further subdivided into romance novels, westerns, crime novels, science fiction, fantasy fiction, thrillers, and literary novels.

A Novel Definition

To nineteenth-century writer Ambrose Bierce, the novel was simply "a short story padded." To my mind, that's a valuable (though sardonic) definition, because thinking about a novel in those terms can help to take away some of the doubt and fear you may be having if you're considering this kind of undertaking. While it is absolutely true that writing a novel is no easy task—bestselling crime author Mary Higgins Clark characterized the first four months of writing one of her novels as "scratching with my hands through granite"—approaching the novel as simply another form for telling a story may be just the incentive you need. If you have a lot you want to say and need some room in which to say it, the novel may be right for you. (Be courageous and read on.)

Novels, which currently attract more writers than any other literary form, are believed to have come into existence around 1200 B.C. Two notable examples from Egypt at that time are *The Predestined Prince* and *Sinube*. Following a number of novel-like stories written in Japanese in the early part of the first millennium (including, most notably, *The Tale of Genji*), the stories that eventually became the *Arabian Nights' Entertainments,* or *The Thousand and One Nights,* were begun. These stories were eventually established as a group between the fourteenth and sixteenth centuries and were read widely in Europe early in the eighteenth century. In 1605, Miguel Cervantes published the first part of *Don Quixote.* By the time Daniel Defoe's *Robinson Crusoe* came into the world, in 1719, the modern novel had come into its own. By the end of that century, it had become a major literary form.

While there are several elements that are key to every type of novel—theme, characters, plot, setting, and dialogue—different authors have different ways of mixing these ingredients together. Some lean on a story line, which then determines the characters who will populate it. Others begin with a character or two in mind, and then develop a story to wrap around them. Some can't stop thinking about a particular piece of conversation, perhaps an angry exchange between a police officer and a motorist that they overheard, and that is the impetus for their story. Other writers experience an event or a place that sets their inventive minds in motion. The elements of a novel can come together in so many different ways, but it's necessary that every element be strong and work smoothly with all the others.

What's Your Theme?

Early in your writing, you'll want to think about your novel's focus, or theme. What is the purpose of your tale? What is the main point? Every novel has a theme, which is either stated or, more often, unveiled along with the story. Often the theme involves an insight about relationships or about life that the characters in the story discover through the situations they encounter and the ways they react to them.

For example, in William Styron's *Lie Down in Darkness,* a novel about a young girl and her difficult family who face great pain and tragedy, the theme is that love must endure if people are to endure. Jon Hassler's wonderful novel *North of Hope* centers on a priest who goes home after twenty years of missionary work to find there are few believers left in town, as well as people he loved facing problems at every turn. The theme, we discover by the time we reach the book's end, is that faith—of varying kinds—can see people through their greatest despair.

How Do You Decide on a Theme?

A theme may already be roaming around in the back of your mind, or there may be an issue that's important to you that you don't yet realize is a theme but actually is one. For example, you may have a child who plays in the local soccer league, and her team has never won a game. But your daughter just loves getting up on Saturday mornings to meet her teammates and play as hard as she can—and she loves the big pancake breakfast that your family shares after every game. You really admire how she gives her sport her all—even though it's clear she's not going to end up with a trophy or a plaque. Here is a theme for a novel—winning isn't everything.

Themes are all around you. Check your personal life, check your beliefs, check the newspaper. Have you recently read about a fire that caused dozens of strangers to help the victim? Your novel could revolve around the point that disaster can bring out the best in people. Or maybe you know about a young couple who went through endless struggles to adopt an orphan—a terrific example of "love conquers all."

As you think of different themes, jot them down and consider them. Which one really resonates? Which feels like the right one for conveying something that's important to you? You probably won't want to actually write the words anywhere in your story, but by settling on a theme you'll give your novel direction and purpose, and have the basis for your characters, setting, and plot.

Themes often involve abstract ideas. The following list is based on Merrill Goddard's *What Interests People and Why*.

- Love
- Hate
- Fear
- Vanity
- Wrong-doing
- Morality
- Selfishness
- Immortality

- Superstition
- Curiosity
- Veneration
- Ambition
- Culture
- Heroism
- Discovery
- Amusement

About Characters

For me, characters are the essence of a novel. If I don't understand them, enjoy them on some level (you definitely can enjoy a great bad guy), find them believable, and keep thinking about them long after I've finished reading their story, the most powerful theme or plot line or setting really means little. Three-dimensional, intriguing, standout characters can make or break a novel.

Characters, of course, don't have to be people. They can be robots or animals or toadstools or ghosts. But whoever or whatever they are, they have to come across as real. As you're bringing your characters to life, try to think of them as actual people (or robots or whatever) with a history, a personality, and a will of their own.

Types of Characters

Most novels contain two types of characters—major and minor. Major characters are the ones we learn all about and grow to love or hate. They're complex, convincing personalities with a paralyzing fear of dogs and a weakness for Belgian chocolates; they are impatient driving a car and happiest when at the beach. They're in most of a novel's scenes and are the focus of the plot. They're the characters we can't wait to encounter again when we happily curl up with the book we can hardly stand to put down.

FACTS

Generally, major characters include two key figures: the protagonist, or principle character around whom much of the story flows, and the antagonist, or the character who tries his or her utmost to make the protagonist's life hell.

The following list, which is by no means inclusive, provides some excellent examples of successfully written and memorable main characters.

- Rhett Butler in *Gone with the Wind* (by Margaret Mitchell)
- Cassandra Mortmain in *I Capture the Castle* (by Dodie Smith)
- The whale in *Moby Dick* (by Herman Melville)
- Charles Ryder in *Brideshead Revisited* (by Evelyn Waugh)
- C3PO in *Star Wars* series
- Mr. Scrooge in *A Christmas Carol* (by Charles Dickens)
- Catherine in *Wuthering Heights* (by Emily Brontë)

Minor characters, as their name implies, receive much less attention. Some play such small roles that we hardly get to know them at all—they populate the pages just to bring tea or give travel directions or be a clerk in a shop when a main character comes in. But some minor characters can play a bigger part, supporting a main character in something he's trying to accomplish or acting as his opposite to point out his features and flaws. Minor characters can also be used to propel the plot. For example, the novelist may supply a victim for the villain in order to show

how bad the villain really is. For characters like this, you'll need to develop a fairly complete profile so that readers come to know at least a good number of things about them.

The Plot Line

The characters in a novel can't exist in a vacuum. To become three-dimensional to readers, they must be placed into situations that let them act and react, move forward and backward, learn, live, and grow. In other words, they need a plot—they need something to happen to them.

> "Plot grows out of character. If you focus on who the people in your story are, if you sit and write about two people you know and are getting to know better day by day, something is bound to happen."
> —Anne Lamott, author of *Bird by Bird*

Plots in novels run the gamut and then some, but most have five essential elements:

1. The introduction of the characters.
2. A trigger event that disrupts the life of the main character and sets the story in motion; often the trigger event causes conflict or a problem that the main character must resolve.
3. A series of events that the main character goes through on the way to solving the problem.
4. A climax, or moment of great intensity, when the main character either succeeds or fails at overcoming the problem.
5. An anticlimax, or resolution, in which calm returns to the main character's life.

The plot is the story and the elements are its structure. If you think about novels you've read, you can probably identify their structure, or the plot points as they're sometimes called. Think about the Charles Dickens's classic *Oliver Twist*:

1. The introduction: At the beginning, we meet Oliver as a baby, his just-dead mother, the parish beadle Bumble, and the other characters who inhabit the poor farm where the orphan Oliver is sent to live.

2. The trigger event: A hungry older Oliver makes the dreadful mistake of asking for a second bowl of porridge and is sent away to work for a casket maker, where he is badly mistreated.

3. The events: Oliver runs off, joins a gang of young thieves who work for a master thief named Fagin, gets caught in his first attempt as a pickpocket, is taken home and cared for by the man whose pocket he tried to pick, is recaptured by Fagin, shot, taken in by the people whose house he tried to rob, stalked by Fagin, and reunited with his first benefactor. (Whew, what a childhood!)

4. The climax: The girlfriend of one of the thieves overhears a plot between Fagin and a man named Monks to keep secret Oliver's true identity (Oliver is the son of his benefactor's late best friend), and to keep Oliver from getting the money he should have inherited. The girlfriend is killed, the thief hangs himself, and Fagin is hanged after revealing where the papers are that prove Oliver's heritage. (Whew, again!)

5. The anticlimax: Oliver is adopted by his benefactor, receives his inheritance, and lives happily ever after.

The Subplot

Minor characters should also play important parts in various conflicts and plot points. Moreover, both the main characters and the secondary characters can be involved in subplots.

Subplots interweave with the main plot to give additional information or reinforce information about characters. In Elizabeth Strout's *Amy and Isabelle,* the plot revolves around a mother and her daughter, and how their relationship changes over the course of a year. But as we see Amy and Isabelle struggling to understand and forgive each other, we learn, from several subplots, more about both women from the friends they spend time with. By helping one friend through the disintegration of her marriage, Isabelle is finally able to open up about an early love affair that affected her entire life. Through daughter Amy's relationship with a sometimes-wild girlfriend, we learn that though Amy is experimenting and pushing at her mother-imposed boundaries, at heart she knows the right thing to do. The outside relationships of both mother and daughter enrich our understanding of these main characters.

Chronological Disorder

As the plot and its subplots carry the characters along, they generally move in a direct, chronological line to the story's conclusion. But some authors like to play with time by introducing flashbacks or through a nonlinear plot line.

QUESTIONS?

What is a flashback?
A flashback (usually presented as a sudden memory) is a literary device that reveals an event that happened earlier in the story. It is an effective way to give readers information that helps them better understand a character or a plot point.

A nonlinear plot is simply a plot that is presented to the reader out of chronological order. That is, the story may jump back and forth in time to relate characters to events in the past or future, or it may even begin with the end: Readers are greeted with a dying man, and then shown the course of events that brought him to his end. Linear and nonlinear plots are both excellent formats, but the nonlinear plot needs extra attention to make the time or character jumps work.

When working with a nonlinear plot, write out the sequence of events in chronological order. No matter how broken up chronologically your novel may be, the story that you are writing is still embedded in time. Keeping the progression of events clear in your head will help you get your story across to the readers.

More on Dialogue

Dialogue is just as important in a novel as it is in a short story (refer to the section on dialogue in Chapter 2, "The Short Story"). In addition to unveiling characters, dialogue reveals and furthers the plot line. For example, it is a particularly effective device in crime and suspense novels. From the interaction and exchanges of characters, bits of the story are intricately woven together. Bad guys and good guys actually tell us how and where things are going as they talk to each other and themselves. Crime novels often contain a good deal of dialogue because it links the many people and actions that are key to solving the crime.

Good dialogue must be clear, believable, natural, not too long, unpredictable, forceful, and snappy. That's some tall order. But just think about exchanges you've read and enjoyed that made you stop to think about or savor what was said. You know who's talking. You understand what they say. They speak in a way that suits and illustrates their character. They speak the way real people speak, with some long, complete sentences, some sentence fragments, some *ohs* and *wells*. They sometimes say outrageous things, or get excited or angry or sad. They speak to the point. And they're not boring.

Practice Writing Dialogue

To practice writing good dialogue, try the following exercise. Pick one of these topics (or one of your own creation) and spend five minutes writing dialogue for the characters. Try to concentrate on creating natural but interesting conversation. Mix sentences and sentence fragments, and don't let each character go on for too long. When you've finished, read what you wrote out loud.

- A couple has just been mugged; they're scared but not hurt. What would they say to each other?
- Three longtime friends are spending the day golfing. Write up an exchange.
- A woman is watching her young child play in the park. What is she thinking to herself?

Interview with Literary Novelist Susanne Pari

Accomplished, creative authors stir together theme, characters, plot, setting, and dialogue until they cook up a winning combination that satisfyingly tells their tale. By studying their styles and frameworks, and by practicing your craft, you'll develop your own sense of story and find the combination that works for you. The following interview with literary novelist Susanne Pari will provide you with more helpful hints and answer other questions you might have about writing a novel.

Susanne Pari began her writing career as a journalist and has been published in the *Christian Science Monitor* and the *Boston Globe.* After working on her first novel, *The Fortune Catcher,* for seven years, she saw it published in 1997 to outstanding reviews. *The Fortune Catcher* sets a compelling love story against the backdrop of the Iranian Revolution.

CW: Susanne, would you say that reading is an important element of writing? Have you always been a reader?

SP: Reading is absolutely a prerequisite for learning craft; it's amazing how much is absorbed about style, plot, and character almost effortlessly by reading other writers. I don't come from a literary family, so the books I read as a teen were not of the best caliber. Still, I read everything I could get my hands on: mysteries, spy books, romances.

• • •

CW: Did your interest in reading eventually lead to your becoming a writer?

SP: As I got older, the Russian literary masters, especially Tolstoy, became my favorites; I was very influenced by their storytelling. I would say my interest in writing began with my interest in storytelling, because, to me, that's what fiction is: storytelling. Long before I understood that I wanted to write fiction, which didn't occur to me until I was in my twenties and already a journalist, I had an inexhaustible desire to listen to people's stories—even the most mundane—and to make stories up in my mind. I don't mean just daydreaming. I mean daydreams replete with beginning, middle, end, and a great deal of dialogue. Daydreams I revised over and over. I didn't realize this was a little weird until a friend pointed it out to me.

Somewhere along the way, several of my editors at newspapers where I worked and at journalism school where I obtained a master's degree suggested that I might consider writing fiction. Truth be told, I was not a very good journalist; "just the facts" was not enough for me. Later, in my thirties, when I had already begun writing fiction without any sense of craft, I attended the Squaw Valley Community of Writers' Conference, where I met my mentor, Molly Giles, who led me into the world of fiction writing and fiction writers.

• • •

CW: Susanne, your novel *The Fortune Catcher* is set in Iran. Does that mean you needed to do a lot of research before you could begin to write your story?

SP: All works require some amount of research. It could be gathering historical information or studying the map of the town where your characters live or asking your mother to tell you a story from her childhood. I am a stickler for accuracy. I allow only my characters and their private thoughts and scenes to be total fiction—everything that takes place in the "real" world must be authentic. *The Fortune Catcher* takes place during the aftermath of the Iranian Revolution. While I relied a great deal on interviews with people who experienced the Revolution firsthand, I always checked their stories against news articles and nonfiction books. Amnesty International was also invaluable; they provided me with videotapes and statistics I couldn't have found elsewhere. I also do research on my characters. I have several psychologist friends to whom I put questions regarding behavior.

• • •

CW: When you begin to work on a manuscript, do you have the whole story already set in your mind? Do you work from a pretty well developed outline, or do characters and actions come together as you write?

SP: First, I have an idea—a germ—for a story. It's a very concise, unblurred idea that looks in my mind like a movie trailer. There are a couple of main characters who begin at some point and end at another. For some reason, the ending of the novel is what appears most clearly to me. The writing of the novel is about getting to that ending point. Beyond this, I don't outline. Sometimes I wonder if I should, and there have been occasions when I tried to—usually when I was in the middle of a novel and steeped in hundreds of pages that made no linear sense. But I've found that, for me, outlining takes me out of the story; I prefer that the characters lead me through the maze. I don't mean that these characters come from somewhere other than my own confused brain, but I have faith that if I understand them psychologically, their actions, which drive the story, will become apparent.

• • •

CW: What inspired the idea and characters in *The Fortune Catcher?*

SP: My imagination, which is based entirely on my experiences in life. It's sort of like that *Fiddler on the Roof* song: "A little bit of this. A little bit of that." I may begin with a character who is based on someone in real life. Then as I write, the character's traits diverge, either in experience or demeanor, from that real person. For example, in *The Fortune Catcher,* the main character, Layla, is based on me. You might say that her ideology is the same as mine. However, her experiences aren't mine at all. Like Layla, I lived in Iran as a child, my husband is my best friend from childhood, my mother is American and part Jewish, BUT my mother is very much alive, her family never disowned her, my father's family didn't treat her badly, my own grandmother was not a fanatic, though she was very devout, I didn't go back to Iran after the Revolution, and I wasn't tortured.

For me, the characters are what drive the plot. Sure, the germ of a novel or a short story is a dramatic story, but the characters are the pistons that drive the engine of plot. This is why I tell my students to write their characters "in full": get to know them first by writing, without stopping or revising, as if they were describing a new friend whom they're getting to know little by little. Most of this writing will not appear in the final draft of a story, but without this kind of analysis, characters tend to be two-dimensional and therefore uninteresting to the reader.

Character analysis also often leads to the discovery of plot. For example, a writer may have an idea to write about a young woman who is forced into an arranged marriage, endures years of unhappiness, and finally develops the strength to divorce. This is a story that could take many twists and turns and offer a lot of dramatic dialogue and touching scenes, but without a full analysis of the main character—I mean, getting to know her as if she exists, right down to the color nail polish she prefers and how much salt she puts into her food—the story would fall flat. Once a writer knows her characters inside and out, the story is formed and informed by them, by their reactions to situations the writer places in their paths; they make the story believable by their thoughts and actions.

It might sound unlikely and perhaps eccentric to place so much faith in the power of imagined characters, but the creative mind is complex and it works quickly and sometimes mysteriously if one gives it freedom from inhibition. Of course, characters are the writer's creation; they're not supernatural beings who whisper in your ear. But fiction writing is not like active thinking; the creative mind works on a different, perhaps unfamiliar, level. The beginning writer must have a little faith and just write, write, write—the story will appear as if by magic. Though we all know it's not magic at all.

•   •   •

CW: Once you know your characters inside and out, how do you get them to speak? What does it take to create great dialogue?

SP: Listening. Eavesdropping shamelessly. Talking to yourself. Talking out loud as your characters. Being in that imaginary scene with your characters, sipping their coffee, swallowing their saliva, feeling their goose bumps, smelling their air. For me, if I enter the scene in my imagination, the dialogue comes easily. I love writing dialogue—pages and pages of it. But once it's written, dialogue must be edited heavily. Truth be told, dialogue on the page is NOT like dialogue in real life. It is sparser. It is like the difference between the transcript of a conversation, with all its *uh*s and repeated words and dangling phrases, and a summary of the same conversation written by a third person. *The Art of Dramatic Writing* by Lajos Egri is an excellent guide to understanding how dialogue should be written.

•   •   •

CW: Susanne, are there certain things you need in order to write at your best?

SP: No distractions. And I don't only mean distractions that come from without, like phone calls, doorbells ringing, dirty laundry, weeds in the garden, but distractions that come from within, like believing you have to answer the phone and the doorbell, wash the laundry, or weed the garden.

•   •   •

CW: What's a typical day of writing like for you?

SP: I wake up naturally, sometimes as early as four-thirty, but it could be as late as six, make a cup of tea, and go directly to my writing room. When I'm writing the first draft of a novel, I don't get up from my chair until I've written at least one thousand words—however awful they are. When I'm revising, I designate certain blocks of manuscript to edit on a certain day. When I'm done, I go back to bed for a few hours. The afternoon is for living in the real world.

* * *

CW: Can you tell me what the hardest thing about writing is for you— and the best?

SP: The hardest is believing that I have something worthwhile to say. My goal is always to tell a story that has meaning, that opens up an unknown world, or that helps me express my views, even to take a personal journey to understand certain issues. The best thing is making up the ideas. And reaching my goal.

* * *

CW: *The Fortune Catcher* is such a creative work. Would you give me your take on the meaning of creativity?

SP: I think of it as opening up my mind to all its strange and wondrous ideas, and not being afraid or embarrassed to share them with others. We all have creativity; it's whether we're brave enough to meet our imaginations head-on that makes the difference.

* * *

CW: Can you recommend some things that beginning writers can do to encourage their creativity and work on their skills?

SP: Take writing classes offered by sensitive, kind writing teachers. Take workshops led by sensitive, kind writing mentors. I have no tolerance for harsh criticism—it is destructive. Your writing is your heart; it should be handled with care. That's not to say that a beginning writer should only receive glowing praise for every word she writes. Criticism is essential to revision, and revision is essential for publication. A class or a workshop should help a writer discover flaws in the manuscript—flaws are a fact of life and of writing, and if you can't accept that as truth, you are writing for the wrong reasons. A teacher, mentor, and classmates are there to assist the writer in much the same way a nurse is there to help the doctor. But if a writer leaves a workshop session feeling the way she did after gym class in middle school if she wasn't athletic, then the workshop isn't doing her any good. Classes and workshops should inspire writers to revise or to submit their writing.

• • •

CW: What about rejection? It seems that all writers, if their aim is to have their work published, have to deal with this at some point.

SP: When I worked for a newspaper, I also submitted pieces to other papers and hoped they would get chosen for publication. Sometimes they did and sometimes they didn't. When they didn't, I was crushed. I told myself I would never subject myself to that kind of scrutiny again. Then, a short time later, I would have another piece and no choice but to submit it. If my pieces were accepted, I was ecstatic for about a half hour—being published is not all it's cracked up to be, but that's another issue.

Rejection is a big part of being a writer, most profoundly where fiction is involved. In fact, once I began writing fiction, I couldn't bring myself to submit anything anywhere. Fiction comes from the heart, the soul, whatever you want to call that very deep and private place that is what I think of as a creative womb. When a writer offers a stranger—an editor—the fruit of this womb, it's like offering your child for evaluation. And if rejection is the result, it hurts like hell. But there is no getting around it. If you don't submit your work, you'll never see it in print, if that's what you're after; if it's not, more power to you, just write.

I can say with complete assurance, though, that rejection can be gotten used to. The more you submit, the more you come to understand the mechanics of rejection: that it is based mostly on the subjective opinion of one human being. If an editor isn't interested in arranged marriages, chances are she won't be interested in your story if it's about arranged marriages; after all, she only has time to read the first few paragraphs, if that. Or maybe the editor published a story about arranged marriage three months ago; her magazine won't let her do it again so soon. Or maybe she's been in an arranged marriage herself and can't face the intricacies of it on the page. Or maybe she has a stomachache from her sushi lunch with a whiny author and her foul mood compels her to lash out and say no to someone, and your manuscript happens to be on her desk.

When rejection comes, don't blame yourself or your writing. Move on and submit to the next editor on your list. The more rejections you collect, strangely, the more committed you can become to your writing. You begin to separate the act of submitting from the act of writing, instead of having one influence the other.

When I was ready to submit *The Fortune Catcher* to a publisher, I was fortunate to have a good writer friend who had been critiquing my work for years through the writing group we both belonged to. Her name is Amy Tan, and when she realized I was ready to submit my manuscript, she sent it to her agent, Sandra Dijkstra, who then took me on as a client. After months of revision, Sandy submitted the first one hundred pages and a short synopsis of my novel to about twenty book editors. Two of them were interested in buying the book and they bid against one another. In the end, I went with Warner Books. Mind you, it was not as quick and easy as it sounds. I had submitted parts of the manuscript to other agents earlier and been rejected. I had even submitted it on my own to Sandy some years before, and she had rejected it.

Interview with Science Fiction Author James Morrow

James Morrow has been called "the most provocative satiric voice in science fiction" by the *Washington Post* and described as "the man [who] defines fantasy" by the *Chicago Tribune*. He received the Nebula Award twice, for his novella *City of Truth* and his short story "Bible Stories for Adults, No. 17: The Deluge"; and the World Fantasy Award twice, for his novels *Towing Jehovah* and *Only Begotten Daughter*. In addition to his award-winning works, James has authored *Bible Stories for Adults, This Is the Way the World Ends, Blameless in Abaddon,* and *The Eternal Footman.*

CW: What is your perspective on science fiction?

JM: Because science fiction has such a broad perspective, it's a good medium for diagnosing the ills of our society and commenting on them. In my own case, the commentary is satiric: I like to hold a funhouse mirror up to nature, in the tradition of Mark Twain and Kurt Vonnegut.

• • •

CW: Can you talk a bit about some of the ways you've gotten ideas for your stories?

JM: The science fiction writer is forever asking "What if?" That's the question through which I've conceived most of my fiction: what if?

In one of my first stories, "Spelling God with the Wrong Blocks," I asked: What if a community of robots decided they were the products of Darwinian evolution rather than human intervention?

This doesn't mean that a science fiction author's impulses are entirely cerebral. I think the genre is more autobiographical than is commonly supposed; you have to pay a lot of attention to your own life, your own surroundings. A friend of mine manages a large farm where I live in central Pennsylvania, and I've used that place as a springboard for two stories so far.

• • •

CW: When you begin to work on a story, do you already know how it's going to unfold?

JM: Let me begin that answer by making a distinction between "plot" and "story." By "story" I mean a novel's overarching narrative line, which generally entails the efforts of a main character to achieve some devoutly desired goal, or to avoid some oppressive responsibility. I couldn't begin writing a novel unless I knew the basic story ahead of time and had a rough sense of how it should play out over the course of three acts and a climax. To focus my thinking, I always prepare an outline. For me, this step isn't optional. The outline tells me whether I'm really in possession of a story, as opposed to a mere succession of situations.

By "plot" I mean the particular machinations and turns of fate through which the story "happens." In military terms, story corresponds to strategy and plot corresponds to tactics, but I'm a pacifist, so I won't pursue that analogy. Unless you're writing a convoluted murder-mystery, a certain amount of ad-libbing is probably desirable. Many of the most satisfying plot twists in my stories emerged during the writing process. I could never have charted them out ahead of time.

When it comes to the overarching story, however, the fiction writer has to be a puppet-master, even a god. If you can't force your characters through their paces, you should get out of the deity business and find another line of work.

•   •   •

CW: Jim, would you tell me what you enjoy most about the writing process?

JM: Both the easiest and the best thing about writing for me is the rewriting process. For me, there is no joy like taking a moment that "almost works" in a novel or story and turning it into an experience that wakes and shakes the reader—by "moment" I mean anything from a single sentence to a whole scene. But this takes lots of time, lots of drafts. I feel very fortunate in that I love doing this, and I'm always surprised when I meet writers who take little interest in the power and magic of rewriting. Sit me down in a café with a sharp pencil, a cup of coffee, and a fresh printout of a rough draft—and I'm a happy man.

The other side of that story—the hardest thing for me—is forcing that rough draft into existence, nailing together the architecture of a scene. Should I begin by describing the setting, or should I start with a line of dialogue? Should I offer up a philosophical observation from the narrator at the outset, or does the narrative flow demand a more immediate moment? From whose viewpoint should the action unfold? It's actually a little scary, because if you make bad or lazy decisions at this stage—if you begin a scene or chapter in the wrong key—the mistake compounds, and you end up living for months and months with material that should never have seen the light of a computer screen. But that's why God invented the seventh draft.

•   •   •

CW: Can you suggest some ways that writers can improve their skills?

JM: Learn a new word every day. Master all the pitfalls of English style: dangling modifiers, preposition pile-ups, the overuse of "that" and "which," and so on. Read omnivorously, and explore beyond the bounds of your chosen genre. If you're drawn to science fiction, spend some time discovering the joys of the realistic psychological novel—you'll be a better science fiction writer for it.

CHAPTER 4

Books for Prereaders

What do you do when your readers are too young to read? You rely on illustrations, interactive components, and catchy words and sentences. Successful books for babies and toddlers capture their attention and help them learn about the world.

It's Not Child's Play

Many new-to-the-form writers think that writing a children's book will be an easy way to launch their writing career—books for kids are usually much shorter than books for adults, some even have only a few words, so they must be much easier to write, right? While it's true that several categories of children's books contain mostly pictures, writing for children can be quite a challenge. Not only do authors need to have the skills and understanding of an adult, but they must also be able to see things from a child's point of view—through the awareness of an on-the-move, curiosity-crazed toddler or the eyes of an experimenting, wondering teen.

ESSENTIALS

The best children's books are not simply adult books taken down a notch or two; they speak with a voice their particular audience connects with and understands. They, too, are works of literature.

Today's—and many of yesterday's—children's books are not just fluff. When you think of a children's book, you may be imagining a few pages of pictures of brightly colored birds and elephants, with a bit of silly copy here and there. But many children's books—for young ones as well as teens—can focus on social, emotional, economic, racial, environmental, and many other important issues that teach and encourage children as well as entertain them.

To create successful books for children, authors need to keep in mind who they're writing for. To tune in to that audience, writers think back to their own childhood and try to remember their favorite toys, colors, games, and interests—and also their emotions, language, and feelings. Of course, very few of us can remember much about our earliest years, but for those who think they want to write for the very youngest, watching them and learning what fascinates, upsets, and pleases them can help adult authors get the feel of what it's like to be a child. Reading classics that have been beloved by generations of youngsters is also a great way to learn what's important to children. Remembering your own favorites, and what it was about them that so caught you up in their world, will help to focus your fiction.

FACTS

Until the mid-eighteenth century, there were few books written specifically for children. One of the first people who recognized the demand for children's books was John Newbery, a bookseller after whom today's prestigious Newbery Award for children's books by American authors is named.

Children's Book Categories

Children's books are generally divided into categories determined by the readers' age. Some authors specialize in only one area, because that's the time period they remember best and feel most at home with. Others create for two or three age spans, comfortable writing about and being in touch with a wider audience. Still others pick a particular category because that's the one their own children fall into—it's an age they know well because they live with its (perhaps unsettling) inhabitants every day. If you think you're interested in writing for children, try to stay open to the different possibilities, not only in audience but in format. Children everywhere love to get their hands—dirty or not—on great fiction, nonfiction, poetry, and plays.

Books for Babies

While it will be years before infants can read, they very much enjoy the sounds of words being read to them. Parents who want to provide a rich, sensory environment for their newborns and babies look for books that appeal to the newborn ear. Many of the best contain rhythmic words and sounds that interest and stimulate or that reassure and soothe, helping babies relate to and bond with their family. Books for babies are often illustrated collections of lullabies, nursery rhymes, and tales that can be read to or sung to the very young. Two outstanding examples of baby books are Linda Saport's *All the Pretty Little Horses,* a lullaby book, and Kay Chorao's *The Baby's Lap Book,* filled with fifty favorite nursery rhymes.

Books for Toddlers

Once they're up and running, toddlers are into everything, including listening to well-worded and nicely illustrated stories that catch their ear and their eye. Because these kids may not sit for long, books for toddlers usually focus on a very brief story or subject and have lots of large, bright pictures that children can quickly take in. To encourage development of language skills, simple words tell toddlers the story, often incorporating rhyme and repetition that children can learn from.

One very good example of a book for toddlers is *Goodnight Moon* by Margaret Wise Brown. This book is a personal favorite; I give a copy to greet every new baby in my circle, knowing it won't be long before he or she is enthralled by the perfect words and drawings in this classic bedtime story.

Including Mom and Dad

Books for toddlers often focus on a familiar and important relationship for young kids—the one between baby and parent. A longtime favorite with toddlers is Jean Marzollo's *Close Your Eyes* (unfortunately now out of print but most likely available at your library). Rhyming words and dreamlike illustrations by Susan Jeffers tell the story of the pleasures and problems a loving dad encounters as he tries to get his active toddler off to dreamland. The simple, compelling, and mesmerizing words entice parent and child to cozy up for a calming bedtime read.

SSENTIALS Toddler books that focus on this key relationship also speak to children when the characters come from the animal world. Good examples of little books about animal families are *Little Bird Biddle Bird,* written and illustrated by David Kirk, and *Guess How Much I Love You* by Sam McBratney.

Think Format

Some books for toddlers are not so much stories as introductions to words and concepts. Some are even wordless and offer brightly colored illustrations, sometimes on board-book pages that can stand up to serious loving. Many books by Richard Scarry are popular with one- and two-year-olds for their silly animal characters and the simple words they present. Scarry's *Best First Book Ever* is a treasure chest of 700 words that toddlers can hear, see illustrated, and learn about in short or longer bursts.

Another bestselling children's book—remarkably, more than sixty years after it was first published—is *Pat the Bunny,* a tiny tome from Dorothy Kunhardt that invites crawlers and toddlers to learn words by patting and playing with them. Each page encourages kids to participate in learning while enjoying the fun of sniffing a scented paper flower, playing peek-a-boo with a scrap of cloth, and patting the fuzzy bunny. The text is simple, with sentences of four and five words.

Picture Books

When most people think of children's books, it's the picture book that comes to mind. Aimed at nursery school and early elementary school goers, picture books usually contain more words than books for toddlers—the average is 1,000 words, though some are 150 words or fewer. In picture books, the burden of meaning and interest is laid on the illustrations. You may be thinking that this rules out the category for you (as well as books for babies and toddlers), but writers of picture books don't necessarily have to be illustrators as well. While many writers for young children do provide the artwork (see the interview with noted picture-book author and illustrator Leslie Tryon at the end of this chapter), publishers will often match up artist with author to provide the visual dimension. However, even if they're not accomplished illustrators, picture-book authors do need to think about how their words can be set to drawings and create a story that is complete on its own yet has action and characters that can be illustrated. As they write, these authors need to be picturing their words.

Picture books generally have more of a story than books for toddlers. Children who have developed a bit of a vocabulary will enjoy following a character through a simple adventure or event that they can relate to—a birthday party, a mishap (like the one in Mr. McGregor's garden), a day at the beach, or the captivating actions of a bug. While children may not yet be reading the words, they will come to know them as they hear the story and look at the pictures. Then, as they gain skills, they'll be able to master the words and read the book for themselves.

Picture-Book Requirements

Because they have so few words, picture books (this includes books for toddlers) must incorporate just the right ones. They must be able to tell the story, appeal to and be understood by little listeners, and take children to interesting places. They also can't be wasted. Like the short story for adults, a picture book needs to get right to it—hook the listener quickly, move steadily through the simple and few-in-number events, then finish up with a satisfying conclusion.

Most picture books are thirty-two pages long and usually don't have more than 100 words on each page. Some picture-book pages have many fewer words, and sometimes just one or even none. But no matter how many words there are, there must be room for a picture; in fact, some authors feel that there shouldn't be more words on a page than can be comfortably read while the picture is being looked at. To keep the story moving, it helps if each page's words function like a mini-cliffhanger or tease so that readers can't wait to see what happens on the next page. In Jose Aruego's sparsely worded *Look What I Can Do,* two caribou try to outdo each other, and the drawings are so funny that you can't wait to see what these two carefree characters are going to attempt next.

As to topics, picture-book subjects should be child-oriented and within the realm of the age group's understanding. Everyday doings, stories about animals, fairy tales and fantasy, stories about families either like or very different from the reader's own are all worthy topics. Picture books can include some drama or conflict—young ones enjoy the grouchiness of a grouchy ladybug (Eric Carle's *The Grouchy Ladybug*) and the bravery of the mischievous monkey who winds up in the hospital (H. A. Rey's *Curious George Goes to the Hospital*)—but remember that some youngsters can be frightened by difficult subject matter, both in words and in pictures. To encourage children and support a positive outlook on life—even though it doesn't always work that way—it doesn't hurt to have a happy ending.

A Few Personal Favorites

The following is a list of the picture books I've found outstanding. They are great inspiration for aspiring children's book writers and, of course, for any little kids that you know.

- *Where the Wild Things Are* (and *In the Night Kitchen, The Nutshell Library,* and everything else) by Maurice Sendak
- *Bread and Jam for Frances* (and all the other Frances books) by Russell Hoban and Lillian Hoban
- *Strega Nona* by Tomie de Paola
- *The Story about Ping* by Marjorie Flack and Kurt Wiese
- *The Little House* (and *Mike Mulligan and His Steam Shovel*) by Virginia Lee Burton
- *The Runaway Bunny* (and the other books) by Margaret Wise Brown
- *The Little Engine That Could* by Watty Piper
- *Blueberries for Sal* (and all his other books) by Robert McCloskey
- *Harold and the Purple Crayon* by Crockett Johnson
- *Curious George* (and the other books in the series) by H. A. Rey and Margaret Rey
- *A Tale of Peter Rabbit* by Beatrix Potter
- *Alex and the Terrible, Horrible, No Good, Very Bad Day* by Judith Viorst
- *The Story of Babar* (and the other books in the Babar series) by Jean de Brunhoff

Interview with Picture-Book Author and Illustrator Leslie Tryon

Leslie Tryon is a freelance writer and illustrator (as well as a dancer, children's playwright, and choreographer) who lives in Carmel Valley, California. Since her first children's book about Albert the duck, *Albert's Alphabet,* won the American Library Association's Notable Book Award and the International Book Publishing Award from the American Institute of Architects, she has been delighting youngsters everywhere with her tales of Albert's adventure-filled life. Her rich, vibrant artwork and engaging stories draw eager readers and listeners to her many books, including *Albert's Birthday, Albert's Field Day, Albert's Halloween, Albert's Thanksgiving, Albert's Play, Albert's Ballgame,* and *Albert's Christmas.* Leslie is the recipient of the Ezra Jack Keats Fellowship Award and the illustrator of *Dear Peter Rabbit, Yours Truly, Goldilocks,* and *With Love, Little Red Hen,* written by Alma Flor Ada.

CW: Leslie, can you tell me how your interest in writing and illustrating children's books first developed? Is it something that's been a passion of yours for a long time?

LT: I wrote and illustrated my first story when I was nine years old. I wrote lots of little rhymes and poems, too. I simply had stories to tell and saw writing as a means of getting them out of my head. But I wrote these stories and did the little illustrations without an eye toward publication. It was a closet activity. Over the years I filled a big fat three-ring binder, then a file drawer, then two file drawers with them. My parents knew I was always carrying on like this; then, when I married, my husband knew it, too.

At some point I decided to share some of my little stories with a friend, a librarian who told me that what I had written fit nicely into the field of children's literature. I submitted some of my illustrated stories to a competition for the Ezra Keats Fellowship (at the University of Minnesota) for a promising writer. I won! When I visited the wonderful Kerlan collection at the university, I knew indeed that I was in the right place. I also won a *Highlights* [a children's magazine] grant to attend a summer writer's workshop in Chautauqua, New York. This was additional support for the argument that I was becoming a children's book author—a revelation that was actually a little difficult to work into my life as a dancer. I had always been and always knew that I was a dancer who wrote and illustrated stories; but now the question was, could I consider myself an author/illustrator who danced? Why not, I argued with myself. After all, it's all the arts.

• • •

CW: Did you read a lot when you were a kid? Did reading encourage your interest in writing and the arts?

LT: I grew up—literally!—in a lending library. My parents had a community lending library in the room behind our jewelry store in Burbank, California. Customers would come into our store to either get their watches fixed or to check out a book! We had a three-by-five card for each book, and the book had a corresponding number penciled into a blank space in our jewelry store rubber stamp. Each book was stamped inside the front and back covers with:

Tryon Jewelers
811 Victory Blvd.
Burbank, California

I still have many of these books, and I treasure them.

So, my reading material was in that collection of about two thousand books. We had wonderful art books as well as the Durant series with all those great old black-and-white photographs. The complete works of Shakespeare with the Rockwell Kent drawings. Series of Steinbeck, Pearl Buck, Lloyd C. Douglass, Mark Twain, James Thurber. My mother loved poetry, so we had plenty of poetry books. My father loved Zane Gray and C. S. Forester's Hornblower series. Dickens. *The Arabian Nights. Through the Looking Glass* and *Adventures in Wonderland.* We had fiction and nonfiction. I could go on, but you get the picture. I was surrounded!

•   •   •

CW: Your childhood, your background, sound so interesting, and very focused on the creative arts. Did you continue with dancing, or did you eventually decide to focus on writing and illustrating?

LT: I'm a dancer, but one can only do that for so long; eventually you've got to think about doing something else. My father had always told me that he thought I had a talent for art, so I decided I would go to college and study commercial art. That's what it was called back then, now it's called graphic art; I guess they felt that the word *commercial* sounded too antiart. But the very fact that they called it commercial art appealed to me—I thought that you could probably make money doing something that called itself commercial. I trained to be an art director. I have no training in illustration. But I'm an illustrator—go figure.

My first commercial freelance job was for the *Los Angeles Times,* an assignment to do an editorial illustration for the Book Review section. "Are you sure you want ME for this job?" I asked Art Seidenbaum, the editor who gave me the job. He did. I worked for Art for many years after that, but I felt I was still an artist in training.

As for writing, I've been singled out by different teachers and professors as a good writer, but I haven't taken any writing classes. I feel I learned a lot about writing by writing. I'd read something I wrote and I'd think, that's terrible! Then I'd rewrite and rewrite. It seemed like a natural process.

•   •   •

CW: Leslie, how did your first book come to be published?

LT: I mentioned before that I went to a *Highlights* writer's conference in Chautauqua, New York. At that conference I had the opportunity to listen to a panel of editors over a period of days. I especially liked the comments of Jon Lanman, and also enjoyed hearing James Giblin and Patricia Gauch. Six months later I made plans to go to New York with the purpose of finding an editor. I was ready to beg. I brought five books I had done, each one written and storyboarded. My plan was to give each editor I had an appointment with a different book, thereby avoiding the problem of multiple submissions.

I was not prepared for the response I received—they all liked my work and they all could see publishing me! They all wanted *Albert's Alphabet.* Since the ball was now in my court, I went with Jon Lanman at Atheneum for two reasons: first, he was the editor I could learn a great deal from and could see working with over the years; and second, he was the one I had given *Albert's Alphabet* to first. I signed a contract for that book in 1989, the book was published in 1991. Jon and I are now about to publish our fifteenth book, and Jon is asking what we're going to work on next.

•   •   •

CW: When you sit down to work on a book, what are the essentials you need?

LT: For writing: pencil and ruled paper. For illustrating: pencil and plain paper, a crow quill pen and permanent ink, Windsor & Newton watercolors, gouache, and Prismacolor pencils. After I have done considerable work on paper I enter my writing into the computer. I used to hate computers but my editor at the *Los Angeles Times* taught me a great lesson. The *Times* made a unilateral changeover to computers in the late seventies. Art was traumatized. He was the old hunt-and-peck, two-fingered typist; he hated computers, too. But after six months of learning to use the computer, he told me that he had to confess it made him a better writer. In the old days of journalism, he would type a story. When he reread it he would always find a sentence in some distant paragraph that would be great as a lead, but he wasn't about to rekey the whole story just to make that one change, so he let it go. Computers gave him the opportunity to make changes like that right up to the last minute. Lesson learned.

• • •

CW: Leslie, where do you get your story ideas—your characters and plot?

LT: Ideas are like pigeons in the park—there are way too many of them, more than you could ever feed. How to recognize and distinguish among an insignificant idea, a fleeting idea, a medium-size/fairly good idea, and a whopper of an idea is where the job lies. According to my editor, I seem to think in terms of "concept." Some ideas are like bumper stickers, but others jump immediately into a concept. This holds true for characters as well. A good story seems to tell itself, but there are some things you must know about your character and the setting to help get you started.

My duck character Albert came into being in Indiana. My husband was taking classes there, and I was teaching a drawing class. We lived in an apartment within a duck reserve—there were ducks everywhere! I gave a fantasy assignment to my students and did it along with them. Since I was surrounded by ducks (big white Pekin ducks), I drew ducks. And because I went to a gym every day to do my stretches, I decided to bring the gym together with the ducks in the first Albert representation, which I called "Duck Press." When we got back to California, I decided to give Albert—who is named after my beloved tap teacher—a legitimate job, building an alphabet for the school playground.

• • •

CW: Do your stories develop as you work on them, or do you follow an outline that you create first?

LT: I simply step back and watch my character work it out. In my first book about Albert, I gave him the job of building an alphabet for the school playground. I knew that Albert was a hard worker and I knew that he would finish the job on time (because that's the way I work). In his enthusiasm for building things, he got a little carried away and used up all his supplies before he was anywhere near finishing the task. Now I had tension. Since Albert is also resourceful, I knew that he couldn't just pop down to the hardware store and buy more supplies, so I forced him to look around and work with the materials he had on hand. He's a recycler. At this point in the story, he had to work against the clock (he had to finish the job by three o'clock) and against a shortage of materials.

There were times when I had an idea but it didn't fit Albert's personality, so he respectfully declined. Your character will almost always tell you what he or she wants to do or say. When this happens, my husband usually asks, "Were you talking to me?" He asks that question daily.

• • •

CW: Even if your characters tell you what they want to say, what do you do if the right words just won't come?

LT: I write anyway. There was a handy technique in the movie *Finding Forrester*. When the young writer couldn't get started, he copied a paragraph from another writer just to get the juices flowing. I use a technique like that from time to time—when I hit a block I write something humorous and short in the form of a little poem or an essay. It's a way of saying "Lighten up! Stop taking yourself so seriously. Shut up and write!"

• • •

CW: As you're writing, are you thinking about the illustrations at the same time, or do you wait to do the drawings until you have a completed manuscript?

LT: What I do comes from a single consciousness—I hear the words and I see the pictures. I force myself to write the story first. Then, only when I feel the story is clear enough, I do a storyboard. At the storyboard stage I lay out the whole book. The storyboard tells me if my visual transitions are working, if my pacing has slowed to a stop; it shows me all the troubled waters. I have never used the first storyboard I created for any book. The second version is light-years better; all the major problems have been worked out. The third through the fifth help me with the fine-tuning. At that point I'm usually willing to show it to my editor. It's very helpful that I have been working with the same editor since 1989; he understands the way I work and I have learned what he expects. And I've learned to ease up on myself a bit because I know he doesn't expect a perfect book when he first reads it.

• • •

CW: Do you do any research for your books, either for the story or the illustrations?

LT: I do research all the time. I have an extensive library at home. I am also on a first-name basis with all the librarians at the downtown library—they have been a huge help to me over the years. I don't use the Internet, although I know that Google is an excellent source. I'm still most comfortable looking in a book. I also do a lot of photography when I visit a location, just to joggle my memory later on. Since I use actual animals as characters in my books, I have a photo file on each real animal. I never draw from a photo but I use them as references so I'm accurate with markings.

• • •

CW: How do you scale your work to the particular age group?

LT: I don't. The work I do seems to find its way into the general K–3 area, but I don't think about it when I'm working.

I do volunteer with little ones—Tuesday mornings, in a first-grade classroom; ten years with the same teacher. I have learned so much about six- and seven-year-olds in that classroom—those finite differences between the lower-grade levels. I know these things about grade level and I always gear my presentation to each group but it never enters my head when I'm creating a book.

• • •

CW: Leslie, what's a typical day of writing like for you?

LT: I'm an early riser, four-thirty to five in the morning. I feed the cats, change their water, clean out their litter box, then make my first cup of espresso (I have two cups a day, then I move on to green tea). I write early in the morning; it's a wonderful, quiet time to write. My husband and I walk two miles every morning, too, and in the spring and summer there's an hour of watering the garden following our walk. (I would spend four or five hours working in the garden if I could get away with it.)

A word about writing, though—I write throughout the day. I write when I'm gardening, when I'm cooking, when I'm illustrating, when I'm driving the car, when I'm working out the choreography for a particular tap step because I said I would have it for the Monday night tap class. It never stops—I'm always trying to solve a word problem, thinking of a good transition, adding a detail I had not thought of, seeing a whole new viewpoint, and so on. It's relentless. A front burner/back burner sort of thing, I suppose you could say.

•   •   •

CW: Is that the hardest part of writing for you—that it's always, relentlessly on your mind?

LT: The hardest part is knowing when to put the work aside and let it cook for a while. And knowing when not to revise but to begin again. Most of all, it's knowing when to stop.

•   •   •

CW: What do you enjoy most about writing?

LT: I love knowing that writing is something I could do if I had no home, no possessions, no family; if I were on an island, if I were deaf, dumb, and blind. It's like a wonderful secret, a gift that's always there.

•   •   •

CW: Will you talk a little bit about what you're working on now?

LT: I'm in the research phase of a young adult novel at the moment. I'll probably spend a year gathering my information. I've written about twenty thousand words—I'll most likely throw them all away, but they're a means of getting something out—anything! A beginning. It's a topic and a story that I must get to in my lifetime, but who knows if it will ever be published. I may have a better chance than some, only because I am already published, but, frankly, it's not relevant—I would do it anyway. That's another thing I love about writing.

•   •   •

CW: Can you explain what being creative means to you?

LT: I like to make the comparison to a light switch. When you flip the switch up, the lights come on. When you flip the switch down, the lights go off. When you begin a creative life, you flip the switch up and the lights come on; what you learn very quickly is that there's no off switch. Dance, writing, illustration—they are all creative arts. Being creative is a great comfort; you are never bored. And I'm really not fit for any other kind of life.

* * *

CW: What would you tell beginning writers or writers who want to work on their skills?

LT: Write! Read! I'm not trying to be glib; it's really as simple as that. A reader who reads endless piles of science fiction is probably going to try writing science fiction since the format is so familiar.

I read very little fiction, I'm mostly attracted to nonfiction. My books, although they are fictional picture books, always include a greater percentage of nonfiction material. My book *Albert's Field Trip*, about a trip to an apple farm, is all factual, nonfiction information.

* * *

CW: Do you have any other words of advice? Any secrets you can share?

LT: Write every day.

Write letters with a pen and paper; it's a great way to learn about being economical and getting to the point. When you're writing in longhand, you're encouraged to not go on forever.

Write postcards. See if you can really write something interesting in such a small space. Try leaving readers with a question, something provocative that they can't wait to ask you about when you return.

Test your memory. Describe your childhood bedroom, describe your kitchen and the breakfast activity. Describe your daily chores. Take the reader along with you on a childhood outing.

Rewrite. Borrow an old rhyme or poem and write your own version in the same format. (I do this a lot with ten- and eleven-year-olds; they do a great job.) For example:

(the original)

Young lambs to sell! Young lambs to sell!
I never would cry young lambs to sell,
If I'd as much money as I could tell,
I never would cry young lambs to sell.

(the rewrite)

Tests to take! Tests to take!
I never would cry tests to take,
If God would just send a small earthquake,
I wouldn't have all these tests to take.

• • •

CW: You've given a lot of great advice here. What's the best advice anyone gave to you?

LT: I've been so fortunate, I've been given so much good advice it's difficult to narrow it down to "the best." My parents said, "Choose your friends carefully." That was a good piece of advice. They also said, "You're very passionate about some things; figure out how to paint it as well as write it." In other words, write what you know. Or, at least learn a whole lot about your subject if it isn't native to you.

My editor taught me about "early days." Patience, in other words. Publishing can drag on forever. When you have a series character, it can take years for the character to catch on.

Be honest with yourself and your readers. Don't sugarcoat if it isn't true.

Writers write! Don't talk about it, think about it, dream about it, talk about that one and only precious book you might write someday—just shut up and do it!

CHAPTER 5

Books for Children and Young Adults

Do you still remember your favorite books from childhood? Do you still read fairy tales? Do your teenaged kids inspire you to write? Then maybe you should explore writing for children and young adults.

Easy Readers

Once children start to read, they're eager for books that are similar to those read by grown-ups, not the picture books they read when they were "little." Easy readers are meant to suit the transition from prereader to reader, and to give growing kids a sense of pride in their new abilities.

FACTS

The standard for easy readers is sixty-four pages, but some have fewer. An average word count is 1,500, but, again, some go well below that number. And, like in picture books, illustrations are very important.

Though newly sophisticated, beginning readers still enjoy stories that revolve around animals and insects, fairy tales, everyday situations, adventures, and family. With a bit more room, easy readers often contain a slightly more complex story, but it still must be easy to understand and appropriate for the age group.

To make children's reading experiences successful, easy readers tell their stories in short, uncomplicated sentences. That doesn't mean they can't include interesting words or words that are a bit of a stretch; these books are no longer the "See Spot. See Spot run" texts of the past, and can be a great way for youngsters to build their vocabulary and have fun with words. But it does mean that writers must keep an eye on the number of words they string together, so that new readers aren't frustrated or struggling. Like picture books, easy readers need to capture kids' attention from the start, move right through the action, and end on a satisfying note.

Best of the Easy Readers

Some publishers have series in the easy-reader category—a few of these are the Dorling Kindersley Readers, the Bank Street Ready-to-Read series, and Simon & Schuster's Ready-to-Read books—but there are several excellent classics to study for their appealing, often humorous stories and their great starts and finishes. Take a look at *Amelia Bedelia and the Baby* by Peggy Parish and Lynn Sweat, *Nate the Great* by Marjorie Weinman Sharmat, *Little Bear* by Else Holmelund Minarik, *Are You My Mother* by P. D. Eastman, *Green Eggs and Ham* by Dr. Seuss, and *Frog and Toad Are Friends* (and other Frog and Toad adventures) by Arnold Lobel.

The Captivating Dr. Seuss

Theodore Seuss Geisel, otherwise known as Dr. Seuss, was a writer extraordinaire of children's early readers. Geisel was born in Springfield, Massachusetts, in 1904. After graduating from college, he headed to Oxford University in England to seek a doctorate in literature, then returned to the United States to work for a leading humor magazine called *Judge.* Geisel submitted both humorous articles and cartoons to *Judge,* as well as cartoons to *Life, Vanity Fair,* and *Liberty.* On a shipboard trip to Europe in the thirties, the rhythm of the ship's engine became the inspiration for his *And to Think That I Saw It on Mulberry Street*—which was rejected forty-three times before a friend finally published the book. Geisel then went on to produce an Oscar-winning documentary and an Oscar-winning cartoon, on which a book character was later based.

After reading a report that detailed illiteracy among schoolchildren and discovering the fact that many children had trouble learning to read because their books were boring, Geisel's publisher sent him a list of 250 words that he thought were important for first-graders to know. He asked Geisel to use them in a book, which he did—the much-loved *Cat in the Hat,* which contains 220 of the words. Several years later, Geisel accepted a challenge from a fellow author to write a book that used only fifty words. The result was the classic *Green Eggs and Ham.* The beloved "Dr. Seuss" eventually wrote and illustrated scores of books that teach children well with rhyme, rhythm, and fun.

Chapter Books

Once kids are more comfortable reading, they're ready for the chapter book. Here the story is divided into sections or chapters, like an adult book, and the plot is more developed. Chapter books can run to eighty pages and be presented in ten to twelve or more short chapters. Generally the chapters are brief enough so that a youngster can complete one in a sitting.

In chapter books, subject matter again runs the gamut, but children in elementary school are ready to tackle more emotional and dramatic topics. Relationships between friends, animals, or people in difficult situations; family upsets; humorous exploits— all are fodder for books that children will want to spend time with.

Characters, too, are more developed and dimensional in chapter books. A favorite character-driven book of many grade-school kids, and one to study as an excellent example of the type, is *Sarah, Plain and Tall* by Patricia MacLachlan. This Newbery Award–winning story focuses on Sarah, a woman from Maine who crosses the country in the late nineteenth century to become the wife of a Midwestern farmer and mother to his two children. As the newly created family gets to know one another, each member confronts the sorrows of loss and the joys and invincibility of love.

In Beverly Cleary's *Dear Mr. Henshaw,* another Newbery Award winner that gets its heart from the main character, an unhappy second grader named Leigh finds that corresponding with an author, and then with himself, helps him through difficult times that many young children can relate to. A second Cleary book, *Ramona, Age 8,* follows Ramona, a boisterous and charmingly annoying girl, as she takes her first school bus ride, deals with a bully, wrangles with her sister Beezus, and runs full-tilt through other familiar childhood situations. Other chapter books to study include *The Bears on Hemlock Mountain* by Alice Dalgliesh and *The Girl with 500 Middle Names* by Margaret Peterson Haddix.

One big difference between early readers and chapter books is that illustrations are no longer as critical. While many chapter books still contain beautiful drawings and paintings that enrich and enliven the pages, grade schoolers no longer need the extensive text reinforcement that pictures provide. Once children are reading fairly easily, the story and its actions become their focus.

Other Chapter Book Favorites

Two current authors have written several books that are incredibly popular with older chapter book lovers: J. K. Rowling and Lemony Snicket. For excellent examples of the kinds of stories that sing for children this age, read and study the Harry Potter books by J. K. Rowling: *Harry Potter and the Sorcerer's Stone, Harry Potter and the Chamber of Secrets, Harry Potter and the Prisoner of Azkaban,* and *Harry Potter and the Goblet of Fire.*

Also enjoy and study *The Bad Beginning, The Vile Village, The Reptile Room,* and *The Ersatz Elevator,* Lemony Snicket's books chronicling the adventures of the Baudelaire children.

Books for the Middle Grades

When children reach the upper elementary grades and junior high, books they enjoy often revolve around their "more grown-up" concerns, though adventure, mysteries, and animals are still appealing topics. Many children in this age group also enjoy delving into books that take them to other worlds, including works with historical themes and science fiction sagas. Around this time, there's often a growing interest in nonfiction fare. Fact-filled books that provide wide-ranging, compelling information in a readable, nonpreachy style are high on many kids' lists. Colorful illustrations still dot the text, and kids enjoy getting an occasional look at their favorite characters and story settings.

FACTS

While there's no standard length for middle-grade books, often they run from 96 to 128 pages. A good number of popular works, though, are much longer, from 200 to 500 pages or more.

One book that middle-grade children have been happily curling up with for some time is C. S. Lewis's *The Lion, the Witch and the Wardrobe.* Fantasy, animal characters, and adventure converge in this classic's pages. Middle graders are transported to the land "beyond the wardrobe," where magical happenings take place. Other perennial favorites that offer up otherworldly doings are Madeline L'Engle's beautifully crafted *A Wrinkle in Time* and Norton Juster's captivating *The Phantom Tollbooth*.

Like the teenagers they will soon become, many middle graders like to read about kids with experiences much like their own. The ups and downs of leaving childhood are a prominent focus for many books aimed at this audience, including issues that relate to school and teachers, family and home life, independence, feelings, and change. Younger children in this category still enjoy the familiarity of stories that feature animals, though the animals may be experiencing very human and very unsettling emotions. Older kids appreciate fast-paced stories filled with action and adventure that speak to their rush to become part of a more grown-up world.

The Best of Books for Middle Graders

The following are excellent sources of inspiration for those who want to try their hand at writing books for the middle grades.

- *Stuart Little* (and *Charlotte's Web*) by E. B. White
- *Black Beauty* by Anna Sewell
- *Charlie and the Chocolate Factory* by Roald Dahl
- *Alice's Adventures in Wonderland* by Lewis Carroll
- *Harriet the Spy* by Louise Fitzhugh
- *The Little Prince* by Antoine de Saint-Exupery
- *Little Women* by Louisa May Alcott
- *The Secret Garden* by Frances Hodgson Burnett
- *Snail Mail No More* (and *The Cat Ate My Gymsuit)* by Paul Danziger
- The Baby-Sitter's Club series by Ann M. Martin
- *Anne of Green Gables* by Lucy Maud Montgomery
- *Heidi* by Johanna Spyri

Young Adult Books

When kids reach the end of junior high and enter those never-a-dull-moment teenage years, the fiction that often interests them is very similar in nature to the cross section of novels that is available to adults. Themes that deal with romance (but not explicit sex), values, fantasy, friendship, and family surface often, and stories can contain complicated situations and evoke strong feelings. High-school interests, including sports, drama, various clubs and hobbies, the outdoors, dances, history, technology, and travel—and friends, friends, friends—are often incorporated in the plot. And, of course, the protagonists are always teenagers.

Because the maturity level of teens can range widely, there are still many books that touch only lightly on difficult issues. Many teen novels concentrate more on wacky behavior and humor.

Joan Bauer's *Hope Was Here* is a good example of the kind of books that appeal to and are read by teenagers. The story chronicles sixteen-year-old Hope, who helps her aunt Addie, the woman who raised her when her mother ran off, to run a diner for a man with leukemia. The plot is filled with situations and issues that are important to many teens as they move uncertainly toward adulthood—romance between Hope and another diner worker and between Addie and the restaurant owner, concern about friends and loved ones, self-image and self-awareness, change, the future, happiness, and plenty of food.

In *Monster,* by Walter Dean Myers, sixteen-year-old Steve Harmon faces charges of being the lookout for a man who shot a convenience store owner. Did he do it, or was he just at the wrong place at the wrong time? The unusual recounting incorporates movie script format, journal writing, and text as readers learn about Steve's life before the murder and how he feels as the trial goes on. The compelling look at a troubled time and the teen-oriented language make this a novel many older teens want to read.

On the lighter side, *A Year Down Yonder,* Richard Peck's 2001 Newbery Award winner, chronicles the story of fifteen-year-old Mary Alice as she spends a year living with her very quirky grandmother. The kids at her new school think she's a "rich girl," she's forced to live in a hick town after growing up in Chicago, and her grandmother keeps committing one outrageous act after another. The lively, engaging story is filled with incidents and emotions that today's teens can relate to even though this teen novel is set in 1937.

When writing for teens, it's particularly helpful for authors to think back to their own high school years. The intensity, growth, and frequent absurdity of the time can be hard for adults to recapture, but spending time around teens can bring those memories back.

Model Works of Teen Fiction

There are many great classics to guide you in writing for young adults. Here are some titles you might find useful:

- *The Catcher in the Rye* by J. D. Salinger
- *Anne Frank: The Diary of a Young Girl* by Anne Frank
- *The Outsiders* by S. E. Hinton
- *Lord of the Flies* by William Golding
- *I Know Why the Caged Bird Sings* by Maya Angelou
- *A Separate Peace* by John Knowles
- *Great Expectations* by Charles Dickens
- *Emma* by Jane Austen

Nonfiction

Though children of all ages love to curl up in a parent's lap or a window seat or on the floor of their clothes-strewn room with a great story, many also have a big appetite for information. Even the littlest ones are eager to learn about cars and trucks and cats and dinosaurs, and a lot of other things. Nonfiction books provide hours of pleasure to children as they increase their knowledge and search out new worlds to explore.

Writing nonfiction books for children can be an exciting pursuit. Not only is it challenging and satisfying, but it can also be a great way for writers to "break in" without having to handle the complexities of fiction's plot, characters, dialogue, and setting. If you enjoy research, expository writing, and introducing readers to a subject that's exciting to you, you may want to try your hand at writing nonfiction.

No matter which age category you're considering, there are a few keys to compelling nonfiction for children:

- The text is straightforward but lively and well paced.
- The subject is one that's suitable to the age group.
- The author teaches but doesn't preach.
- The information is well researched and accurate, and doesn't water down or cover up difficult facts.
- The book doesn't cover too much territory—it focuses on one battle, rather than an entire war, or monkeys, rather than all jungle animals.
- The subject is one that deeply interests you—you don't have to be an expert already, but you should be interested enough in the topic to immerse yourself in researching it.
- The text lends itself to photographs or illustrations that provide additional information.

Choosing Your Subject

Just about any topic can be the basis of an intriguing book of nonfiction. For toddlers just beginning to learn words and numbers, a counting book, a book about colors or letters, or a book that depicts familiar objects and their names should be well received if it offers a fresh, appealing approach. Pictures are very important to these books—there are generally not very many words—but incorporating just the right words in just the right way helps to widen young ones' understanding of their world.

If you're unsure if children will take to your subject, try it out with parents and children you know, talk to preschool and elementary-school teachers, and visit libraries and bookstores to see what children this age are sitting down with.

Nonfiction picture books and easy readers focus on topics as wide ranging as you can imagine. Just about anything goes here—nature, cars and trucks, animals, history, families, places like the zoo, jobs, interests, cooking, getting a new sibling, going to the hospital, or traveling. If you choose something that interests you, and it's within the readers' scope, it's likely that four- to eight-year-olds will enjoy learning all about it.

FACTS

For first-rate examples of winning nonfiction, check out books by these authors:

- For preschoolers and the early elementary grades: Vicki Cobb
- For the nine-to-twelve set: Jean Fritz
- For young teens: David Macauley

During the middle-school and high school years, preteens and teens are ready for books that dig deeper into their subject matter; nonfiction works for this age can run from 25,000 to 40,000 words or more. Important events in history, studies of different cultures, biographies and autobiographies of people from many backgrounds and times, scientific exploration, geography and aeronautics, psychology and physiology are all of interest to this age group's inquisitive minds. Information that relates to readers' own lives—for example, facts about a famous athlete who competes in a sport they practice, information about their ancestry, or what the times were like the year they were born—is particularly enjoyed.

CHAPTER 6
The Screenplay

Many authors with a good story to tell sometimes choose to tell it not only with words but with pictures—moving pictures. Writing for the movies can be an exciting way to express your ideas, the ultimate in the fiction writing principle of showing rather than telling.

Writing for the Movies

How do you know if the screenplay is the right format for presenting your story? One way to think about it is to ask yourself if you enjoy writing dialogue. True, you need interesting characters and plot, but dialogue is the most important part, especially if you are writing a movie that you know is unlikely to have a large budget for special effects. Dialogue makes the movie interesting—it moves the action of the screenplay forward and fleshes out the characters. Screenwriters must remember as they write that their script will be seen and heard—and not read—by their audience.

Another point to consider is if your story is very cerebral—if the plot involves characters who do a lot of thinking and a little talking but don't get involved in much action. Every screenplay doesn't need a hold-on-to-your-seat car chase or a battle scene or a baby being born, but it does need some movement and some points of visual interest. The novel might be a better choice for an inner-directed plot, and the short story or the short movie the right pick for an idea with a smaller scope. (See the interview with Academy Award–winning scriptwriter and director Bert Salzman on page 86.)

One other thing to think about is whether you feel you're a visual person. Novelists, of course, need to describe their scenes and characters to make them come alive in readers' imaginations, but they don't need to structure their story so that it lends itself to visual presentation. Everything about a screenplay is connected to an audience's watching it, so screenwriters must be comfortable with both words and pictures. In essence, the screenplay's form and the way it's written differ completely from a novel's because the screenplay is focused on being made into a movie.

Screenplay Versus Novel

Like the novel, a screenplay is based on theme, characters, plot, setting, and dialogue. It also requires gripping conflict and pacing that doesn't lie down on the job.

A conflict is made up of a series of crises, straining points in the conflict that cause a realignment of forces or some change in the character. The plot is created by the selection and ordering of these crises. In each scene's internal crisis, an action is taken or not taken, or a decision is made or not made knowingly by the characters.

—Irwin R. Blacker, screenwriter, teacher, novelist, and television documentary writer

The format of a screenplay is completely different from that of the novel. It is structured in three acts and generally runs between 110 and 120 pages; that's because scripts under 100 pages or over 120 are less likely to be bought and produced due to economic reasons. Shorter films, which run closer to an hour and a half than two hours, are sometimes shunned by moviegoers who think they won't get their money's worth. Longer scripts can require an enormous budget to film, making them less attractive to production studios, no matter how good the story. If you hope to have your script end up being shown at the Cineplex, you'd be well advised to keep it to the feature-length standard of between 100 and 120 pages.

FACTS

Did you know that one of the reasons most movies run two hours or less is so that they can be shown in theaters many times a day? Long movies can't be shown as often, lowering the theater's revenues.

Another big difference between the novel and the screenplay is that the author provides a line of information at the beginning of each scene. This information, called the slug line, tells the reader about the look, time, and setup of the scene. Lines of description about what's happening in each scene are also provided, making a completed screenplay a blueprint for filming a movie as well as a vehicle for telling a story.

"HOW TO WRITE A SCREENPLAY" BY MURRAY SUID, SCREENWRITER

I graduated from UCLA's graduate school of screenwriting and learned enough to have four of my screenplays optioned. My professors, along with the working screenwriters who taught many of my courses, would probably hate me for condensing all their precious lessons into just a few words. But if I can save you two years and many thousands of dollars, I don't mind.

1. **Get a high concept.** This is the seed idea from which your entire project will grow. Usually, a high concept includes the protagonist, the main problem, and the key action, and it's described in twenty-five words or less. Brevity in describing your concept is crucial, at least with films aspiring to be popular. This is because television marketing requires having a story that can be quickly told. Examples of high concepts are:
   - An out-of-work male actor dresses up as a female to win the part of a lifetime. (*Tootsie*)
   - A young couple fall in love on a ship bound for disaster. (*Titanic*)
   - A stumblebum fighter gets a chance to compete for the championship of the world. (*Rocky*)
   - A monomaniacal robot comes from the future to kill the woman who might become the mother of the savior of humanity. (*The Terminator*)

2. **Write a treatment.** Describe your story in one or a few pages, presenting all the main characters and the major plot points. This prose piece is told in the present tense and is mostly narrative, but it may include a few lines of dialogue.

3. **Outline your story.** This may be done in one of two ways. You can write a step outline that consists of a numbered paragraph for each important scene. The alternative is to create a story deck consisting of three-by-five index cards, each briefly describing a scene, usually in fewer than ten words. The advantage of the story deck is that you can easily add, delete, or rearrange the order of the scenes.

4. **Get to know your characters.** During the time you spend writing, you will continue to deepen your understanding of the characters. But ahead of time, you might make short biographical sketches. Or you might simply talk about the characters with friends.

5. **Write the first draft.** Keep your outline or story cards close at hand and work scene by scene. Keep the descriptions brief. Because dialogue is so important, you might read aloud the speeches as you work.

   As for how to get the words down, although some of the world's greatest screenplays have been written using a typewriter or word processor, because the screenplay is rigidly formatted the most efficient way to produce one is using special software, such as Final Draft.

6. **Table-read the script.** Unlike prose pieces, which are meant to be read by the "end users," that is, the readers, dramas are meant to be read by actors, who serve as intermediaries with the audience. A key step in producing a polished script is having it performed. Most screenwriters prevail upon friends or colleagues to read aloud their scripts. This is known as a table reading. In order to get a better grasp of the material, the screenwriter should probably not be one of the readers.

7. **Sell the script for a million dollars.** Ah, but this is another story.

In Three Acts

Most screenplays are built around the framework of three acts. Act I is generally a quarter of the script, Act II is usually half, and Act III is the final quarter. So for a 120-page script, the first thirty or so pages will comprise Act I, the next sixty Act II, and the last thirty Act III.

FACTS

Each page of a screenplay is equal to approximately one minute of screen time. That means a standard-length script of 120 pages will become a movie that's about two hours long.

The most important part of the screenplay is the beginning—the first ten pages of Act I. They must dazzle. They must immediately grab the reader's (and later the viewer's) attention. They must also do a lot of legwork—introduce the main character, establish the story's setting, let readers know the type of movie they'll be watching (comedy, thriller, science fiction, western), and get the story going. If you've seen the beautifully photographed film *Out of Africa,* you'll remember that the main character begins the story with the line "I had a farm in Africa," and viewers immediately see, as the setting shifts from a woman sitting at a writing table to a hunting scene from her youth, that the story will be a remembrance, and from the clothes and the lush scenery and the music and the introduction of a flirting male character that this will be a story of relationships in a distant time and place.

Approximately twenty to thirty pages into most scripts, a plot point is introduced. This is an event that occurs within the story that sends its characters off in a new direction. In *Out of Africa,* the female lead, who hasn't married and is feeling condemned to a small life in the place where she was born, arranges a marriage to a friend, and the two leave their homes in Denmark to start a life together in Africa.

Following the first plot point, Act II turns up the tension. During Act II, the characters confront and deal with many issues and the conflict increases. In *Out of Africa,* the lead characters fall in love, war causes change, a business fails, and the lovers find that they can't live happily together.

Approximately three-quarters of the way through most scripts, the major issues come to a head in a second plot point—the climax, where another unexpected shift takes place. In *Out of Africa,* after the main characters sadly decide to go their separate ways, the male lead is killed in a plane crash.

For the last quarter of the script, in Act III, the denouement, or resolution, takes place. In these pages, any remaining issues are worked out and wrapped up. In *Out of Africa,* the female lead returns to Denmark and begins to write about her experiences, bringing the story full circle.

Scene Elements

A screenplay generally contains dozens of separate scenes that are put in a particular order that best tells the story. Each scene is usually short, from a few lines of description and dialogue to four or five pages long, and focuses on a particular incident. One scene should flow smoothly and clearly to the next, and end with the words "CUT TO" (to indicate a jump to the following scene) or "FADE OUT." Each scene is also marked with a slug line, providing information about the setting and time, and with a few lines of description about what's occurring in the scene. (To see a sample scene from a screenplay, refer to Appendix A.)

Every scene has a lot of work to do. It should:

- Move the story forward.
- Move the main character closer to or further away from the goal.
- Add to readers'/viewers' understanding of the character.
- Have a beginning, a middle, and an end.
- Be a logical and necessary part of the story.
- Show how the characters involved feel.
- Be compelling—contain either conflict or the foreshadowing of it, or show an unexpected alliance between opponents.
- Keep viewers eager to learn what happens next.

Scene Sequences

Series of scenes stitched together, called sequences, work as a unit to get across a particular message about action that takes place in one setting. In the Steve McQueen prisoner-of-war movie *The Great Escape,* one sequence toward the end of the movie shows each of the different characters making his way through the escape tunnel. One scene that focuses on one of the men is followed by another and then another. Together, these scenes depict how the mass escape is carried out.

How scenes are sequenced is very important to the finished product. In the classic murder mystery *Witness,* the male lead and the female lead are from completely different backgrounds, the woman an Amish widow and the man a Philadelphia police officer. In a scene where they dance together in her barn, we feel there's a chance that their growing relationship could develop into something lasting. But in a following scene, where the policeman's violent side can't be suppressed, we understand that it's impossible for him to live with her according to the strong, nonviolent principles that govern her life. If the scenes had been reversed, we would have known too soon that their relationship was doomed, and given up our interest in it.

Many screenwriters like to establish the sequence of their scenes using three-by-five-inch index cards. On each card they briefly detail what happens in that scene. Then they pin the cards up so that the entire story is laid out in front of them. Using the cards, writers can better visualize character development, see if the action is flowing smoothly and the conflict increasing, and determine whether the story needs ramping up, toning down, or additional exposition. They can also experiment with changing the sequence of scenes to see if different positioning makes for a better story. Some writers use a different color card for the scenes in each act.

Here's an example of what might be detailed on one card:

Act I/Scene 2
- Joan opens the garage door from inside the car, pulls into the garage.
- Gets out, looks worried, starts to unload groceries.

- As the garage door starts coming down, Bob slips under it, unseen.
- Joan turns away from car, is surprised by Bob, screams, drops groceries.
- Bob pulls out flowers from behind his back, grabs Joan in a huge embrace.
- They fall laughing to the floor.

Exposition

Exposition is the telling and the showing of the story. In classical tragedies, exposition was handled through the Greek chorus, a group of onstage performers who acted as commentators on the action. But today, in movies, exposition is carried out in several ways: through dialogue between the characters, through a narrator, through words shown on the screen ("San Francisco, 1936," or a newspaper headline), through music and songs, and through dramatic action (if a sleazy-looking guy is walking slowly along the edge of a playground full of children, we know something bad is about to happen). The best kind of exposition isn't accomplished by factual statements but by subtly yet dramatically integrated details.

SSENTIALS

"In Hollywood, the story gets you in the door. The first question a producer asks is not who the movie's about but what it's about. A compelling story gets you into the room, strong characters keep you there. Without a strong story to guide them, your characters, though they may be fully developed, will wander aimlessly around until the producer yawns and thanks you for your time."
—Christopher Keane, novelist and screenwriter

It is most often characters who tell us who they are and what's going on. But they don't generally just turn to the camera and stop the flow of the action (although some comedies do use—sparingly—the technique of a character speaking directly to the audience). Characters carry out exposition by giving us information through their interaction with their environment and with the other characters. For example, a woman might have a dialogue-free scene in which she forwards the plot by carefully putting on makeup in front of a mirror and then casually tucking a pistol into her purse. Or a frustrated woman might argue with a child, revealing deep-seated anger for her mother. Or a man might have a best friend with whom he has a drink every Friday after work, someone who's known him for a long time and draws out every juicy bit about his life. Good character-driven exposition tells us everything we need to know in bite-sized pieces and with a delicate hand instead of a hammer's blow.

Learning the Lingo

If you are interesting in taking up screenwriting, make sure you are familiar with the following terms:

- **Back story:** Information about a character's past that helps viewers to better understand the story.
- **Crisis:** A point in the plot when two or more forces confront each other.
- **Denouement:** The period that follows the climax, when any remaining issues are resolved.
- **Exposition:** The parts of a script that show what happened previously and identify the characters and the time and place of the action. Exposition shouldn't be spelled out by the characters—it should be an invisible part of the story.
- **Log line:** A compelling one- or two-line description of a screenplay that sells your idea.
- **Master scene:** All the action and dialogue that occurs within one setting at a particular time; preceded by a **slug line** (see below).
- **McGuffin:** An object that moves a story forward: For example, a clue, such as Cinderella's glass slipper, or something desperately wanted by a character, such as the Ark of the Covenant in *Raiders of the Lost Ark*.
- **Plot point:** A particular occurrence within a script when something happens to change the direction of the story.
- **Scene:** One event in a screenplay, with a beginning, a middle, and an end; a scene often contains a crisis or confrontation and always advances the story.

- **Shot description:** A description of the action in a scene. For example: "Trina, twenty-five, dressed in nurse's scrubs, enters the hospital corridor briskly, headed for her patient's room." This information follows the **slug line** (see below) and is given in lowercase letters.
- **Slug line:** Identifies the time and location of a scene. Follow these guidelines:

  - INT. (interior) and EXT. (exterior) indicate whether the scene is taking place inside or outside.
  - Provide the scene's location: BARN, BEACH, or LIVING ROOM, for example.
  - Indicate the time of NIGHT or DAY.
  - You may want to suggest the type of camera shot—CLOSE, MEDIUM, FULL, or LONG—to film the scene, although the director has the final word on these kinds of decisions.

  A slug line for one scene might read INT. LIVING ROOM—NIGHT. The slug line information is always given in capital letters.
- **Storyboard:** Sketches of a script's scenes that the director uses to plan the making of the film.
- **Synopsis:** A brief summary of a script, generally only a few paragraphs long.
- **Treatment:** A breakdown of a story that describes it in just a few pages (ten to twenty is standard). Often a producer who is considering a script will ask to have a treatment written to sell him or her on the story.
- **V.O.:** Voice-over—commentary by a character or narrator that is heard from offscreen or that is set up as a character's thoughts.

Interview with Screenwriter Bert Salzman

Bert Salzman is a painter, screenwriter, and film and TV director. His short film *Angel and Big Joe,* starring Paul Sorvino, won an Academy Award for Best Live Action Short Film as well as eight other festival awards. Bert has created numerous short films for the educational-film market and wrote, directed, and produced several television shows in the

United States and France. He also wrote and directed the Canadian feature film *Just Jessie*.

•   •   •

CW: Bert, you've had quite a career. How did your interest in writing screenplays develop?

BS: As a child, I was always the one who told stories. I grew up with my brother in a Jewish orphan home, and when it came time for telling stories at night, I would be chosen and make them up. A teacher there said I should be a writer, and that burned a place in my mind. I think I have a natural ability; I've been graced with the ability to imagine stories and see characters.

After working for a short time in an ad agency, I decided to become a painter, and I went to study with a German expressionist painter, George Grosz. Right behind the Art Students League where I took classes was an ABC-TV studio, and I went there during lunch and watched the rehearsals. It was fascinating. Then a friend bought a 16mm camera and film and we decided to make a film. So I wrote a script about an experience I'd had with a woman, a brief love affair. The film, which I called *Forget Me Not*, was about a beautiful moment the woman and I had had together, and my later realization that one beautiful moment doesn't always add up to one hundred beautiful moments. It was a lovely little film.

Then my friend was hired as an assistant to work on a commercial film, and I went along as a second assistant. I began to do lighting and camera work; then I helped with a little story, and gradually I began to write for documentary films.

•   •   •

CW: When you first began to write screenplays, what guided you?

BS: I learned how to write screenplays by reading screenplays, and by reading fiction. I also went to the movies a lot, all the time. I loved movies by the Indian filmmaker Satyajit Ray and the French filmmakers Renoir and Truffaut. They were my models.

But I actually learned more from bad films than good ones. When you see a bad film, you can analyze where the filmmaker went wrong: story elements, direction, casting, and so on. You develop your ideas from your own unique and innate sense of place and character, your unique sense of rhythm in dialogue.

I also learned a lot about writing from reading Aristotle's *Poetics*. Someone told me that if you want to learn how to write, it's imperative to read that, so I ran out and got a copy. Aristotle talks about structure as the key to writing fiction, about how to build conflict, how to bring it all together, the catharsis and the denouement. Aristotle would have definitely known a good screenplay from a bad one. I recommend that all writers go through the *Poetics* and learn that structure. Without it you can get lost.

• • •

CW: Can you talk about how you've come up with some of your ideas for stories and characters?

BS: One of my short films is called *Miguel: Up from Puerto Rico*. It's about a boy from Puerto Rico who lives in New York City. His mother gives him a dollar to buy a special fish—this is a long time ago—on his way home from school for his father's birthday. She tells him not to lose the dollar. Miguel goes to school, then he and his friends stop at a fried-food shop, wishing they had money to buy something. When Miguel gets to the fish store he realizes he lost the dollar, and he hurries back to the fried-food shop. There he discovers that his friend found the dollar and treated the group. All that's left is a quarter, which the friend gives to Miguel. Miguel is dismayed.

Then he gets an idea. He gets a cord and a curtain rod and a safety pin from home and runs to the river to catch a fish. But all he catches in the messy Hudson River is an old doll. On his way home he stops at the fish store to see if there is anything he can buy for a quarter. The owner says only three sardines, but then a woman customer walks in who speaks only Spanish. The owner asks Miguel what she's saying, and Miguel tells him. So the owner asks Miguel to hang around, to translate for his Spanish-speaking customers, and at the end of the afternoon he gives Miguel a huge fish to take home for his father.

Where did this idea come from? As a kid, I once went to Central Park and saw some kids fishing for minnows. So I made a fishing rod and tried to catch a fish but caught nothing. But I so wanted to please my stepmother that I stole a jar of minnows from another boy and ran home and gave it to her. But she wasn't pleased. She took one look at it, said that it was disgusting, and flushed the minnows down the toilet. I was dismayed and never forgot it. That was the basis for my movie—only the film has a happy ending.

For my ideas I go through my treasure trove of insights and remembrances for a theme and then spin a story around them. All the characters in my films are mostly aspects of me, or aspects of people who have been in my life.

• • •

CW: What do you think are the ingredients for a memorable character?
BS: You can't have a winning film without a winning character. The audience must be able to empathize with your main character. For example, a great movie character is Rocky. In the beginning of the film, we're not sure we like him, he's kind of ignorant, he's a tough guy with the Mob. Then he stops at a pet shop and talks to the doggie in the window. And suddenly you begin to see another aspect of the character, and it's a magical moment. Through Rocky's shyness and timidity you begin to love him, and by the end of the movie you do love him. He's a winning character. You never lose interest in a Rocky.

• • •

CW: Do you have any tips on writing strong dialogue?
BS: I'm very lucky, I just hear the musical cadence of dialogue in my head. Real dialogue has overlapping and repeated phrases, it's like poetry. I've read books about how to hook dialogue and studied American films from the thirties and forties, but I just hear it. Characters just appear in my head and then they speak.

• • •

CW: What else is very important to you in addition to winning characters?
BS: Ambiance is very important in films; it sets the tone of the story. Ambiance is created with sound effects, music, pacing, slow or quick edits, character movement, and place. I don't write a story until I feel the ambiance is there. Ambiance first.

Contrast is also helpful. For example, the silence of the desert followed by a cut to someone walking along a noisy city street with big signs. You need to feel a mood, and the mood will create the tone of the film.

• • •

CW: How do you work out the sequence of scenes for your films once you have your idea? Do you use index cards?

BS: I start by sketching the basic story idea and theme, including profiles of the main characters. I think, *What would it be like if . . . ? What would happen if . . .?* Then I start blocking in scenes on three-by-five cards, noting each scene on a different card. I pin the cards on a wall, juxtaposing and building. I also develop the main characters on cards. When the cards tell the entire story, then I begin writing the screenplay. I take Scene One and write the dialogue and the action. Then I take Scene Two and write the dialogue and the action, and so on. Then I repin the cards on the wall so I can scan back and forth and see the whole story. If need be, I change the cards until I feel the story has continuity and I hear it as a melody. I build bridges wherever I need a little one to take me from one scene to another. Maybe just some expository dialogue to make a clearer connection.

• • •

CW: Bert, many of your films are short films. What are the main differences in writing a short film as opposed to a feature-length film?

BS: In a short film you have to set your characters and conflict up very quickly. It takes too long to reveal characters through dialogue. I use what's called interior monologue voice-over early on: "My name is so and so, I'm a migrant worker . . ." This starts the story and also sets the tone by the way the character tells the story. Somewhere down the line I might use interior monologue again, because it gives expository information again and heightens the conflict. If you want to tell a big story in a short film, that's the way to do it.

• • •

CW: When you're working on a film, do you do a lot of research or just let your creativity flow?

BS: I don't do much research, because facts come into conflict with the poetry. I want to talk about human beings, about their fears, their sorrows, their beauty, their aspirations. If something doesn't seem factual after the film is written, I can reshape it then, but not at the beginning.

Daily life is my research. Being creative is dropping all definitions, which results in emptiness. In this emptiness, if you just wait long enough, something will come up, an insight. There's a deep well, the muse, whatever you want to call it, that you've got to learn to trust. Give it an open field, and something will arise.

* * *

CW: Are there any special things you do to invoke the muse?

BS: I try to break down the barriers in my mind. I always put on music to help set up the ambiance, I make sure I'm rested, and I drink coffee so I'll be awake. I let things speak to me, come up from nowhere.

* * *

CW: Do you have some words of advice for up-and-coming screenwriters?

BS: Trust yourself. When I wanted to break away from making documentaries, I realized that if I didn't take a chance on myself, no one was going to. My first fiction film, *Joshua: Black Boy in Harlem,* which I financed myself, was seen by Columbia Pictures—and they offered me a six-picture deal. Believing in myself paid off. If you don't trust in yourself and invest in yourself, you're never going to win.

Writers should also remember that no one will ever write a character or a story the way they do. What they write is unique.

CHAPTER 7

Functional Nonfiction

D o you need creative-writing skills to write a travel piece, a press release, or other kinds of functional writing pieces? Of course you do. To capture readers' interest, works of nonfiction also require a creative, imaginative touch—in fact, they're really just another way to tell a story.

Dispelling the Fiction

Just like fiction, good nonfiction is original and innovative. Nonfiction genres—essays, political or people columns, how-to books, travel articles, memoirs, humor pieces, literary criticism, biographies and autobiographies, and business documents—are exciting vehicles for creative expression. (For information on writing nonfiction for children, see pages 70–72.)

Many authors come to nonfiction writing because of an interest in a particular subject, such as travel, or a recent election, or a piece of family history. The topic so interests them that they want to learn everything they can about it, and then share what they know with others. But not everyone who picks up the newspaper or scans the travel-book table at the bookstore is immediately interested in an unknown writer's trip to Santorini or in learning about a stranger's take on local politics. So nonfiction writers have two important jobs—to inform and enlighten, and to write so compellingly, so creatively, and with such a fresh approach that they capture the attention of readers who might not otherwise keep reading.

In choosing a nonfiction topic, be sure it's something that grabs your attention as well as a subject you think will appeal to readers. Nonfiction works can teach, delight, connect with, and entertain readers, but exciting nonfiction needs the author's personal and passionate commitment.

Because they function as teachers, commentators, and reporters, nonfiction writers must be accurate and base their stories on fact. Research, then, is key to this type of writing. Nonfiction research can involve hours at the library or on the Internet, reading through old family letters or scrapbooks, interviewing experts, studying business or legal documents, tracking down relatives, or testing directions for building a chair. It can even involve self-research, for a memoir or an autobiography. Writers who enjoy uncovering information rather than dreaming it up may find one of the nonfiction formats right to their taste.

Those who enjoy expressing their opinions may also be drawn to nonfiction writing. News reporters, of course, must present the facts just as they happen. But other nonfiction writers have the luxury of also saying what they think about the facts. Columnists, biographers, memoirists, and movie critics can present the truth funneled through their own take on life. Nonfiction writers often develop a distinctive voice that draws readers not only to what that they say but to how they say it—think of humorists Dave Barry and Garrison Keillor, E. B. White in his essays and anecdotes, *Angela's Ashes* author Frank McCourt, and National Public Radio's personal essayist Marion Winik (see her essay of advice on page 115).

To sum it up, writing nonfiction may be for you if you:

- Enjoy research, learning, and discovery.
- Are avidly interested in a particular topic.
- Are a good observer and listener.
- Have strong opinions you want to express.
- Have an exciting, fact-based story to tell.
- Enjoy writing from information rather than imagination.
- Can present facts dramatically and descriptively.
- Can be both objective and subjective in your writing.
- Have the desire to share experiences and knowledge with others.

Remember: The process of writing a functional piece can be just as creative as writing a poem, a short story, or a screenplay. All forms of writing give your creative muscles a good workout and add to your knowledge, your skills, and your growth.

While there are many, many forms of nonfiction writing, the following pages will provide information on several popular and important areas: letters to the editor, press releases, and travel pieces, as well as other forms of functional writing.

No matter what genre you choose to work with, keep in mind the following techniques for creating exciting nonfiction.

- **Personify:** Treat inanimate objects as though they were alive.
- **Dramatize:** Surround your subject with action and interest.

- **Compare:** Use similes and metaphors (see Chapter 17, "Rhetorical Devices").
- **Make it relevant:** Connect with the reader's experience.
- **Intrigue:** Pose a question at the start and then answer it later on.
- **Unleash emotion:** Write with passion and from the heart.
- **Include unusual information:** Surprise or astonish with the truth.
- **Reveal your bias:** Let readers know your unique point of view.
- **Teach, don't preach:** Stay off that high horse.

FACTS

Use dialogue and description to present facts dramatically. Just like fiction writers, who use these devices to show readers their imagined characters and world, nonfiction authors can incorporate intriguing conversation and vivid depictions to enliven their factual accounts.

Functional Forms: Personal, Analytical, and Promotional Writing

Many nonfiction forms, in addition to providing information, serve a specific purpose: to respond, thank, analyze, argue, express an opinion, influence, or promote, among others. Many of these writing forms we come across in our daily life. For example, we read ads that try to influence us to buy a certain product or take a particular action. And we write thank-you notes (or at least our mothers told us we should) when someone does us a favor or provides a service. Functional forms of writing include everything from letters to the editor to complaint letters, book reviews and other types of reviews or criticism, opinion pieces, campaign speeches, and advertising and marketing materials—all excellent vehicles for expressing your creativity.

Letter to the Editor

With most types of personal, analytical, and promotional writing, the aim is to convince the reader to accept your opinion or message. Sometimes you also try to get the reader to take action, for example, to take a stand against a government policy. Writing to persuade or put forward your opinion on a topic that's important to you can be exciting and involving, and can also be an excellent way to break into print. Many authors have begun or boosted their writing careers by having a letter to the editor or a review published and noticed—longtime *New Yorker* movie critic Pauline Kael began her career by reviewing movies for free. Some authors have also gone on to develop their letters and opinions into much longer articles or even books. While you won't be paid for writing a letter to the editor or an unsolicited movie review, if your piece catches an editor's eye and gets published, you'll have a clipping to accompany your next for-pay article proposal.

ESSENTIALS

If a local or global issue is important to you, writing a letter to the editor of your hometown newspaper or a larger, national paper can be a great way to share your ideas with others. If your letter is printed, you may persuade thousands of readers to join your cause.

The best letters to the editor are written in a clear, strong voice. The letter focuses on one specific issue and relates all information to that point. Letters to the editor can include both facts and opinions. For example, you can quote statistics on teen-related car accidents while you state your opinion that the minimum driving age should be raised. You can also outline action that the reader can take if he or she supports your idea. For example, you could urge readers to write to their state representatives and senators to advocate the raising of the driving age in your state.

Some letter writers like to reveal that they have a connection to the issue, to add clout or to provide readers with their particular perspective. A person writing about raising the minimum driving age might explain that her friend's car was struck by a truck driven by a teen driver, and point out the difficult aftereffects that the writer witnessed firsthand. Or a writer with a strong opinion about the state of local schools might add credence to his claims by letting readers know that he's a teacher. But writers who simply want to let others know their opinion and not their bias can write powerful, compelling letters as well.

Here are some important points to keep in mind when you write a letter to the editor:

- Choose a topic that you feel passionate about.
- Remember your audience—include details and opinions that will interest others.
- Use a strong, clear voice and vivid, descriptive language to assert your idea.
- Express your opinion in a reasoned, nonconfrontational way.
- If you use quotes, be sure to include your sources.
- Urge readers to support your idea or take action on its behalf.
- Edit your letter carefully for typos, spelling, and grammar.

After you write your letter, test it with a friend or colleague. Ask for suggestions that might make the letter clearer or more powerful. After you make any revisions and mail your letter off, watch the letters page to see if it's printed. Then keep watching to see if another writer responds to your letter. You might strike up a challenging correspondence. And that might give you the opportunity to write another letter.

Interview with Letter-to-the-Editor Writer Shirley Ledgerwood

Shirley Ledgerwood, a longtime college composition and literature instructor, has published numerous letters to the editor on a variety of subjects in California newspapers.

CW: Shirley, what have you learned are the most important points to remember as you're writing a letter to the editor? Are there things you can do to increase the chances of a letter's being published?
SL: There are three keys to writing a strong letter to the editor. First, brevity. This is by far the most important thing—be brief. Most letters that are published are less than 250 words long. Editors appreciate a short letter, and they probably won't publish a longer letter even if it's very

good. Editors know that readers won't read a long letter, or maybe they'll read only the first paragraph. Readers' eyes flick over the letters section and they're looking for white space. People are usually in a hurry when they read—they may have time to read only one letter.

The second thing is unity. A lot of people don't understand what this is. It means, stay on the subject, don't ramble. Your first sentence is the most important—it contains the central idea of what you want to put across—and every sentence after it, every paragraph, should refer to that sentence.

The third thing is be specific. Don't generalize. For example, don't say, "People should be good to each other." Say instead, "I've noticed lately that people on the street are being good to each other. For example, I've seen a man pick up a woman's purse and return it to her after she dropped it, and I saw a man turning in someone's lost keys to a police officer."

Whatever you're writing about, don't get too personal. Though editors occasionally will publish this kind of letter, they shouldn't. If you have a gripe—and most people write letters to the editor because they have a gripe—be careful how you talk about the person you're criticizing, your opponent. For example, don't call a person who is for capital punishment a murderer. Don't attack the other side with scurrilous remarks. Be dignified.

The Press Release

Many fields of business, from high tech to retail to real estate, need the skills of the creative writer to promote and publicize their goods and services. Advertising campaigns, marketing communications, and public relations events all are important ways in which organizations catch the public's eye. From TV and newspaper ads to campaign buttons to press releases and brochures, creative copy can influence what people buy, wear, and do.

One promotional tool that is often used by businesses is the press release. This information source lets newspaper editors and others know that a new product has just become available, an important conference is going to be held, or a significant event has taken place. Press releases help to promote awareness and put the business being touted in a positive light, increasing the chances that the public will buy its wares.

Get the Reader's Attention

Writing a press release that doesn't get tossed in the trash takes skill and thought—and creativity. Your release most likely will have competition from a number of others to grab an editor's eye and his or her available print (or airwave) space. So your news should be truly newsworthy, and so interesting and inviting that an editor will use it as the basis for an article or review.

FACTS

Did you know that many famous creative writers and artists worked in advertising or public relations at one point in their careers? These include Sinclair Lewis, Sherwood Anderson, Dorothy Parker, Cornelia Otis Skinner, and writer and comedian Bob Newhart.

In promotional writing, as in other types of nonfiction writing, the first sentence carries the burden of getting the attention of the reader. For example, to grab the spotlight for one of its new lines from among all the computers that are out there, Apple crafted a press release that began, "In a move that makes the world's fastest personal computers faster, Apple today unveiled an all-new Power Mac G4 line. . . ." The fastest computer made faster is definitely something worth reading about.

Provide Information Quickly and Economically

Once you've got the editor's eye, you want to provide all the essential information quickly, in what some editors call the inverted pyramid—the who, what, where, when, and why of the release at the top and the less critical information farther down. This approach can be effective if the editor reads only part of your piece, or needs to cut information to make an article fit the available space.

In your release, make every word count. Provide information, but use your word-crafting skills to evoke images that make the reader see the product or event. Great press releases use strong visual language. In copywriter and novelist Annalisa McMorrow's press release, she uses powerful description to invite readers to learn more about a fashion-oriented line of note cards and prints. McMorrow intrigues and entices by revealing that the cards depict "a wayward ankle strap [that] falls daintily open; a stiletto heel [that] prepares for the next forward stride."

Find an Interesting Tie-In

Eye-catching press releases also take a fresh approach. A new laundry detergent or the opening of another nail salon may not be exciting to an editor or the public on its own, but when put in an intriguing light, either can be the perfect basis for an engaging story. In his *Careers for Writers*, Robert Bly tells about a young publicist who was looking for a great hook to promote an acupuncturist. The man discovered that it had been ten years since former president Nixon had made his groundbreaking trip to China. His lead, and his story, put a new slant on what could have been just another report on a small business. His release, which was widely picked up, stated, "Ten Years After Nixon's Visit to China, Acupuncture Comes of Age."

To catch editors' eyes, press releases need to be fresh and inventive. But to do their job they also have to be accurate. Always double-check all the pertinent information: times and dates, street addresses, phone numbers, Web site addresses, the spelling of people's names and places.

Keep in Mind

Here are some pointers to remember when writing a first-rate press release:

- Use visual and sensory language to create images and mood.
- Watch out for clichés.
- Put the most important information at the beginning.
- Find a fresh approach.
- Write to the audience who will be reading your release.

- Be sure all the facts are correct and current.
- Make the release irresistible with an exciting title and a grabber of a lead.

Interview with Business Writer Annalisa McMorrow

Annalisa McMorrow is a copywriter, journalist, and business writer. She began her career as a staff writer for the alternative weekly newspaper *The Village View.* For several years, she interviewed celebrities, panned a wide array of truly bad movies, and wrote reviews of rock concerts featuring performers such as Duran Duran. She has written press releases and other business copy for a wide variety of clients. Her articles have appeared in magazines including *Parenting, People,* and *Eye,* and on Web sites including Worth.com and Zippidee.com.

CW: Annalisa, what do you feel are the most important points to think about when you write a press release?

AM: As with any type of writing, I think it's important to start with a *bang.* Grab the reader's attention as quickly as possible with an interesting fact, a fascinating statement, or even an unusual question.

•　•　•

CW: In addition to using current terms and lots of description, is there anything else you can recommend for making business documents engaging?

AM: Using humor can make a difference. Sometimes, you can tell that a writer has had a lot of fun with a piece. This generally makes for a fun and interesting read, even if the subject matter is rather dry.

•　•　•

CW: So you would recommend having fun, being very creative, even if you're working with functional business pieces.

AM: Absolutely. Plain facts bore people, especially facts that are stated in a bland manner. Most journalists understand this. In fact, some of the most creative writing I've seen has been in the business section of the newspaper. Those writers know that if they write in a boring manner, they're going to quickly lose their audience.

• • •

CW: Do you generally have a pretty firm concept going before you start to write a marketing or Web piece?

AM: I gather all of my information and then piece the parts together like a puzzle. When I started writing a recent travel piece for a Web site, I chose the different places I wanted to mention, then wove them together, adding the lead and the ending after I had written the body.

• • •

CW: Can you offer some suggestions for new writers to break into business and Web writing?

AM: Start small and think locally. One of my first jobs, while I was living in Los Angeles, was to write restaurant and bar reviews for a book about Los Angeles nightlife. I also interned on a local weekly newspaper, and then was promoted to staff writer. It was thrilling to see my words—and name—in print each week. From there, I collected clips and was able to move on to the national level.

The Travel Piece

If one of your passions is experiencing up close and personal the many wonders the world has to offer, it won't take you a New York minute to decide that travel writing is where you can shine. Recounting a travel adventure can be an exciting way to let loose your creativity while connecting with others who share your continuing urge to get up and go. It can also be a great way to explore personal or global issues that are important to you, meet people with different backgrounds and interests, and experience other cultures.

While many travel articles provide the lowdown on exotic destinations, a good number of travel writers choose less expensive and more accessible spots to focus on. Travel pieces can detail not just the makings of dream vacations for those with the means to cruise the Caribbean or be whisked by Concorde straight to Paris. They also share information about more down-to-earth—and still immensely appealing—

attractions, making it possible for travel writers of all resources, interests, and hometowns to find intriguing locations to write about.

FACTS

Travel writing (including humor, roundup, how-to, advice, personal essay, and so on) can be grouped in two ways: service-oriented or "destination" pieces, which provide the "what you need to know" traveling information; and more literary pieces, which provide important information by telling a story. This chapter will concentrate on "destination"-travel writing.

Destination Articles

Destination articles are written for travelers who are considering a trip to a certain locale and are interested in obtaining tips and advice from someone who has already been there. Many such articles concentrate on frequently visited tourist destinations but offer a fresh outlook, detail an overlooked but intriguing spot, or cover the latest restaurants or attractions. Rather than a simple recitation of the facts, service articles should stir up readers' interest and encourage them to say, "Now, that's a place I want to visit."

Doing the Research

Because the information in this kind of article is intended to help readers with their travel plans, it's essential that all the details be correct and current. That means research—often a lot of it. Depending on the breadth of the piece, you may need to provide the skinny on getting there, where to stay, where to eat, where to shop, how to get around, what the weather will be like, motels that will accept canine travelers—the works. This can be done through a variety of sources.

Before You Go

Before you head out the door, you can request brochures or information from appropriate tourist or travel organizations (including the nearest embassy or consulate if you're writing about a foreign country);

review cultural, geographic, historic, and other material available at the library; and speak to friends or colleagues who recently visited your chosen travel destination.

If you know in advance what the focus of your article will be, you can also obtain information from target sources. If you're going to be writing an article on traveling in England with a baby, you may want to talk to a pediatrician, check out current equipment that's available for tot toting, and talk with new parents who have recently been brave enough to travel *en famille*. If you have a contract to write a piece for a particular magazine or newspaper, you'll want to look for information that will help you focus your piece to their audience. If you're writing an article on traveling with a baby in England for an upscale magazine, you may want to query English four-star hotels to see which provide babysitters, infant strollers, and massages for mom and dad.

Look at road maps and atlases and browse through the newspaper archives for general background information. The Internet, of course, is a huge source of facts and photos. You may also want to consult travel guides for their ideas on must-see sites and places to stay.

While You're There

Visiting your destination of choice is, of course, an exciting part of writing a travel article. But once on location you'll have work to do. In addition to experiencing the place, you'll need to search out the *whys* and *wherefores* of what makes it an excellent spot for travelers to visit.

Good note taking is essential. You'll want to write down details about everything you see—not only scenery and structures but sounds, smells, colors, how the light falls, the mood, the feel of the place. Remember, your job as a travel writer is to not only provide the facts but to provide them vividly and in a compelling way. Descriptive, sensory language will add much to the appeal of your piece.

In addition to taking notes, you'll also want to collect brochures, fact sheets, bus schedules, event flyers, museum admission information— anything that will add to your knowledge base. It's also a good idea to talk to people in the area, to gain their perspective, tips, and advice. If you think you'll quote residents or experts in your article, be sure to get the correct spelling of their names.

Structuring Your Article

Adventurers turn to destination articles for the *who, what, where, when,* and *how* of being in a particular part of the world. That means you need to provide those essentials within the description and story of the piece. You also need a great "hook" to interest readers in the first place, and a closing that reinforces the central idea.

The best travel pieces start with a lead that captures the reader's attention and sets in motion what the article will be about. Kathryn Brockman's story in the *San Jose Mercury News* that compares spending time in a Kenyan game reserve with a "safari lite" stay at the Animal Kingdom Lodge in Orlando, Florida, begins, "A cloud of dust trailed our mini-van as we hurtled over large stones, then dropped into potholes on our journey into the heart of Kenya's national parks." In seconds, we're right there in Kenya with Brockman, and we want to know more about her trip. Another tantalizing beginning, from an article by Larry Bleiberg in the *Dallas Morning News*, teases, "Every day, a tiny outpost of England comes to a handful of U.S. airports." What will that be? We need to read on to find out. (If you're wondering, it's the better-than-U.S.-airline food, service, and amenities the author enjoys by traveling on British and other foreign flights.)

Things change. Museums switch to off-season hours. Restaurants go belly up. Hotel rates rise. If an article you write is published several months after you wrote it, you will need to verify the facts or include a disclaimer that the information was correct as of the time of the writing.

Sometimes leads just naturally spring to mind, but other times they'll show themselves once you've begun writing. However you find your lead, your following paragraphs should all relate to it, and your closing should circle back to it.

In between the lead and the conclusion, you'll need to transmit the information the reader is looking for:

- **Location:** Where in the world the point of interest lies (this should happen in the first few paragraphs).
- **Season:** The time of year the article refers to.
- **Reason:** Why the reader should go there.
- **Author:** Who the writer is and his or her viewpoint (someone on a trip with an alumni group, a first-time traveler to the Far East, etc.).
- **Useful facts and tips:** Trains or planes to take, relative costs, don't-miss sights, problems encountered—everything you feel will help a fellow traveler get the most out of a trip to that spot.

Some facts are best presented in bulleted form—say, how and when readers can access each of the ten-best places to picnic in the area—but the majority of travel articles are presented in the form of a narrative. Anecdotes showcasing high points or unusual aspects of a trip will also give readers a good feel for the writer's experience and what they might come up against or enjoy if they make the trip. Captivating, can't-put-'em-down travel articles interweave facts, description, quotes, dialogue, and anecdotes told through the writer's unique perspective.

Try It Yourself

A convenient—and inexpensive—way to try out travel writing is to focus on places close to home. Putting a fresh face on a familiar location or discovering something unusual about something seemingly ordinary can intrigue a local newspaper editor as well as your neighbors. Parks, historic buildings, private homes, and new restaurants or attractions can all be the center of appealing travel pieces. Pretend you're a visitor to your area and take a close look around. What's the history behind the sculpture in the center of town? Does the café that draws a crowd every summer evening serve an unusual dish? Are the beautiful homes you see ever open to the public? Do the research and write the article.

Interview with Travel Writer
Louise Purwin Zobel

Louise Purwin Zobel is the author of the bestselling travel-writing authority *The Travel Writer's Handbook,* now in its fifth edition. Louise's articles on travel have also been published in such magazines as *Parents, Modern Maturity, Better Homes and Gardens, Travel Age West,* and *The Writer.* A frequent speaker at national and international conferences, as well as on radio and television, Louise currently teaches online travel-writing classes for WritingSchool.com and is a consultant to private writing clients. She has traveled to all fifty states and to over a hundred foreign countries.

CW: Louise, has your writing career always centered on travel writing, or did you come to this field via another one?

LPZ: I was a communications major at Stanford and began working at United Press's Pacific Division headquarters in San Francisco. Then I started freelancing magazine articles for various publications, writing about houses and gardens, family living and relationships, schools, community affairs. After my husband and I took our four children to spend a summer in Europe, I wrote an article called "We Could Hardly Afford to Stay Home" that was published in a magazine called *Medical Economics.* Before I even received my copy of the magazine, doctors from all over the country began bombarding me for more information. This alerted me to the idea that travel writing isn't just about beautiful sunsets and luxury hotels—readers want to know how you did it, how much it cost, how it all worked out. And thus began a new offshoot of my freelancing.

•　•　•

CW: And it grew from there?

LPZ: Yes. I had been speaking and teaching on various writing subjects at conferences and on university and college campuses, and I had also gone back to Stanford and gotten an M.A. in communications, including a magazine-writing class. I was very involved in many areas of writing. When the Sacramento branch of the California Writers Association asked me to speak about travel writing, I put quite a lot of work and time into the speech, and it went well. So I thought I should get a little more mileage out of it and wrote an article for *Writer's Digest* magazine, and it received a lot of fan mail. And that led to the first edition of the *Travel Writer's Handbook,* which Writer's Digest Books published. That book has sold about 82,000 copies, and it's now in its fifth, up-to-the-minute edition.

* * *

CW: How do you choose the places you write about?

LPZ: Quite often I'm invited as a guest or invited to speak at a faraway conference. Other times I have an assignment to cover. And other times I guess I like to see places that I haven't seen or that I especially enjoyed before, or that sound so appealing I just can't resist. I have been to every continent and seen most of the world's "musts" and many of its offbeat places. I'm especially interested in archaeology—Roman and Greek ruins in the Mediterranean countries. Actually, I suppose I like almost everything, so a lot of factors go into deciding when to go where.

* * *

CW: What sort of research do you do—and do you do most of it before you leave on the trip?

LPZ: I always do a great deal of research—being there is never enough. I do library research before, during, and after the trip. You really need research to do research—you need to know enough to ask your informants the right questions and to look for specific answers in print and in online reference materials. Although much of what you find won't appear in the finished piece, the knowledge behind the words gives depth and credibility to the article. Also, many times a story can be reslanted for additional publications using some of the leftover research material.

* * *

CW: Louise, do you take a lot of photos while you're on an assignment? How important is it for a travel writer to be a good photographer?

LPZ: It's not critical to be a good photographer—I married one!—but it certainly is a big help. A travel writer should at least be able to take a good-enough photo to show the editor what is available, but there are, of course, many ways to get photographs if you don't take any. Now, with digital cameras and the different printing technologies, a lot is possible.

* * *

CW: What would you say is most important for writing a strong travel article?

LPZ: Be sure you know what you're trying to say—you need to write what I call a great "capsule sentence." And be sure you know the audience you're writing for—study in minute detail the articles published by your target publication. Those are critical points.

A few years ago, when I was teaching an adult seminar, a writer who was taking the class told me about a sale she had just made. She was in Hawaii and writing about her trip, and her husband teased her about the writing class. The manager of the hotel where they were staying overheard them talking and asked to see something she had written. She took out an ode to a Hawaiian sunset, and he immediately bought it to feature on his menu—and he gave her a sizable check.

Again and again I tell my students and private clients that there is no such thing as "just writing." We are always writing for somebody—whether it's a postcard or a best-seller—and it behooves us to know who that somebody is.

· · ·

CW: Do you have any other advice you'd like to mention?

LPZ: Don't be afraid an editor will steal your idea and assign it to another writer. In all the years I have been a writer, only once did I feel that a very sleazy publication stole a writer's idea. I think the same idea just occurs to many people at the same time.

Another point is, you don't have to travel to exotic places to find interesting stories. Once, when I wrote an article on travel writing, I advised readers to look for stories close to home, even if they'd been done many times before. "Add a new twist," I said. "How about the homes of all the writers who have lived in your town?" Within a month I saw half a dozen published articles about writers' homes in various cities in Northern California.

CHAPTER 8

Literary Nonfiction

The memoir and literary criticism represent the literary side of nonfiction writing. These works tend to be more self-conscious than reader-directed, and demonstrate a higher level of concern for the literary aspects of writing.

The Memoir

Derived from the French word *mémoire,* meaning "memory," the classic memoir is the recollection of a particularly vivid and important time in the author's life. The earliest memoirs date back to the fourth century, when writers described the intense religious and psychological experiences they underwent. More recent memoirs have offered up remembrances of the full range of situations that affect the human condition, and the most current tend to expose deeply personal and often painful times.

What makes authors want to share their private thoughts and experiences? It seems that this kind of storytelling could be embarrassing or shameful, since it allows complete strangers to read about intimate details and perhaps difficult or even sordid situations that the writer was part of. Restaurant critic and gourmet extraordinaire Ruth Reichl says she was very worried what people would think after she published her collection of memoirs called *Comfort Me with Apples,* which details a love affair, the demise of her first marriage, the lowdown about cooking luminaries she worked with, the death of her father, and her romance with the man who became her second husband. Other authors, too, have found it hard to expose their lives to scrutiny and have been fearful of hurting people whom they mention in their work. Revisiting painful times can also be traumatic.

QUESTIONS?

Is a memoir an autobiography?
In a sense it is, because it details part of the author's history. But an autobiography is the whole story, the author's whole history. It generally covers everything from one's birth and childhood to the present time and is written toward the end of one's life.

But many memoirists say they thoroughly enjoy—and gain a great deal from—writing about their past. They relive pleasurable moments. They rediscover someone or something that once was an important part of their life. By writing a memoir, they are able to confront lingering issues. They can connect with other people and share common experiences. They can better understand their own life and what drives others. They can move ahead by looking back. And they can discover they don't need to be living an extraordinary life to have something important to say.

The memoir focuses on a selected time of particular meaning and impact. Memoirs can be written by authors looking far into their past, but many memoirists are young and recount significant recent events. The memoir can be a fertile field for writers of every age and background, and a powerful way to write about important memories without taking on the sometimes overwhelming task of writing an autobiography.

Try to Remember

Because memoirs are personal histories, they need to be honest to honor the real-life people depicted in the story, and to make those people real and believable. They also need to be honest because they deal with facts.

If you're wondering how you're ever going to remember the details of something that happened years ago, try these ideas for bringing it all back:

- Interview (in person or by phone, e-mail, or snail mail) someone who would be familiar with the situation or at least the time period you are writing about—a family member, friend, neighbor, colleague, teacher, coach, or activity leader.
- Search through old files and records, including photos, home movies, letters or postcards, diaries, even bills or statements from the time.
- Look up important documents such as marriage or birth certificates, grant deeds, or car purchase papers.
- Spend time at the library checking up on relevant historical, geographical, and cultural information. Try books, magazines, newspapers (newspaper offices also contain files of back issues), audio- and videotapes, and online sources.
- If it's possible, revisit the "scene of the crime." If you can't, try to visit a similar place. For example, if your memoir centers around an incident during college, visit a nearby college to bring back the feeling of being a student.
- Sit quietly and try to visualize the time. What did you like to wear? Who were your friends? What did your home look like? What was going on in your life? In the world? Write everything down or speak into a tape recorder.

Stitching It Together

Because a memoir is actually a story, it also needs to be structured and developed, like a novel or a short story. Often writers feel their memoir will just take shape as they write it, but a memoir needs to be built with a sense of order to link and sequence the many memories involved. Memoirs should also be seeded with information about the particular time to give the story context.

Memories are imperfect. Readers of your memoir may recall things differently, but remember that *your* memoir is *your* story as *you* best remember it. If you're honest in your recollections, you'll preserve an important time with your personal truth.

Writer, editor, and teacher William Zinsser says that good memoirs are "a careful act of construction." To tell their story well, they skillfully and clearly weave together three key elements: summary, exposition, and drama.

Summary

Summary information gives readers the background of the story and gets it started. Sometimes this is done with just a sentence or two of introduction. In other memoirs several paragraphs detail the time, place, and circumstances of the memory. Characters are also introduced as part of this information.

E. B. White, in his "Afternoon of an American Boy," gets right into his story with a straightforward summary of when and where it takes place and who it will be about:

> When I was in my teens, I lived in Mount Vernon, in the
> same block with J. Parnell Thomas, who grew up to become
> chairman of the House Committee on Un-American Activities.
> I lived on the corner of Summit and East Sidney, at No. 101
> Summit Avenue, and Parnell lived four or five doors north of
> us. . . .

The thing that made Parnell a special man in my eyes in those days was not his handsome appearance and friendly manner but his sister. Her name was Eileen. She was my age and she was a quiet, nice-looking girl. . . .

Exposition

Exposition is story development. Through exposition, we learn everything we need to know in order to understand the particular point or the moment that's going to be the focus. There's no set length for this memoir element, and often it alternates with drama (see below) throughout the story to provide additional information or to analyze something that just happened. Exposition takes places through narrative and dialogue and can include cultural, geographic, historical, personal, and other kinds of information.

In "Afternoon of an American Boy," White takes us through his relationship with Parnell and his sister, as well as his confession that he both admired girls and was terrified of them at the time. His relationship with his sister is also important to the coming crisis of the story:

My bashfulness and backwardness annoyed my older sister very much, and at about the period of which I am writing she began making strong efforts to stir me up. She was convinced that I was in a rut, socially, and she found me a drag in her own social life, which was brisk. She kept trying to throw me with girls, but I always bounced.

Drama

Here is where the story reaches a significant moment, and the description and action slow down to concentrate on it. Sometimes characters will speak to add reality to the situation and to add punch to the narration.

In "Afternoon of an American Boy," once White has provided the background, he moves on to the main event:

One day, through a set of circumstances I have forgotten, my sister managed to work me into an afternoon engagement she had with some others in New York. . . . My sister had heard tales of tea-dancing at the Plaza Hotel. She and a girl friend of hers and another fellow and myself went there to give it a try. . . . Incredible as it seems to me now, I formed the idea of asking Parnell's sister Eileen to accompany me to a tea dance at the Plaza. . . . The fact that I didn't know how to dance must have been a powerful deterrent, but not powerful enough to stop me.

Following his decision to ask Eileen to a dance, the young White makes his move, and, miraculously, Eileen accepts. But it's a disaster. The grown author remembers the horror of trying to adapt his "violent sister-and-brother wrestling act into something graceful and appropriate." Years later, he *analyzes* the event—through an imaginary conversation with Parnell in his later role as the chairman of the House Committee on Un-American Activities. White confesses not to being a Communist Party member or a member of the Screenwriters Guild, but to taking Parnell's sister to a tea dance when he knew he couldn't dance.

Evaluating Your Work

Once you have your story down, you'll probably want to let it sit for a while and then, refreshed, take a close look at it. You may even want to read it aloud, to yourself or to someone whose opinion you respect, to see if the words let you conjure up a picture and to get a sense of the flow. Try to determine if everything hangs together—if the descriptions and dialogue travel smoothly from one point to the next. Also check if all your remembrances are necessary for the main point. Sometimes a piece of information that is meaningful to you will establish itself in your memoir but really shouldn't be there, either because it isn't relevant or because it doesn't move the story forward. Check that you've provided enough context so that people who aren't familiar with the circumstances can still understand the story. (For more on evaluating your writing, see Chapter 16.)

See how your work compares to some of the most memorable memoirs written to date. Included is a list of some favorites.

- *Walden* by Henry David Thoreau
- *The Road from Coorain* by Jill Ker Conway
- *The Year of the People* by Eugene McCarthy
- *In My Father's House* by Nancy Huddleston Packard
- *The Boys of Summer* by Roger Kahn
- *Memoirs of a Catholic Girlhood* by Mary McCarthy
- *Life on the Mississippi* by Mark Twain
- *Memoirs* by Pablo Neruda
- *Pilgrim at Tinker Creek* by Annie Dillard
- *Angela's Ashes* by Frank McCourt

Literary Criticism

Literature, in all its forms, gives readers great pleasure. But it also extends a challenge: to think about the themes, issues, and relationships on which it is based. As we read, not only are we told a story, but we're given information, opinions, and thoughts about the big questions of life.

> Although . . . in ordinary usage 'criticism' implies finding fault . . . in fact most literary criticism is . . . chiefly concerned with interpretation . . . and with analysis. . . . A critic can see excellences as well as faults. Because we turn to criticism with the hope that the critic has seen something we have missed, the most valuable criticism is not that which shakes its finger at faults but that which calls our attention to interesting things going on in the work of art.
>
> —Sylvan Barnet, *A Short Guide to Writing About Literature*

While many readers consider the issues that literature brings up by discussing them or thinking them through, some readers like to contemplate them by writing a critical or analytical work. This work can focus on a particular book, essay, or article, or an issue that relates to a written piece. For example, a critical essay might discuss how a particular work reflects the time in which it was written, its meaning in current society, its implications for the future, what it says about the author, what it says about relationships. Works of criticism are generally arguments that seek to answer important questions using facts and persuasive reasoning. They can also include the author's personal experiences with the issues. Literary criticism can be especially creative because the author brings a unique viewpoint and interpretation to the topic.

FACTS

"Thinking is an integral part of writing. . . . the essayist—the creative nonfiction writer—must also be a thinker, a critic, and a social commentator. . . . This is the coveted privilege of the essayist. . . ."
—Lee Gutkind, author of *Many Sleepless Nights*

Find a Worthy Subject

With this form of writing, it's vital to choose a subject that deeply moves or concerns you. Sometimes an author will be interested in a particular topic long before he or she begins to write about it, and will have years of information and experience to bring to the argument. For example, Ocean Howell, the critic interviewed below, first became interested in urban issues because he experienced the power relationships involved in urban spaces through his years as a serious skateboarder. Over the years, he learned about and developed ideas about public spaces that he brings to his theories and arguments.

WORDS OF ADVICE ON WRITING

Marion Winik is a personal essayist and commentator whose work airs regularly on National Public Radio's "All Things Considered." Her witty, insightful prose has also appeared in such publications as the *Utne Reader*, *Glamour*, and *Texas Monthly* and in newspapers and anthologies. Marion's latest book, *Rules for the Unruly*, grew out of an invitation to return to her high school to address the recipients of an award for academic excellence. Marion's other works are *The Lunch-Box Chronicles: Notes from the Parenting Underground*, selected by *Child Magazine* as a parenting book of the year; *Telling: Confessions, Concessions, and Other Flashes of Light*; and *First Comes Love*, a *New York Times* Notable Book. She lives in Glen Rock, Pennsylvania, with her husband, Crispin Sartwell, and their numerous children.

Wherever I go, whatever I do, there is just one thing people want to know from me, one question that always comes up no matter what the context: How did I get on "All Things Considered?"

The story begins in December 1990, when my friend Liz Lambert looked up from reading one of my essays in the *Austin Chronicle,* our town's alternative weekly. "Mare," she said in her West Texas way, "you should read these thangs of yers on NPR."

"Yeah, Liz," I said, "and you should be president of the United States."

But not two weeks later, I got a postcard from NPR correspondent John Burnett, who had also been reading me in the *Chronicle*. Later we would become elementary-school parents together, but at the time our kids were in diapers and we'd never met. He asked if I'd like to come over and record a couple of the essays, and offered to take the tape to Washington and see what people thought.

I called him immediately, but not fast enough: His wife said he'd been sent to Iraq to cover Operation Desert Storm. Oh, great. Now the only thing between me and my big break was Saddam Hussein.

John finally came home and recorded me in late spring of '91. I taped a piece about dealing with the Texas summer, and another about raising a child in a Jewish-Catholic intermarriage. Luckily my demo arrived during an early May heat wave in Washington and it went straight on the air.

That was ten years ago, and not long after that, I heard from a literary agent who wanted to help me publish a book of my essays. That was four books ago. So there are two morals of this story. One is: Liz for president! The other is, the whole thing started with me publishing essays for almost no pay in a local alternative newspaper. This is why I always tell people who are wondering how they can begin getting published to aim low—think small—go local. I spent years sending essays to major national magazines and saw them come back in my SASEs like clockwork. To get started, I had to look for a lower foothold.

There is always somebody who is interested in your work. At first, it may be your family members, compadres in a writing group, the audience at an open-mike reading. Well, fine. Take any audience you can get and work from there. Get it out there, get feedback, and maybe someday you'll also get a check. But if you start by looking for the big check, you may never find anything at all.

—Marion Winik, memoirist and radio commentator

FACTS

"The writing that the critic does . . . is not a dispassionate and objective evaluation based on more or less universal criteria, but rather a spontaneous response prepared from a host of personal and professional experiences."

—Robert L. Root Jr., *Working at Writing*

Read Up on Your Subject

In addition to being passionate about a subject, a critic also needs to enjoy research and critical reading. You'll want to view what you read as a kind of puzzle. For example, if you decide to analyze a piece by the writer William Faulkner to see what he tells readers about the post–Civil War breakdown of traditional Southern values, you may want to study several interwoven issues—race relations of the time, Faulkner's background, and the history of the area in which Faulkner grew up—to see how they affected his philosophy and his writing. Literary criticism often involves making connections and drawing conclusions through context.

The Literary Analysis

To analyze a literary work, here are some general steps to follow:

- Choose a thought-provoking topic that is particularly meaningful to you and that you think will interest readers.
- Read widely on the subject.
- Choose the work you're going to analyze.
- Read it several times, trying to understand the ideas the author put forward.
- Write down key points and phrases. Identify important relationships.
- Summarize your theme and develop your key points and theories.

ESSENTIALS

To summarize, try asking questions. For example, what's behind a particular character's need for respect and position? Work until you feel you have enough information and a compelling argument.

- Outline your essay.
- Write a first draft.
- Keep thinking about your topic, and make changes as you develop new ideas or arguments.
- Revise and edit until your position is clear and well supported.

Interview with Literary Critic Ocean Howell

Ocean Howell is an associate editor with Jossey-Bass Publishers and the managing editor of *Board Leadership,* a journal focused on issues of governance. His works of theory-oriented criticism have been published in a variety of journals and magazines, including San Francisco State University's *Urban Action.*

CW: Let's start by your defining theory-oriented criticism—what exactly does that mean?

OH: More traditional literary criticism, like reader-response theory or "close reading," tends to treat a work of literature as a self-contained world. Traditional criticism also maintains rigid distinctions between "high culture" and "low culture," the former being the only kind of culture that merits study. The critical approaches that are loosely called "theory" seek to place any cultural production—a novel by Rudyard Kipling or a commercial for laundry detergent—in its larger socioeconomic context.

What does Kipling's writing tell us about British imperialism? What does a laundry detergent commercial tell us about gender roles? The theory approach maintains that we live immersed in culture, and that distinctions between high and low, legitimate or illegitimate, are not only arbitrary but serve to reinforce existing power relations, like class. For example, what interest is served by maintaining that baroque music is high art and mariachi music low art? Some of the critical approaches that fall under the general rubric of "theory" include psychoanalysis, structuralism, poststructuralism or deconstructionism, feminism, Marxism, and postmodernism. Some of the major theory figures are Marx, Freud, Lacan, Foucault, Derrida, Judith Butler, Edward Said, and Slavoj Zizek.

• • •

CW: Do you have a particular subject area that you focus on and, if you do, how did your interest in it develop?

OH: I'm very interested in urban studies. I suppose my interest originally got started when I was pretty young—I was a serious skateboarder as a kid, and so I was always thinking about streets and public spaces, particularly about the power relations involved in streets and public spaces. I started to read about urban history, planning, and politics. I was initially interested only in how our streets and public spaces came to be the way they are, but my interest quickly expanded into architecture and planning.

• • •

CW: When you sit down to write a critical essay, do you pretty much know what you want to say? Do you develop an outline first and then work from that?

OH: I never make an outline, but I always have a good idea about what I want to say before I start. I know what my conclusion will be and the major points I have to make to prove it. I guess you could say I start with an outline in my head—I know where I'm going. But once I begin, I immediately realize I've left something out, and I start exploring tangents. The outline in my head gets me started toward my conclusion, but I can still explore all the possibilities and potential problems of my argument without losing focus of my end goal. You find out which ideas you should expand and which you should ditch.

I think that to write well you have to start with a well-developed idea but also "write as you go." If you adhere too rigidly to your initial idea, you won't be able to correct the inevitable mistakes in your initial thinking. But if you just write as you go, without an idea, you waste a lot of time on tangents before you find your focus.

• • •

CW: Do you do a lot of preparation, a lot of research, before you begin to write?

OH: I usually do a good amount of research to gather all the relevant information. The best resource is a good library. For the last piece that I wrote, about defensive architecture and public space, I started with my local library and then went to the Urban Design Library at the University of California at Berkeley, then to various local agencies like the Planning

Department and the Department of Public Works. I use the Internet a lot, but usually only for simple information, for example, to check a date—was a firm founded in the late forties or the early fifties? Did World War I end in 1919, 1920, or 1921?

* * *

CW: Did you start out writing critical essays, or did you come to this field from another area of writing?

OH: I started out writing skateboarding articles. I also write short stories. But my first analytical piece that was published was a review of a book of poetry for the now-defunct *San Francisco Review of Books*. I went to high school with the editor and years later ran into him and ended up discussing books with him all night. At the end of the night he suggested that I write something for the *Review*. Unfortunately, personal contacts are very important in getting work published.

* * *

CW: What would you say is the hardest thing about doing this kind of writing?

OH: Starting. I find that it's really difficult to convince myself to actually sit down and commit to getting an idea out. Getting it out can be wrenching. But once you've started, it's just a matter of refining what you already have. Once I have an idea down, I'm not very self-conscious about it, I just work with it to make it as tight as I can. But when I'm starting, I second-guess myself a lot. I never procrastinate so much as when I first have to articulate an idea.

But it's great when, after staring at something for so long without progressing, I have some flash of insight. It's definitely exciting. Sometimes, after banging my head for a long time, I suddenly come to understand my subject better or see a new angle on an old argument.

* * *

CW: Is there something you do to help these flashes along? To start the words and ideas flowing again?

OH: If I'm not just being lazy, if I've been giving the work all my attention and I determine that I'm having a legitimate block of some kind, I try not to beat myself up about it. I just get the idea out as best I can for the time being. Sometimes that means writing down a few key words or phrases, not even complete sentences. Once I have the idea written down, even if the expression isn't right, I can come back to it later with a fresh perspective. When I get blocked it's usually because I've been working on something for too long in one sitting: It's usually an indication that I need a break. So I go for a walk, make some dinner, have a beer, do whatever I feel like doing for a while and come back to the work when my head is a little more clear. You don't want to keep pushing yourself in that situation. Your judgment starts to get bad if you push yourself for too long and you don't allow yourself some breaks. If you push yourself too hard, you just have to come back later to clean up the mess you've made.

• • •

CW: Ocean, this seems like a particularly creative area of writing; it involves coming up with original ideas and arguments. How do you define creativity?

OH: People often talk about the creative act as coming up with something new, something that breaks out of a system. While the moment when you have some creative insight does feel liberating in a way, I think that the feeling is ultimately misleading. All genuinely creative acts are the products of a profound immersion in a system, not liberation from a system. Joyce, Woolf, and Faulkner developed the stream of consciousness narrative style only after they had mastered the naturalist narrative style. Coltrane could never have developed modal jazz if he hadn't already exhausted the possibilities of bebop, explored every microscopic niche in that system. So I don't think creativity is a product of "free thinking," I think it's the product of zealous diligence. Usually work that is the product of the "free thinking" approach to creativity is sloppy, cheap novelty. The moment of creativity is not a moment of liberation from a system, it is the moment of complete engagement with a system. Once you've internalized a system, then you're capable of creativity.

CHAPTER 9

Poetry

Many believe that poetry is the essence of language, and that all other forms of communication and expression are based on it. But what exactly is poetry? Is it a Shakespearean sonnet of iambic pentameter, Ogden Nash's light verse, or a Mother Goose nursery rhyme?

Defining Poetry

Poetry really does include structured poems, light verse, and nursery rhymes—and more. In fact, one of the most wonderful things about poetry is that it encompasses so many forms. Though many poems follow a traditional structure, experimentation and new forms are not only possible but encouraged. Just about any group of words that tells a story and is put together in lines can be considered a poem. As poet William Carlos Williams said, "[Y]ou can make a poem out of anything. You don't have to have conventionally poetic material."

SSENTIALS

"Poetry is life distilled."

—Gwendolyn Brooks, poet

"Poetry is the search for syllables to shoot at the barriers of the unknown and the unknowable."

—Carl Sandburg, poet

Children's poetry is poetry, too. To write poems for children, think back and remember what it's like to be a child. You need to see the world the way a child does. As in all writing for children, observe what they like to do, how they react to situations, what pleases them, and what they fear. Try to remember your own childhood and what was important to you. Use words suitable to the age group and remember that young children generally love the fun and surprise of rhyme.

The Basics

Though poetry is a diverse and liberating genre, and powerful, moving poetry is much more than just a group of words in lines. It is a celebration of language, a work of sounds, images, color, rhythm, and emotion that expresses a deeply felt experience or idea with the poet's unique voice and in words that he or she shapes to personal dictates. According to William Carlos Williams, "Anything that is felt, and that is felt deeply . . . is material for art. . . . It's what you do with it that counts."

While poetry is a completely personal expression, with varying forms and no required structure, it may help you in your writing to understand some of the traditional elements.

Line and Meter

Almost all of poetry is written in lines. A line can be a complete sentence, but it can also be part of a sentence, with the rest of the sentence on the following line or lines. In longer poems, lines are often combined into stanzas, two or more lines that work like a paragraph in a piece of prose. Each line is made up of feet, or rhythmical units, and each foot contains accented or unaccented syllables.

FACTS

The pattern of accented and unaccented syllables in a line is called the poem's meter. All the lines in a poem can follow the same meter or each can be different.

Frances Mayes, poet, creative writing teacher, and author of *Bella Tuscany*, believes that the two most useful meters in English are iambic pentameter and iambic tetrameter. A line of iambic pentameter contains five feet of an unaccented syllable followed by an accented syllable—as in C. Day Lewis's line: "the FLAGS,/the ROUND/aBOUTS,/the GA/la DAY."

Iambic tetrameter contains four feet of the same, illustrated in Lewis Carroll's line: "The SUN/was SHIN/ing ON/the SEA."

There are several other kinds of feet, however:

- *Trochaic* is a highly emphatic form, with an accented syllable followed by an unaccented syllable.
- *Dactylic* has one accented syllable followed by two unaccented syllables.
- *Anapestic* has two unaccented syllables followed by an accented syllable.
- *Spondaic* has an accent on every syllable.

A line generally contains between two and five feet.

Rhyme

When most people think of rhyme in a poem, they think of end rhyme, in which a word at the end of a line rhymes with a word at the end of another line. But there are many kinds of rhyme. True rhyme, or perfect rhyme, is a rhyme in which the last stressed vowel sound and everything following in the rhyming words are identical, for example, *shining* and *whining*. An internal rhyme is a rhyme in which the rhyming sounds are within the lines of a poem, rather than at the ends. For example: The sun shone *high* its brilliant *eye*. An off rhyme, or near rhyme or slant rhyme, is not a true rhyme, but words in which the final consonant sounds are alike and the words echo each other, for example, *cough* and *huff*.

FACTS

Many modern poems are lyric poems. A lyric poem was originally written to be sung accompanied by a lyre—the English word *lyrics,* the term for the words to a song, comes from this form.

There are also rhymes in which vowels are different and consonants are the same or echo, and rhymes that have similar vowel sounds but their consonants are different. Alliteration can also be thought of as rhyme (head rhyme), since it repeats sounds—consonants usually at the beginning of words or syllables, such as *she/shell/shed*. Rhyme can add a pleasurable, musical quality to poetry—much of poetry is written to be spoken aloud or sung—but not all poets use rhyme in their work.

Genres

There are three major types of poetry: descriptive or dramatic, narrative, and lyric. A descriptive poem focuses on details that depict a scene, a sound, a person, or a feeling in a very immediate way. Often a character will speak lines to dramatize the telling. A narrative poem, such as Longfellow's "Paul Revere's Ride," tells a story or part of one. A lyric poem is any poem that expresses personal feelings and thoughts, and is often written in the first person.

Forms

While poetry can take any form that pleases the poet's eyes and ears, many poems fall into one of the metered measures mentioned previously. However, others follow a form all their own. Here are some recognized formats:

- **Blank verse:** Unrhymed lines of consistent length and meter, often in iambic pentameter.
- **Concrete poetry:** Also called shaped poetry, in which the typography and layout of the words contribute to the poem's meaning; for example, a poem about a bird in flight might have the words placed on the page so that they are in the shape of a bird.
- **Haiku:** A centuries-old, extremely brief Japanese verse form that evokes a mood and often refers to a season or nature; haikus consist of seventeen syllables in three lines—five syllables in the first and third lines, and seven in the second.
- **Epic:** A long narrative poem about a cultural hero.
- **Found poetry:** A sequence of words not originally intended as poetry; found poetry is generally extracted from prose because it contains rhythms or sounds or images that can be expressed as poetry.
- **Limerick:** A five-line poem in which lines one, two, and five rhyme and lines three and four rhyme; most are meant to be humorous. "There Once Was a Man from Nantucket . . ." is a well-known limerick.
- **Prose poem:** A short, often intense piece of writing that is generally structured like a paragraph of prose but uses such poetic devices as repetition and meter.
- **Free verse:** A poem with no pattern of rhyme or line length.
- **Sonnet:** Fourteen lines of iambic pentameter incorporating a rhyme pattern.

Words and Images

Engaging poems are composed of language that is fresh, colorful, sensory, emotional, and meaningful. The words come from the author's understanding and perception and create a mood or feeling that conveys his or her thoughts. That means that the words of a poem must be chosen carefully to produce the image the poet intends. The poet must also arrange the words in a way that both pleases his or her sensibility and provides meaning to the reader or listener.

> "Let's say I want to write a poem in which I describe what it's like when my husband is out of the house and I'm oaming around the apartment without him, enjoying myself. I can sit here and describe that to you in a conversation. But to take something very natural and reconstruct it in a poem, and maybe find a rhyme in it, and words that connect below the surface, and still have it come out sounding as natural as the experience, almost as natural as [a] conversation—there's the struggle."
>
> —Deborah Garrison, poet

While clarity is important, poets often choose particular words for their sound or tone or because they hint at a meaning rather than place it directly in the reader's lap. They also use words to surprise, to entice, or to suit the subject matter or the mood they're working to convey. A poem about a visit to your late grandmother's home might use Victorian language and a stately rhythm. One about street life might include colorful, vibrant words and mix bursts of speed with a slower pace.

Flowery, excessive language isn't always necessary to convey beautiful or compelling images. A poem is usually stronger if it is more sparsely worded and includes only those words that best express the writer's message.

To enrich their poems' meaning, poets often construct word images. These can convey a visual impression, or one of sound, smell, taste, or feel. Images can provide the way for a reader to experience what the author experienced, or evoke a mood that deepens the reader's understanding of the poem. When creating images, poets write from their emotions and feelings and focus on the details that will best illustrate what they wish to express.

Figures of Speech and Figurative Language

When creating images to deepen the reader's understanding of a thought or an idea, poets often use figures of speech and other figurative language. A line in a William Blake poem deepens the reader's understanding by using a simile: "The moon like a flower . . ." Another line in the same poem provides additional insight and pleasure with personification: the moon "With silent delight / Sits and smiles on the night."

Similes, metaphors, and personification enable poets to make what author Frances Mayes calls "figurative images," which surprise, expand the reader's understanding, draw attention to the message, increase reading pleasure, and add dimension by making associations that wouldn't immediately have come to mind. By creating such images, poets establish a new medium of exchange between the writer and the reader.

When crafting an image, the poet, in the words of poet Florence Trefethen, details "something in the external world that the senses can apprehend that is the equivalent of an intangible mood or feeling." To do this, there are a variety of image makers to work with:

- **Alliteration:** The repetition of consonants, particularly at the beginning of words. For example, the letter *s* is alliterated in the following line: "He summoned the sweetness of silence."
- **Allusion:** A reference to or the mention of something from history, the arts, nature, current society, and so on that the reader has knowledge of and that will help the reader better understand the poet's meaning. For example, "like Juliet she waited" is an allusion to a character from Shakespeare's *Romeo and Juliet.*
- **Metaphor:** A direct comparison between two things. For example, "my mind is a clock clicking down the day."
- **Onomatopoeia:** Using words that imitate sounds. For example, *mew* sounds like a cat mewing, and *snicker* sounds like snickering.
- **Personification:** Giving human qualities to inanimate objects. For example, "the sun sprang orange into the lifting haze."
- **Simile:** An indirect comparison of one thing to another using the words *like* or *as.* For example, "his voice roiled like a storming sea, pulling me beneath it."

For more on figures of speech and other rhetorical devices, see Chapter 17.

Putting Words on the Page

That blank page or screen can be intimidating. How do you get started? What are you going to write about? Poet Wallace Stevens said that poetry emerges from a "transaction between reality and the sensibility of the poet." But how do you begin that transaction?

The Idea

Keep an image journal. Write down bits of conversation you hear, advertising copy, lines from letters or books or plays, words you come across in the dictionary, quotes, cartoons, recipe ingredients—any words that carry particular meaning or emotion for you. You may also want to make drawings. These can be of images from dreams or something you observe, or drawings that illustrate words or that convey a particular mood or feeling you experience. Then, when you sit down to write, you'll have a treasure trove of idea starters, and perhaps some of those just-right words you're looking for.

Some writers have the germ of an idea, something that resulted from an observation or a particular event or a memory, a dream, or an emotion. Others begin by choosing a form. Still others have a complete line or a sequence of words in their head that sets them writing. Whatever brings you to the page (see Chapter 10 for more on getting ideas), concentrate on it and go with it. Write down everything you can think of that relates or that comes to mind, even if it doesn't seem particularly good or useful or expressive. You may gets bits and pieces that you like and ideas for revising at the same time. Put it all down. Think about specific words. Take inspiration from other poets or favorite stories. Let your subject guide you as you look for evocative language and the right rhythm. Remember that your words should convey not just your message but the feeling behind them. Try not to censor yourself; write freely and honestly. This is *your* poem.

FACTS

Revise, Revise, Revise

When you've gotten a good deal down, start to revise. (You may want to let the first draft sit for a bit before you do, to approach it freshly.) As you revise, keep in mind the feeling or the circumstance that triggered the poem in the first place. Look for clichés or overly flowery or excessive language. Check that your figures of speech not only make sense but truly express your feelings. Does the poem still interest you? Do you still feel deeply about the subject? Would a different format, a prose poem or free verse, for instance, suit the poem better? Are the words vivid and layered but not obscure? Reading the poem aloud will help you hear the rhythm and the flow and point out where further revision is needed.

Robert Pinsky, the thirty-ninth Poet Laureate of the United States, believes that poetry is a vocal art. "If a poem is written well," he says, "it was written with the poet's voice and for a voice. Reading a poem silently instead of saying a poem is like the difference between staring at sheet music and actually humming or playing the music on an instrument."

Name Your Poem

If you haven't named your poem yet, think about doing it now. This can be surprisingly hard. Since it's the first thing readers see or hear, it can make them curious or make them shrug. Some titles directly state what the poem is about—like Frank O'Hara's "Why I Am Not a Painter." Others give more of a sense or feeling than an explicit statement—like Robert Frost's "Design" or William Bronk's "Where It Ends." Still others name someone or something that the poem addresses—for example, Denise

Levertov's "To the Snake." Titles can also be taken from the first line of the poem, and some poems go unnamed. If you feel that a strong title will enrich your poem, create one that relates to the poem in some way, either through words or images, or pick one that would intrigue your audience.

The Last Two Steps

Read your poem aloud again, and have others read it. Listen to the musical quality as you read—does the poem "sing" for you? Do the words move at the pace and with the tone you had in mind? Does a word stop you? Is the poem stronger in some parts than others? Ask someone who enjoys poetry and will treat your work seriously and respectfully to read the poem, too. You needn't revise based on his or her criticism, but another opinion or interpretation will add to your understanding of the work you created.

Poetry Pointers

Here are some poetry pointers that should get you ready to write:

- Write about something that is very important to you.
- Aim for a fresh, new approach. Even if your subject has been the focus of many poems, you can infuse it with interest by being original.
- Experiment with form, line length, and punctuation—you have "poetic license" to break the rules.
- Construct images that appeal to the senses as well as convey meaning.
- Watch out for clichés and too much sentimentality.
- Revise and revise and revise until you have just the right words in just the right order.
- Read your poems aloud—you'll hear the music or the remaining problems.

"In a poem the words should be as pleasing to the ear
as the meaning is to the mind."
—Marianne Moore, poet

Interview with Poet Louis Phillips

Louis Phillips is a widely published poet, playwright, and short-story author who teaches creative writing at the School of Visual Arts in New York City. Louis has published several books of poems, including *The Krazy Kat Rag; Bulkington; The Time, The House, The Solitariness of the Place; Celebrations and Bewilderments; In the Field of Broken Hearts;* and *Into the Well of Knowingness.*

CW: What is it that you love most about writing?

LP: There have been writers who complain both loudly and softly about how painful it is to write. I say if writing make you unhappy or puts you in deep misery, don't do it. Life is short and filled to the brim with all kinds of other pains. I enjoy writing. I enjoy sitting at my desk and making up stories, poems, plays, humor pieces, or, as the kids today say—whatever! I think writing is one of the best things you can do in life. You don't have to dress up. You make your own hours. You don't have to please anybody but yourself. Of course, you have to be awfully lucky to be able to carve out the time and lifestyle to do it. That's the tricky part. You have to have a vision of who you are and what you want to be and fight for it.

•　•　•

CW: Louis, what do you do if the right words just won't come to you?

LP: Switch gears and write something else. Go to the movies. Or go to bed and let my dreams bring a solution. For this last technique to work, you have to be on good terms with your Muse. Court her wisely.

When you get bogged down or blocked, you should also go back to the source of what inspired you to write the piece in the first place. Go back to the beginning. You can never really repair a story, poem, or play by tinkering with it. When the story goes wrong, you have to start again at the source.

•　•　•

CW: Do you have any special writing tips that you can share?

LP: There is no secret to writing. You write. Rewrite. And work hard. If I had the secret, I would be a millionaire many times over, selling it to people who want to learn how to write.

That said, I do have a few suggestions:

1. Be thankful that you can express your thoughts and feelings in language. There are many people who—because of physical or economic disadvantages—cannot.
2. Read dictionaries. Be curious about the language.
3. Keep a notebook. Write down ideas when they come to you. Copy out in longhand passages of writing that appeal to you. You will be surprised how much you can learn by writing out good poems or good examples of prose.
4. Don't take rejection slips seriously.
5. Remember that the major difference between you and Random House is hundreds of millions of dollars. If you had $100,000,000, writers would send manuscripts to you and ask you to publish them.
6. Be generous to other writers. Writing is not a competitive sport. It is an art and a craft. It is wonderful to share our thoughts and feelings with other human beings. In fact, sometimes we don't even know what we're feeling or thinking until we express our thoughts and feelings.
7. Don't take yourself too seriously. In the long run, we are merely specks in a vast cosmos.
8. Since no one is going to pay you a lot of money for a poem, you might as well write it the way you want to write it.
9. Read, read, read.
10. Do it. Just do it. Even do it in the road. What's the worst thing that can happen? Someone might not like what you write. So what?

•　•　•

CW: All great advice. Have other writers given you special tips?
LP: The best piece of advice I ever had came to me via the novelist Nelson Algren: Never eat at a place called Mom's. Never play cards with a man called Doc. Never sleep with a woman who's got troubles worse than your own.

CHAPTER 10
Getting Ideas

Every piece of writing begins with the generation of an exciting idea— it's what sends you racing to your desk and sets your fingers racing across the keyboard. So what is your idea going to be? What story will you tell?

Ideas Are Everywhere

Story ideas are everywhere, but you need to find one that truly interests you and that's worth writing about. If you don't already have an idea that you want to run with, this section provides numerous ways to help you uncover a compelling idea that you can shape into an engaging story. And guess what? Coming up with that idea is probably not as hard as you think. And guess what else? The best ideas are often the simplest.

ESSENTIALS

Ideas can be found in memories, observations, experiences, encounters, conversations, activities, sensory details, moods and emotions, books and other media, objects, scenery, relationships, weather, fantasy, history—just about everything.

There is no right or wrong way to look for an idea. Different authors use different methods, some spontaneous, some very methodical. There are probably as many approaches as there are creative writers. There are also many, many sources. Be open to everything. Don't disregard anything. You'll discover what works best for you by trying lots of approaches and investigating many different possibilities. And you'll probably discover that you come up with so many good ideas that you have dozens to choose from, and dozens to store away for future projects.

Where to Look

Some authors will tell you: "Write about what you know." Others say: "Write about what you don't know"—sticking to what you know can be limiting and keeps you from learning. Whether you choose to search for your work's foundation in familiar terrain or decide to walk on unknown ground, there are plenty of sources that can stimulate your imagination and start you on the road to that great idea.

Notebook or Image Journal

Way back in Chapter 1 we talked about the need to keep a notebook or journal within reach at all times, to record thoughts, ideas, words or phrases, bits of conversation, impressions, illustrations, feelings, dreams, colors, inspirations—anything that strikes you as interesting or important as you go about your day. So, of course, you've been jotting things down for a while now, and have pages of ideas and starting points to work from. Right? I'm pretty sure you just answered yes, but if you didn't, never fear. You can start keeping a journal or notebook now. As you read, work, converse, relax, study, eat, and write, stay open to possible story starters. Fill your notebook with anything that seems noteworthy. As you add to your stash, you may want to say exactly what about the entry seems important to you and where you were and what you were doing when you noticed or thought about it.

The Media

Magazines, newspapers, radio, TV, letters to the editor, and movies—these sources are gifts. Other writers are out there providing you with all sorts of material that you can use to inspire ideas.

As you already know, reading extensively can teach you a great deal about writing: structure, dialogue, character, plot. It can also give you the seeds for stories, which you then develop according to your own imagination. So read widely. Don't just look at the front page of the paper for dramatic ideas. Look at the business section—the stock market could be an exciting focus to wrap a story around. Look at what the different columnists have to say—a humorous piece could remind you of a crazy situation you experienced, which could be the starting point for a collection of anecdotes. Read the editorial page, the travel section, even the comics. The sports page, the pet page, *every* page is a possible treasure trove of great ideas. Ditto for magazines, TV and radio shows, plays, improvisational games, and movies. A photograph, a quote, a piece of dialogue, a funny phrase, a character's mannerism or an emotion he's experiencing, an announcer's accent, a sound or color could click with your imagination and turn magically into a story idea.

Artistic Sources

Artistic sources include photographs, family albums, home movies, book and magazine illustrations, sculpture, and paintings. Pictures can inspire well more than a thousand words. Often, looking at something beautiful or unusual or colorful or even frightening or ugly can result in another picture or idea appearing in your mind. Again, as with media sources, be open to everything: colors, textures, moods, emotions, memories, associations, settings, sensations.

Daily Life

You may think that going to the grocery story or working in a bank doesn't lend itself to exciting ideas. But that needn't be the case. If you set your creative switch to "on," you'll be surprised at the possibilities. Working in a bank could be the source of a great nonfiction book for children—what happens to your money when you put it in the bank? Or a trip to the supermarket with kids in tow could lead to a magazine article entitled "Ten Secrets to Shopping with Children: Or How Not to Commit Murder in Front of the Mushrooms." Overhearing a conversation between an elderly man and a post office clerk (yes, you are encouraged to eavesdrop shamelessly) might offer up the name of a small town that makes you suddenly think of a story you want to set there. Think about the places and the people you interact with on a regular basis. If you take a look at ordinary events with an eye out for stories, you'll see everyday life in a whole new light.

Music

Song lyrics, from Gershwin to McCartney to Tom Waits, can be the inspiration for novel ideas. And not only can the words stir associations, memories, and emotions, but the music itself can put you in a receptive, creative mood. If you usually listen to country, try opera or rock. Listen to your kids' music or your parents'. Expand your world and your imagination at the same time. Even listening to songs sung in a foreign language can help you conjure up scenarios to go along with them.

Conversations

Keep an ear out for the way people speak. If you catch the sound of a southern accent, it may put you in mind of a story that could take place only in the South. Think about some of the more interesting conversations you have each day. That discussion about revising a software manual? Perhaps you can develop an idea about a programmer who comes up with a computer language through which he can control the work of the Pentagon. Strike up conversations with fellow sufferers waiting in line at the bank. Eavesdrop. Make a point of saying "hello" and "how's it going?" to your children's friends. By speaking to—and, yes, listening in on—as many different people as you can, you may be rewarded with a word or a thought that will set your story in motion.

Dreams

No one seems to know exactly what dreams are, but one thing we do know is that they're fertile fields for ideas. What was that bit about flying from your house to your ex-boyfriend's old school? It could be the makings of an idea for a story about old loves. Or it might be the impetus for a children's book about birds.

ESSENTIALS

Write down your dreams as soon as you wake up (your journal and a pen are, of course, right by your bed). When you think about your dreams later, you may find an interesting idea beckoning.

Old Records

Diaries, family histories, birth announcements. Dusty old files are definitely worth cleaning off. Inside could be some amazing information, from pictures of never-before-seen relations to correspondence that details how things were done decades ago to a pressed flower from a long-ago dance. All can carry your thoughts to new places where exciting ideas may develop. Or, take a trip to your local library to browse through old newspapers and magazines. Who knows, you might breathe life into a long-forgotten story or event.

Beautiful/Horrible/Unusual Settings

Your imagination can be set on fire when your eyes take in a variety of sights. Sit beside a fountain. Look at a burned-out building or forested area. Go to the park or a lake, watch an old house being bulldozed, look at photos of favorite vacations or landscape paintings, take a trip to a botanical garden. Try to observe as many and as varied outdoor settings as you can. Look not only at colors and textures but think about how the setting makes you feel. Peaceful? Dreamy? Aristocratic? Horrified? Sink into the feelings, and see if one of them helps you formulate an idea.

Here are twelve easy-to-get-to spots for idea gathering:

- The coffee shop
- The airport
- Your family room
- The elevator
- A hotel lobby
- The laundromat
- A quiet garden
- The car pool
- The diner
- The park
- A hospital
- A cemetery

Favorite Objects

Spend some time with some of your favorite things. Sitting in your beautifully crafted Shaker rocking chair may cause you to think about how furniture is made, which may make you think about what sort of person made your chair, which may make you think of a story about a troubled teenager who turns his life around by meeting an older woman who handcrafts beautiful chairs. Let your imagination loose as you observe or touch treasured objects.

Favorite Books

Go back and reread some of your all-time favorites—not to steal the plot or make off with a character, but to reconnect with the story's essence and remember what made it so appealing to you. Was it the setting? The time period? Because it reflected a personal experience? Get caught up again in what made those books so special, and think about related stories that might make you feel the same way. You can also make note of special passages or inspiring thoughts in a book you're currently reading.

How to Generate Ideas

Powerful story ideas are waiting to be created. Try some of these helpful techniques to bring them into being. Just remember—be open to everything, and write it all down, no matter how crazy it may seem. It may take a little while, but an engaging idea will come.

You can make characters believable by giving them attributes that real people have: emotions, dreams, goals, habits, skills, flaws, problems, physical characteristics, style, loves and hates, ambitions, secrets, fears, and values.

Play "What if. . . ." What if that woman walking down the street walked right into a bank and held it up? What if a dog could use a computer? What if your friend hadn't gone on that blind date and met the man she ended up marrying? What if the Civil War had been won by the South? Choose several different situations and suppose what might happen.

Play "I wonder. . . ." I wonder if that kid just did something he shouldn't have because his mom is practically dragging him out of the store. I wonder why penguins can't fly. I wonder why that man keeps tugging at his ear. I wonder how animals sense earthquakes before they happen. Let your mind roam freely and come up with possible answers.

Brainstorm with other people. Ask friends and relatives to tell you about memorable experiences. Ask other creative people how they come up with ideas.

Eavesdrop (surreptitiously). Experiences and opinions you overhear people sharing as they go about their daily lives can become the basis of believable stories.

Recast favorite stories in a different genre. Turn a memorable mystery into a fantasy. Turn a fairy tale into a modern-day children's story.

Use a favorite story as a model. Use the story's structure, but change the characters and the setting. Or tell the same story through a different character's point of view.

Let your mind wander. Sit in a comfortable chair, close your eyes, and see what happens. Let your thoughts follow any direction they want to go in. If you hear a sound, concentrate on it. If you get a picture in your mind, notice what's happening.

People-watch. The way a couple hold hands and whisper intimately may set you thinking about an idea for a love story. A tattooed muscle man may set off bells for a crime caper. The emotion you feel when a teenager walks by pushing a baby in a stroller may put you in touch with a character for a young adult novel. Watch not only for how people look but how they hold themselves, interact, the kinds of work they do, how they speak, the time of day they're out and about.

FACTS

"It's easier to write about those you hate."

—Dorothy Parker, critic

"And because I found I had nothing else to write about, I presented myself as a subject."

—Michel Montaigne, essayist

Idea Exercises

To practice, try some of these writing exercises:

1. Make three lists: one of character types, one of conflicts, and one of settings. Combine the different possibilities until one of them strikes a chord.

2. Make two other lists: one of things you love, and one of things you hate. Create a story in which one character loves one of the things you love and another character loves one of the things you hate. (Remember, conflict is at the heart of all stories.)

3. Create some character sketches to see if inventive characters might help you determine a plot:
   a. Write a character bio using one quality from each of three friends.
   b. Think of a memorable movie character and base a new character on him or her.
   c. Choose a dramatic story from the newspaper and develop a character sketch based on the information.
   d. Choose a memorable book hero and make him younger or older.
   e. Create a character description of someone you'd like to know.
   f. Choose someone you know well and change three things about him or her.

4. Write down ten words that come to mind and combine them into a story synopsis.

5. Think about a place you'd like to visit and develop a story that would be perfect to set there.

6. Describe in a paragraph something you love. Then come up with a story about that thing being stolen.

7. Think of a strong emotion. Then think of five scenarios in which that emotion could be involved.

8. Play with word associations. Write down a good number of words and then write what each immediately makes you think of.

9. Animate an object. Have a toy describe what it's like to play with a child.

10. Think about a decision you made recently. Write about why you made it. Create a scenario of what could have happened if you'd made a different decision.

11. Take the first line from a favorite book and base a new story on it.

12. Freewrite. Even if you have no idea what you'd like to write about, start writing anyway. See what appears on the page. One word or phrase may suggest an idea.

Choosing the Best Idea

Once you've tried some of the approaches suggested above, you'll probably be surprised at how many good possibilities you came up with. Now, to choose one to run with.

Before you begin the decision process, let your ideas sit in your notebook or a file folder for a while. You probably won't be able to keep yourself from mulling them over at least a bit, but try to take a break from concentrating on them so you can come back to them fresh. When you're ready, give each one a good look.

Pick What's Interesting

The first criterion is, does the idea really capture your imagination? Does it stir your emotions? Is it something you know you can enjoyably spend a good deal of time working on? Is it something worth writing about? Writers need to be passionate about their subjects, or it's likely the writing will reflect the lack of interest. If an idea doesn't grab you, you probably should put it aside. Or if something about an idea intrigues you though it doesn't excite you, give it some more thought, and try to come up with a slightly different take. It's the idea that you keep thinking about, and that doesn't let you go, that's probably a good bet.

 **SSENTIALS**

"Choice of subject is of cardinal importance. One does by far one's best work when besotted by and absorbed in the matter at hand."

—Jessica Mitford, novelist

Pay Attention to Scope

Second, will the idea generate a work of a reasonable size? Is the subject so broad that you'll need to write a three-volume set to cover it all? That may be taking on too much, and you'll probably want to revise the idea to narrow the focus. On the flip side, is it too narrow? Is it a compelling idea, but will you be able to put enough meat on its bones?

Putting together a very rough outline or synopsis will help you determine this.

To see if your idea will support a good-sized story, try outlining it with cards. Screenwriters and children's book authors do this, but it's a good technique for any genre. Note each key scene on a card and pin up the cards. Too much for one work? Too little?

Consider Your Audience

A third point to consider is if the idea involves a topic that a lot of people would be interested in reading about. If you're writing for yourself, any topic that interests you is a good choice. But if you're writing with the goal of being published, you will probably want to think about ideas that will appeal to a broad spectrum of people.

Keep in mind that if your idea is one that's often the focus of articles or novels or memoirs, it may be very difficult to set it in a new light or distinguish it from other stories like it.

Check the Emotional Factor

Is your idea dramatic? Do you see ways to make it compelling? If you're planning to write a piece of fiction, can you envision engaging characters? Is there an issue to be developed—a conflict around which the story will advance? Stories need drama and tension to keep readers turning the page. Be sure your idea is filled with possibilities for drawing in an audience.

Run with It

When you've weeded out the not-quite-ready-for-prime-time ideas, sum up and write down in a sentence or two the idea you've chosen. Check it for appeal, conflict, focus, and freshness. If it makes the grade, and sets your mind racing, you've probably got a winner. But don't throw away any worthy contestants. Store them away for possible future use.

How They Do It

So where do successful writers get their ideas? Here are some anecdotes that you might find interesting—as well as inspiring.

Author Peter Mayle was in France with friends who took him to a church service where mass was being celebrated in honor of . . . the truffle. Worshippers asked the patron saint of truffles to help them produce a bumper crop, and put truffles in a donation plate to be auctioned off to raise money. The bizarre experience made Mayle wonder if there were other unusual French gastronomical celebrations and festivals. After numerous discoveries, he wrote a book about them called *French Lessons*.

"My keyboard wasn't working quite right and I don't know quite what the problem was. But I thought, 'You know, it's almost as if somebody is in my computer and looking at all my files right now.' And I thought, 'That's quite a scary proposition.' I'm always looking for scenarios that will engage readers as emotionally as possible."
    —Jeffrey Deaver, best-selling crime thriller author

Shay Youngblood, author of *Black Girl in Paris,* loves to cook; took opera-singing lessons; has been an au pair, an archivist, and a model; has worked in a library; has delivered phone books; and has cleaned houses—and drew on all of these jobs and experiences to create her book's heroine, Eden.

When she sits down to begin the next book in her "alphabet" mystery series, writer Sue Grafton concentrates on her heroine, private investigator Kinsey Millhone. Grafton always begins by asking herself two questions: "Who hires Kinsey?" and "What is she hired to do?"

For George Saunders, creative-writing instructor and author of *CivilWarLand in Bad Decline,* inspiration comes from language. Saunders says he needs one good sentence or idea "and then you just stick with the texture of the prose and say I like the way that sounds."

British author P. D. James, creator of the Commander Adam Dalgliesh detective series, starts to develop her bestselling murder mysteries with a location in mind: "For me, it's always the setting," James states. Her best-seller *Death in Holy Orders* is set in a sinister Victorian theological college on the windswept coast of England.

Aaron Sorkin, award-winning writer of the TV series *The West Wing,* wrote most of the screenplay for the movie *A Few Good Men* on cocktail napkins. The script was loosely based on a case that involved his attorney sister.

 SSENTIALS

"You can't say to yourself, 'I think I will have a great idea at 3:47 this afternoon' and then make an appointment with your head. As soon as something floats into consciousness, you've got to grab it."
—Steve Allen, author and comedian

Several of the Beatles' songs, including "A Day in the Life" and "She's Leaving Home," were inspired by items in newspapers and magazines. Others, including "Getting Better," came from what was happening around the musicians. When they asked a friend how he was getting on, he always replied, "It's getting better."

CHAPTER 11
Planning

Now that you've got a solid idea, you probably want to sit right down and start writing. But don't hit the keys yet. Before you begin composing, there are a number of questions you need to answer and a number of steps you need to take.

Developing Your Idea

You've got to take your raw idea and develop it—you've got to let your creativity get to work. Is your idea going to be the basis for a short story or a novel? A children's book? Perhaps a poem? Who is the intended audience? Will it be told in the first person? Is the story one in which you'll be putting forward a personal message, or will you be relating facts and statistics in a neutral voice? Answering these and other questions will get you ready for writing.

FACTS

"Finding the right form for your story is simply to realize the most natural way of telling the story. The test of whether or not a writer has divined the natural shape of his story is just this: after reading it, can you imagine it differently, or does it silence your imagination and seem to you absolute and final?"

—Truman Capote, short-story writer and novelist

Purpose

A piece of writing can have several goals, but it's a good idea to have one in mind when you're writing. Your goal may be to teach a skill, share an important experience, explore a specific topic or relationship, write a bedtime story that will soothe a restless child, argue a point, critique the plot of a movie, thank a policeman for helping you in a crisis, or any other particular purpose. It's a good idea to write your purpose down and pin it up as a reminder to stay on track.

Scope

In Chapter 10 you were advised to size up your idea—is it big enough? Too big? At this point you can think about it in more detail. For example, you may have refined your idea from covering all of a famous local politician's life to just the years that she's been in office, but as you shape your idea now, you may want to narrow it even further. Instead of undertaking a book, you may want to start exploring the topic with an article about just one of the many ways in which the politician improved life in your community. If the article turns out well, you can expand on it with another article or perhaps a book at that point. Or you may decide that you're ready now to undertake a big project, and that concentrating on the politician's entire term in office is the best approach. Try to suit the breadth of the project to both the material and to your time and interest.

Format

You may have gone into a project with the idea of writing in a particular genre, for example, a poem or a play. But thinking about format now may produce a different approach. A crazy time from your teen years might be the basis of an exciting memoir, as you originally thought, but it could also be the topic of a very funny poem.

You may even want to use the same idea as the foundation of two different pieces. Think about how your idea might work with several different formats. You can always change your mind after you start writing.

Audience

Who you're writing for can affect the words you use. For example, if you're writing a nonfiction book for toddlers, you'll need to know and use vocabulary and concepts they can understand. Likewise, if you're submitting an article to a niche magazine, you'll want to slant your wording toward that audience; for example, use certain food terms for a cooking-light magazine's readers. You should also keep in mind what kind of background information your audience might need in order to understand your point. For instance, if you're writing a book for beginning gardeners, you need to explain terms that experienced gardeners would probably know but beginning gardeners might not. Books for beginning readers will need shorter sentences. Books for teens should incorporate language and information they can relate to.

Characters

If you are writing fiction, you should also start thinking about your characters. Creating well-written, believable, and interesting characters can make all the difference. The characters' story will evoke interest, create suspense, and draw the readers into the plot.

> "If your writing is unfocused, your reader may be out of focus too. When you can't see the target, you don't know where to aim. . . . Clarifying your audience will clarify your thinking and your writing."
> —Patricia T. O'Connor, author of *Words Fail Me*

Make Your Characters Real

As you create your fictional population, remember that the best way to help readers get to know them is through their personality and behavior rather than their physicality. You will probably want to include some kind of physical description—hair and eye color, body type—when it comes time to set your people down on paper. But what will really bring your characters to life will be what they're like: how they talk, how they interact with others, what they think about, what their tastes are, what their fears are, their favorite things, their weaknesses, the way they react emotionally. These are the things that will make them seem real and be fascinating to read about.

A Character Is Born

Here is an example of how I found my protagonist for a short story I was writing years ago. I knew I wanted to write about the difficulties of adolescence, and immediately saw a teenage girl named Kate. I somehow knew that Kate's best friend had moved away just days before Kate was to start high school. I didn't have a friend named Kate when I was fourteen, but I had experienced the strong emotions of the age and had always liked the name *Kate* for its spunkiness and strength. Kate grew into a character who had many of the interests, qualities, and fears that my friends and I had when we faced our very first day of high school.

If they don't appear out of the blue, characters can be created from your past, your present, your likes and dislikes, your fears, your job, newspaper accounts, your friends, your family, just about anyone or anything. A character could have your husband's way of lining up the dishes by size before washing them. Another character could have your mother-in-law's arrogant demeanor. Your good friend's love of bubble gum–flavored ice cream could be another character's dietary downfall. Let your mind range freely as you create and develop characters.

Character Explorations

Fictional characters can also be compiled by focusing on people outside your usual turf. One of my favorite pastimes is people watching; observing people going by can be a great way to develop ideas for characters. When you see someone who intrigues you, try giving this person an identity. What's this guy's name? Where was he born? Does he speak with an accent? Has something just happened to make him smile that way? Does he keep adjusting his tie because he's nervous? Does he always wear dark-colored clothes? Is he meeting someone he hasn't seen in a long time? Does he walk so gracefully because he's an athlete? Do you think you would like him as a friend? Imagining personalities and traits by playing "I wonder . . ." and "What if . . ." while studying passersby; you could even have imaginary conversations with them—it's a great way to develop intriguing characters.

QUESTIONS?

Where do characters come from?
According to Alice Walker, author of *The Color Purple* and other novels and short stories, "If you're silent for a long time, people just arrive in your mind."

One caveat: If you base characters directly on friends or family members, you will probably want to change something about them to distinguish them from the real, live people. Those in your immediate circle might be very defensive and unhappy if they recognize themselves in your pages—especially if you show them in an unflattering light.

Show, Don't Tell

To clue readers in on what your characters are like, try to show them rather than tell the reader about them. Telling can be boring and doesn't give readers a chance to connect their own feelings and thoughts to your words. If you write, "Mark really liked to ride his motorcycle," you're just giving basic information. If you write, "Mark smiled as he walked up to the Harley, his long day in front of the computer disappearing with every step," you let readers associate their own experiences with Mark's love of adventure. You also give them much greater reading pleasure. Details that relate not just to sight but to smells and sounds as well—the irritating timbre of a character's voice, the pleasantly sweaty smell of a sleeping child, the stale breath of a cornered killer—add another layer of depth to your creations.

EFFECTIVE AND NOT-SO-EFFECTIVE CHARACTERIZATION

An Example of Effective Characterization
It took Anthony forever to come to grips with what he was going to wear. The brown suit was too conservative. He wanted to look a little more casual, maybe even a little hip. Not the green sweater either. Frankie always told him he looked like a lizard when he wore it. The tan jacket. It would have to do. He slipped it on and tried to force down the twist of hair that always went its own way. Giving up, he grabbed the card with Jenna's address on it and, with a smile beginning to surface, rushed out the door.

An Example of Less-Than-Effective Characterization
Anthony spent a lot of time deciding which clothes to wear. He could wear the brown suit, the green sweater, or the tan jacket. He chose the tan jacket. After he put it on, he tried to comb his hair, but it wouldn't lay flat. Sighing, he picked up the business card with Jenna's name on it. As he left the house he smiled because he was looking forward to seeing her.

A Final Caveat

As you show your readers who and what your characters are, work hard to avoid stereotypes: the tough cop, the timid secretary, the arrogant doctor, the prostitute with a heart of gold. These characters are more like caricatures, and readers won't believe them. Plus, by offering up stereotyped figures you run the risk of offending your audience. Be particularly aware of age, sex, cultural, and ethnicity issues.

Conflict

Characters travel down the road projected by the plot—a string of events that takes them from the beginning of the story to the end. Like road builders, authors connect section after section of their concept so that characters can travel along them to reach their destination. But usually that traveling doesn't go smoothly: conflicts—head-on collisions of events—often beset and besiege the protagonist. These conflicts can be internal, within the main character; or external, conflicts the main character has with another person, an animal, an object, a force (like the force of time), the government, or nature.

When adding conflict to your story, don't overload characters with too many quirks or problems. You don't want to add so many conflicts that readers—and characters—can't catch their breath.

In Emily Brontë's *Wuthering Heights*, Heathcliff is continually at war with his feelings—with his love for Catherine and his jealousy of those she gives her heart to. In L. Frank Baum's *The Wizard of Oz*, the trigger event is a tornado that takes Dorothy far from her home and leaves her to face a tin man, a witch, a wizard, and a lion as she attempts to return home.

Conflict is the basis of the drama of a story, and what pulls readers in emotionally and gets them to turn the page. A well-paced and well-developed plot should contain enough times of conflict to produce tension and emotion in a continual escalation, but also times of calm when things go more smoothly.

Here is a simple plot, provided by Gary Provost, teacher and author, in *How to Tell a Story:*

> Once upon a time, something happened to someone, and he decided that he would pursue a goal. So he devised a plan of action, and even though there were forces trying to stop him he moved forward because there was a lot at stake. And just as things seemed as bad as they could get, he learned an important lesson, and when offered the prize he had sought so strenuously, he had to decide whether or not to take it, and in making that decision he satisfied a need that had been created by something in his past.

Point of View

Author and poet Frances Mayes believes that "Apart from the use of significant detail, there is no more important skill for a writer of fiction to grasp than . . . the control of point of view."

Any story that's told is told from a particular perspective. While you're planning and shaping your story, that perspective may be obvious—if you're going to create a memoir, you'll be writing the story from your own point of view. But some ideas present a question: Who is going to be telling this story? If there are three main characters involved, which of them will be providing the information? Will all three take turns? Or will an external narrator speak to the reader? Who tells the story and how it is told have a major effect on the tone of a story and greatly affect its meaning. Since readers can receive information from only one viewpoint at a time in order to understand the situation and identify the characters, you need to decide which point of view will work best with your story and intended audience.

There are three main points of view to choose from:

First person. The first-person point of view is used when an external narrator or a character in the story tells it. This viewpoint incorporates the words *I, me, my, mine, we, us,* and *our* and provides information that only the narrator or the particular character would reasonably have. Telling the story from a personal point of view, the narrator or character can observe all the action and tell readers about his or her reactions and feelings.

Second person. This point of view uses the words *you* and *your* to tell the story. With the second person, the reader is actually addressed and involved in the action: "You walk up the stairs and turn to face the window. You see the frail boy walking carefully up the street." While the second-person viewpoint does engage the reader, it can be difficult to carry through a long piece of fiction. It's an excellent choice, though, for several nonfiction formats such as training manuals and travel guides.

Third person. There are actually two different third-person points of view. Third person limited tells the story through one character's perspective, and third person omniscient speaks through an "all-seeing eye." In both cases, the speaker is not part of the story, a major difference from the first-person point of view. The third-person narrator uses the words *he, his, him, her, hers, they, them, their,* and *theirs.*

ESSENTIALS

To obtain different characters' perspectives, you can switch between viewpoints. However, you'll need to take pains to make sure that readers are certain who's speaking and that the speaker had access to the information he or she is talking about.

Using the third person, you can go deeply into one character. Third person omniscient gives you a great deal of freedom, because you can speak from your own viewpoint or speak as, or reveal the thoughts of, any character.

In nonfiction stories, there are two other points of view. The objective point of view provides readers with facts and observations. The subjective point of view lets the writer inject personal emotions and experiences.

How can you decide which is the best viewpoint to use? There are several things to consider: Which one seems to bring the story to life? Which character is in a position to best tell the story? Through whose emotions and characteristics would you like the reader to experience your work? Would the story have more impact if an omniscient narrator could see and tell everything? Which voice do you feel most comfortable writing in?

Think about your story's structure and focus, and experiment with several different viewpoints until you feel comfortable with one. Once you start writing, you might discover that a different character wants to tell the story, and you may change to a new voice at that point. You may also find that different pieces work best employing different viewpoints.

Tone

Depending on the viewpoint you use, the voice that speaks will develop a particular tone. Tone is a reflection of the writer's attitude, manner, mood, or morality, and often reflects his or her personality. The tone of a humorous story could be sarcastic or satiric. A letter to the editor noting a strong disagreement with a community issue could be scornful. A memoir could focus on a surprising situation and be ironic.

QUESTIONS?

What is the difference between irony, sarcasm, and satire?
Irony conveys a meaning that is the opposite of the actual meaning. Ironic statements bring attention to words and phrases and show the difference between an ideal and an actual condition. Sarcasm is harsh or bitter irony. Satire employs sarcasm or irony to make fun of something.

Tone does much to attract or repel a reader, and, when consistent, adds much to the telling of a story. In some works, you may want to adopt a neutral tone and simply relay facts or observations. In others, you'll want to write in a tone that reflects and enhances the concept. If you're expressing anger, you may want to use crisp, hard-charging language. If you're gently chiding, you might use carefully chosen words that mock.

Irony

Irony has been used in prose and poetry for many hundreds of years. Scholars believe it was first used in Plato's *Republic,* where the term meant an underhanded way to take people in. When used by Cicero and other Roman rhetoricians, it implied a meaning opposite to the words used. Much later, in the 1800s and 1900s, several authors developed different views about irony—for instance, that it's a way of looking at life and that it develops from perceiving the absurdity of life.

FACTS

Voltaire and Swift are thought by many to be outstanding ironists. Jane Austen, James Joyce, and Mark Twain are also known for their effective use of this device.

Today, irony is often explained as an awareness of the difference between appearances and reality or between actions and their results. For example, people say, "Great weather, isn't it?" when a brutal storm is knocking down power lines and sending branches barreling onto the streets. Or, "That really helped, didn't it?" when the best effort to unplug the drain ends up only breaking the plunger. People also use irony to mock or ridicule: You might say, "You'd lose your head if it wasn't attached" to a friend who's always losing things. Irony generally conveys sarcasm or makes fun of something or someone, and though it can be harsh and biting, it can also enliven writing and make a picture particularly clear.

Irony is used both in speech and narration. A narrator might tell us that a character is a fine, upstanding citizen when we have just read that the character cheated on his taxes. Irony is also seen in situations: For example, a movie character laughing maniacally at another character being slobbered on by a dog, when another dog is about to do the same thing to the character who's laughing. In Laurie Colwin's *A Big Storm Knocked It Over,* editor Jane Louise is trying to get an annoying coworker, Sven, out of her office to no avail. He just stands there and mocks her by telling her what a nice greeting she's giving him. Later, when Sven tells Jane Louise that a book designer is a lush, Jane Louise says, unhappily, "How nice for me." Sven goes on to say, "He's one of those Brit types who has been so enchanted by the sound of his own voice for so long that he goes around bleating like a sheep and expecting everyone to fall to their knees at his every utterance." The exasperated Jane Louise can only reply, "Wonderful. Just my type."

Viewpoint and Tone Exercises

Try the following exercise to practice working with different points of view. Write a few paragraphs about something that recently happened to you, using the first person. Then tell the story again using third person, as though you were an outsider on the scene. Which way of writing feels more comfortable? More involving? Which gives the story more punch?

To work on your tone, try writing a two-paragraph description of a person you observe. Use a straightforward neutral tone. Then, including the same information, write the description again, this time using a humorous tone. Write it again incorporating a sarcastic tone.

CHAPTER 12
Researching

Any piece of writing, be it fiction or nonfiction, may require research. Settings, facts and statistics, character traits, dialogue, and historical references may all need some checking to make sure they're as accurate and reliable as possible, and to give you credibility.

Research Is Fun!

Though the thought of researching may make you groan—you immediately have visions of days slogging through dusty library shelves or in dank basements filled with crumbling boxes—there are so many excellent sources of information available that researching can truly be a pleasure. In fact, some authors get completely caught up in researching their work, and often develop additional ideas that enrich and ignite their work. I'm actually one of them—researching can be fun!

Researching for Nonfiction

Successful nonfiction presents accurate, reliable information—it speaks with a voice of authority. To use this voice, if you're not an expert on your topic, you will need to do some research. Whatever the subject, plan to spend a good deal of time reading, observing, and asking questions.

The library, of course, is where you'll find a lot of the information you're after. Reference librarians are generally amazing sources of help, and can direct you to fact-filled books, magazines, online resources, and audio- and videotapes on your topic. Your local library is a great starting point, but don't forget nearby university or college libraries and local business archives; many allow at least limited public access to their stacks. Many newspapers also make available information in back issues.

In this age of the World Wide Web, online sources of information are extremely plentiful and generally useful. Web sites abound on just about every topic, so take your research online.

People are also great sources of information. If you're researching a particular period in history, you may be able to locate a neighbor, colleague, or associate who has a detailed memory of the time. Or you might try to track down a teacher or professor who specializes in the period. Authors of books on your topic may also be willing to talk with you or direct you to useful information. And be sure to let your friends and family know what it is you're researching—often someone will know a "friend of a friend of a friend" who has just the information you're looking for.

As you do your research, take careful notes and then organize and keep them in a safe place. If you interview experts or record your thoughts, be sure to date and label the tapes and keep them away from heat. Make note of publishing information for books and magazines you refer to if you think you'll be including a bibliography, or for your future reference. You may also want to make sketches of important objects, buildings, or people that will help to jog your memory when you write, or that will provide details for illustrations.

Make It Real

Short stories, novels, and movies can take place just about anywhere: in cities, in the countryside, in any part of the globe, even in outer space or a made-up world. But even a story that takes place in an ordinary house in an ordinary town can be fascinating if the details of the setting are provided with authority and with care. When characters interact with the setting, the story will come alive.

Gather as much information as you can. Even if you're writing a nonfiction book for the youngest kids and will actually write very few words, having in-depth knowledge will help you enormously— it will provide you with a voice of authority and lots of information to choose from.

A good setting not only gives readers a mental picture of where the action is happening, but provides depth and dimension that helps them to understand the characters better. And, just like characters, a story's particular setting can be a key element in the action. Think of Ernest Hemingway's riveting tale *The Old Man and the Sea.* The sea is so important that it's actually part of the title, and it's the setting that enables the hero to wrestle with and vanquish a marlin as he wrestles with his past and finds the courage to go on. The setting is almost a character in the story—it has a tremendous effect on the forward movement the plot takes.

Settings and Genres

For several types of novels, the setting is actually the foundation for the story. In the western, the setting, of course, must be in the American West. In this type of novel, events unfold sometime during the late nineteenth century, and the characters are usually ranchers and farmers who live their lives in small towns and rural areas. Great examples of the western are Jack Warner Schaefer's classic *Shane,* the story of a stranger taken in by a Wyoming family in 1889 who becomes involved in a feud between local cattle ranchers and the homesteaders; and the more modern-day telling of the western story in Larry McMurtry's *Lonesome Dove,* about a last cattle drive north.

The science fiction novel also takes place in a particular setting—an imagined world. Here characters deal with machines and creatures that don't really exist, are able to do impossible things, such as read each other's minds, and live on other planets or on Earth at a future time. Creating a setting for a science fiction tale can be lots of fun, because your imagination is set loose from reality. But though the setting is made up, much of science fiction is actually based on science and logic, so research should be done to create a believable plot and setting. (Extensive research is also necessary for the western, to get the details of both time and place exactly right.)

ESSENTIALS

Most settings require at least some research—otherwise you would need to limit your settings to places you've been and are familiar with.

The following excerpt is from an interview with science-fiction author James Morrow, where he talks about the importance of research in his work.

Science fiction keys itself to the physical universe and our present knowledge of nature's laws. The serious sci-fi writer is therefore obligated to keep up with new developments in biology, physics, and cosmology, and to achieve a rudimentary understanding of these fields. At the very least, he or she is obligated to avoid populist misunderstandings of contemporary science, such as the several trendy but wrongheaded interpretations of the Heisenberg Uncertainty Relation that are currently floating around.

With fantasy, by contrast, nature's laws are up for grabs. They can be suspended or superseded through magic. So, in theory, the fantasy writer has to do less rigorous research than the science fiction writer, although the typical fantasy epic generally achieves its verisimilitude through the author's familiarity with a particular historical era, most commonly medieval Europe. So even though we usually find "science fiction" and "fantasy" lumped together in the bookstores, at a certain point they part company radically, and it makes about as much sense to shelve the two genres side by side as it does to place vegetarian cookbooks next to vivisection manuals.

I've found that if you know nothing at all about some technical aspect you need to understand for a science fiction novel or story, a children's book is often the best place to start. Children's book authors generally have a lot of integrity, write clearly, do their homework, and get their facts straight.

One other genre that grows from its setting is the war story. Like the western needs the West, the war story needs a war. Though characters are also key in these types of novels—many war stories, such as Stephen Crane's *The Red Badge of Courage* and Ernest Hemingway's *For Whom the Bell Tolls,* focus on how the hero or a group of heroes struggle against monumental odds—the sounds, sights, and smells of the struggle put the story in context.

To sum it up, rich, powerful settings:

- Are vivid
- Engage the reader
- Use sensory details, not statistics, to create an atmosphere
- Are believable
- Are evocative
- Are suitable to the character and the plot
- Are rooted in time

A SHORT-STORY WRITER'S EXPERIENCE WITH RESEARCH

I enjoy [research], and actually I find it difficult to know when to stop doing research. But you have to hit a point where you say, okay, I know enough, I can at least make a stab at this. One of my favorite authors, Kim Stanley Robinson, says, "Skate fast over thin ice." Which means, if there's something you don't know, just wave your hands and hope people don't notice it, and keep going.

One of my characters was a police officer in a small town in Texas. I grew up in Texas, but there were a lot of things that I didn't know about the police community there, so I went online, I talked to friends who were policemen, I did the Citizens' Police Academy through the Redwood City Police Department to learn about police procedure. There are a lot of different ways to do research; books are just one way. The best way is to go out and talk to people, which can be hard for writers who are introverts.

The San Mateo County coroner let me go through the room where she actually does the autopsies. People love to talk about their work, and if you ask them, most people will be just extraordinarily helpful. Don't be afraid to ask.

—From an interview with short-story writer Susan Fry (see the rest of the interview in Chapter 2, "The Short Story")

Try This

To get a feel for how to write a setting, try the following exercise. Choose a nearby spot that you're very familiar with. Go there with your notepad and pen and spend some time *experiencing* the place. Pay attention to the people or animals or buildings, the sounds, the smells, the light, how cold or hot it is, how it relaxes or invigorates you, the feelings or memories the spot brings to mind. Run your hands over things, change your viewpoint, close your eyes and listen, cover your ears and observe. Note down everything you see, hear, and smell, as well as your thoughts and feelings. Then write a few paragraphs describing the setting as you experienced it. Remember to show, rather than tell.

Determine What You Need to Know

You can start doing research as soon as you've decided on your story idea. Say you've decided to set a mystery in New Orleans, but you've never been there. You're going to need to learn about the city—what it looks like, how the people speak, exactly where it's located, its attractions, the weather—in order to have your characters live there and make the story believable. Or say you're going to write a memoir about the summer you spent with your grandfather. You remember the trips you took together and the important values he instilled in you, but your recollection of the small town he lived in is fuzzy. If he's still alive, you'll want to ask him a lot of questions to fill in your memory gaps. Or you may need to read through letters he wrote to you over the years, or drive to the town to refresh your memory, or discover if there's a book that covers the local history.

If you write young adult fiction, real-world research is crucial. Go see the latest teen flick, spend some time at the local mall, and visit other teen hangouts. Pay attention to what teens like, what they wear, and how they act.

Once you've settled on your main idea, think carefully about the plot or the focus to determine what you're going to need to research. It's a good idea to make a list of all the questions you need answered, which you'll most likely add to after you start to write. Think about the work from many different angles. Will you need:

- Statistics to support an argument?
- Background information?
- Historical information?
- Advice or analysis from an expert?
- Anecdotes to enliven or illustrate information?
- To interview someone for a personal account or to obtain knowledge you won't be able to find anywhere else?

Make as complete a list as possible of all the information you think you'll need to track down.

Gathering the Information

Next, think about the available resources. These can be grouped into three categories:

- Media sources such as books, magazines, audio- and videotapes, TV, and the Internet.
- People sources, including experts or specialists in particular areas and other people who can provide you with facts, observations, or insights.
- Your own remembrances, experiences, and observations.

"Whatever the authority of facts, everyone does research to prepare for writing, even writers of fiction, even poets, even if the only library they consult is memory. You can't write without it."
—Richard Rhodes, Pulitzer Prize–winning author

Be creative as you think about which sources will be the most helpful. For example, you'll be able to find a good deal of information about New Orleans in an encyclopedia, but a memoir or autobiography by someone who lived in New Orleans will provide additional, and most likely exciting, detail. If you need to dig up family history, interview relatives, but also search through old records, check with pertinent community organizations to see if they published any books that cover the time, read through archived newspaper accounts, and ask friends of your relatives for remembrances or anecdotes. Coming at your research from several different angles will provide you with a full range of rich material to work with.

Prepare to Research

Once you've decided on some sources, prepare any materials you may need to gather the information. You'll probably want a notebook just for research—it helps to divide it up into sections by topic ahead of time. Keeping a file folder and some index cards will help you keep track of and group references. If you plan to interview someone, a tape recorder may be helpful.

If you are going to be quoting some of the people you talk to, or include lengthy excerpts of other people's work, you will need to request written permission from them to do so, and should prepare a permission form.

You may also need to prepare some materials. If you will be conducting an interview, write up a list of questions ahead of time. If you're going to be taking a survey, you may want to prepare a formal questionnaire. If you're going to be requesting information by mail, some places may require a self-addressed stamped envelope along with the request.

Now Start Digging

Go through your list of questions or topics until you've answered each one completely. Take careful notes and include names, phone numbers, dates of contact, publishing information, Web site addresses, page references— everything you need in case you want to reach a source again or refer to it in your work. Label and date tapes after you complete all interviews. Make any drawings—they don't have to be great—that will help you remember information or that an artist can work from. Or take photos or make a videotape. Ask people to spell their name for you. If one expert can't answer your questions, find another one who can. If a source doesn't seem completely reliable, confirm the information by checking a second source.

One word of advice: Even if you don't enjoy doing research, stick to it and gather as much information as you can. Once you start writing, you'll be very happy to have all that material on hand. It's definitely better to have too much than too little, and you'll find it will make your writing much more exciting and detailed.

Doing an Interview

Sometimes the best way to get the information you need is by interviewing an expert or an eyewitness. The thought of asking strangers for their help or insights can be intimidating, but often people will be the best resource for answering your questions. While some experts receive requests for interviews regularly and may not be able to accommodate you, many people will be flattered and quite willing to take the time. If you think certain people have information that will help you in your writing, don't be afraid to ask, either because you think you'd be intruding or because you've never conducted an interview before.

When calling or writing to set up an interview, be friendly and straightforward. Explain your project and what you'd like to talk to the person about, and ask what a convenient time to get together might be. If it fits into the person's schedule, you can offer to take him or her to lunch or out for coffee. A quiet place is best, especially if the person agrees to have the conversation recorded. Do your best to reassure the person that you won't need a lot of time, but if the answer is no, accept it graciously and start to look for another person who might have similar information.

If people seem willing but feel they don't have the time to meet with you, suggest an alternative: either a brief phone conversation or sending them questions that they can answer at their leisure. The Internet can be an excellent way to hold an interview, either with instant messaging or by sending questions that the interviewee can receive quickly and then answer when there's time. Tape recorders are also available that plug into your phone system to record a conversation.

Once you've set up the appointment, make a list of the questions you want to ask. This may be your only chance to talk with the person, so be sure to include everything you want to know. Type up your list and work from it during the interview. This will not only make it likely that you'll get the information you're after, but it will also remind you to guide the conversation back on track if it goes off in an unexpected direction. If you have the time, though, let the person you're interviewing follow a path you didn't choose but that sounds interesting; you might end up with some very special pieces of information.

Recording phone conversations without permission is illegal in some states, so be sure to ask interviewees while the tape is running to confirm that they agree to it. Some recorders can be set to provide a regular beep tone as a reminder.

During the interview, try to stay in the background. Ask each question, then step back and be an interested listener. If the interviewee has trouble getting beyond "yes" and "no" answers, rephrase your questions so that the response needs to be some sort of explanation. Instead of asking, "Did the result of that experiment surprise you?" ask, "What were your thoughts when you realized what the experiment proved?" Try to put the person at ease by smiling or nodding, and by being respectful of what he or she is saying. If you take notes rather than, or in addition to, tape recording, look up every now and then to maintain a connection.

At the end of the interview, check your list to see if there's anything you've missed. Then ask the person if there's anything else he or she would like to add; often an interviewee will think of something particularly useful that wasn't covered and appreciate the chance to bring up something that he or she feels is important.

Sorting and Storing

Whew! Now you're done (at least until you start writing and discover there's lots more you need to find out). Your notebook is full. You've got piles of tapes and index cards. You've got printouts from Web sites. You've made copies of information from books and magazines. Time to go through everything and store it safely and effectively.

Index cards can be sorted in a file folder. If you're going to be writing an article about vacationing in Tahiti, you could separate your material into travel information, weather, beaches, nightlife, and culture. If you plan to write a short story, you could group your information into material that relates to characters, settings, and scenes.

FACTS

To research his new computer-based thriller *The Blue Nowhere*, best-selling author Jeffrey Deaver learned to write a Basic program, took apart and studied his computer, talked to programmers and technology innovators, and mingled with employees from Hewlett-Packard, Xerox PARC, and Stanford University.

If you have loose pieces of paper, you may want to type up the information on your computer or write it in your notebook. Newspaper clippings could be taped to or copied onto sturdy sheets of paper. Clearly labeled tapes should be stored in a box away from heat. Try to make everything as easy to find and use as possible. Color code, use separate binders, create computer files—whatever makes the information accessible. As you go through everything, you'll probably find things that you can safely throw away—information that seemed useful when you discovered it, but on second look seems unreliable, unhelpful, or off the subject, or something cryptic you jotted down that now makes absolutely no sense.

CHAPTER 13
Organizing

Now, after you've done your research, is a good time to firm up your outline or concept and set it down in a way that will help you produce the finished work. Organizing your idea will also let you know if there's additional research to be done.

The Organizational Process

The process of organizing is really the process of thinking through an idea and putting its elements into some order. Some authors like to do this by creating a detailed, formal outline that gives them a complete working blueprint. Others prefer simply sketching out the way the story will progress because they know the details will develop and change along the way. But most writers organize their concept in some way to help them start writing and to give their idea shape.

During the organizational process, you're going to:

- Review all the materials you've collected.
- Decide which areas you want to cover.
- Decide in what order you're going to cover them.
- Make an outline or informal list of key points.

Review the Material

Start by going back over your research notes and any other notes you've made while you were developing your idea and doing the planning. Keep your idea in mind as you organize your notes—in fact, if you haven't done so, you may want to post your idea where you can keep referring to it.

As you look through all the materials you've gathered, a sequence of scenes or information may start to appear. Take notes on your thoughts as they develop. Keep thinking about what you want to say and how you've planned to say it.

Decide Which Areas to Cover

While you did your research, you may have collected information on more areas than you can comfortably cover or on areas that on second thought just don't seem that interesting. As you continue to think about your outline or key points, decide if some pieces are better left out. For example, if you plan to write about the history of your town, you may want to forego covering the construction of the post office, because it actually replaced the small building that was already there and didn't effect any change on the town.

"If I didn't know the ending of a story, I wouldn't begin."
—Katherine Anne Porter, short-story writer

"I write any sort of rubbish which will cover the main outlines of the story, then I can begin to see it."
—Frank O'Connor, short-story writer

Including uninteresting information just because you gathered it, trying to work in something that you find interesting but that just doesn't fit, or covering too much territory in a short piece can keep your work from being its best. If you have trouble deciding what to leave in and leave out, try to think about the idea as though you know nothing about it. What would you like to know as a reader? You can also ask a friend what he or she would be interested in reading about.

Decide the Order

Ordering your topics or scenes will help you to write a smoother, more logical, better-structured story. It will also help your readers to understand and enjoy it.

There are several organizing patterns to choose from, depending on the type of story you plan to write. Choose the one that best suits the material and the way you like to work.

- **Chronological order.** This pattern is popular with both fiction and nonfiction writers—it can work well with just about any kind of narrative writing. Using this method, you set down scenes following a time frame: This happened, then that happened, then that happened.

     If you're writing a memoir about a trip to your daughter's new home right after she returned from her honeymoon, you could describe driving there, then being greeted by the newlyweds, then being given the staggeringly awful painting your new son-in-law brought back from their trip especially for you.

- **Logical order.** This works well with critical pieces and arguments. You start with your viewpoint or what you want to prove, and then present the reasons, facts, and examples that make your case.
- **Rank order.** With this pattern you present information according to an attribute, for example, size: largest to smallest or smallest to largest.
- **Order of importance.** When writing an essay or report, you can list supporting reasons or arguments from what you consider to be the least important to the most important, or vice versa.
- **Sequential order.** This pattern is great for use with how-to materials: to organize the step-by-step process for throwing a clay pot, planting an herb garden, or repairing a roof.
- **Cause–and-effect order.** This organizing method connects a result with the events that came before it. It can help you explain why something happened as well as allow you to predict what will happen because of what has already taken place.

QUESTIONS?

Which organizational pattern would work well for each of the following pieces?

- An article about making croissants
- A mystery novel about the death of a baseball player
- A review of the play *The Producers*
- A biography of famed singer Ella Fitzgerald

Make an Outline

Some authors don't like this step at all—they think it's a waste of time because they've learned that once they start writing, one sentence leads to another and one idea leads to another, and the work takes shape in an intuitive, rather than a structured, way. Other authors really get into their outlines. They make flow charts and diagrams and graphs, or complete poster-size pages of detailed scenes, lead sentences, chapter titles, and character actions.

Whatever your inclination, some sort of outline, even a sketchy one, can be a helpful tool in the creative process. An outline lets you start to set down on paper the story that you've been imagining and developing in your head.

The type of outline you make is a matter of choice. Some authors go with the format many of us learned in school. Here is a typical example:

"Why No One Should Ever Go to a Class Reunion"—working title

I. Why I decided to go
    A. Tenth anniversary of graduation
        1. Background info
        2. Out of school long enough to see changes
    B. See if the "predictions" came true
        1. See if Bob really was "most likely to succeed"
        2. See if Joan is still "most popular"
        3. See if everyone still thinks I'm "best dressed"
    C. See my old boyfriend
        1. Did he live without me?
        2. Is he divorced now, too?
II. Getting there
    A. Remembrances while driving
        1. Last time I saw Jenny and Laurie
        2. Graduation day

And so on.

Others choose to make just a simple list of major points:

- Background info and reasons to go—tenth anniversary, check out what certain people are doing now, definitely find out about Bernie
- The drive there—remembering disasters and high points
- The reunion—changes, good and bad

Others are most comfortable with the index card method. On each card they jot notes about a particular scene or area to cover—the main idea and perhaps a few details—and then put the cards into what seems to be a realistic order following the organizational pattern they chose.

SSENTIALS Choose a method to try; you'll probably be able to tell quickly if it's going to help you with your writing. If it's not looking good, try another way of sketching out your plan. Different writers have different methods that they've worked out over time.

Just remember that however you put it together, your outline's not set in stone; you can be creative in your approach to making your outline, and you can also always change the outline itself. In fact, you can count on changing at least one point in your outline somewhere along the line, because new ideas are going to keep coming to you throughout the writing process. If you're writing fiction, characters may also direct you on a completely different course.

But for now, get something down. Imagine the story—with a powerful beginning, middle, and end. What should come first? What would logically follow? What would tie the story up? Consider what readers would want to know. Think about what you want to say. Improvise. Brainstorm. Create. Then, once you get something down, take a good long look at it. Does the sequence of events make sense? Is everything in chronological order or in the pattern you decided on? Are there gaps in the structure or the logic? Is there interest and tension? What's missing? What doesn't fit? Keep rearranging, adding, and subtracting until you feel a flow and see a strong, inventive story running smoothly and clearly from dramatic start to satisfying end.

The Hook

No matter what the genre, what you write needs to start with something that immediately captures the reader's attention. This "hook" pulls the reader right into the story and sets the tone for the sequence of events that follow. These events provide the conflict, tension, and interest that carry the readers—hungry for every page—to the powerful conclusion that resolves the crisis or brings them understanding and satisfaction.

Group Your Materials

Now it's back to all those research materials you collected (and
organized so well). Take them out again and start assembling them
according to the entries on your outline (or list or cards). You can either
group them on your desk or nearby, titled ("Everything About Art
Museum") and in outline order, or you can make a new list, using the
outline or original list as your foundation. For example, if an entry on
your original outline is "A. Talk about the new museum of art," you could
list that point again and then under it list the information you've
researched:

> A. Talk about the new museum of art
> > 1. Admission price, hours, current exhibit
> > 2. Setting, look of building
> > 3. Interview with curator

FACTS

Mystery writer Jean Bedford outlines her projects in the following
way: She writes a synopsis of the main plot and subplots; writes an
account of the crime, who did it, and why; makes detailed notes
about the circumstances of the crime; and lists main characters and
their attributes.

As you do this grunt work, keep thinking about your idea. Is there a
hole in your outline? For example, should you cover the day before your
detective meets the teenager who becomes her sidekick, so the reader
has more background information? Would a traveler want to know about
the different ways of getting to the hotel? If you think so, then you need
to do more research and add to your outline.

Your outline and your materials will also tell you if you have any
unnecessary elements. For example, though the information you
discovered about a visitor to your town's centennial celebration might be
fascinating, by looking at your outline you'll be able to see that it really
doesn't provide information about the celebration itself, which is the
focus of your article. Weed that material out—painful as it may be—and
save it for another day and another project.

CHAPTER 14
Drafting

O kay, folks, this is it. This is where pen really meets page (or you start to whale on those keys). You've gotten the idea. You've planned it all out. You've done the research. You've organized your information and made an outline. Now you start to write.

Getting Something onto the Page

Did your stomach just take a dive? Don't worry—you're not looking for perfection here. You just want to get the story down. The first draft is nothing more than the groundwork. It will serve you as the foundation of your final work, but it's not set in stone. Further revision is not only possible—it's essential.

Because the first draft is meant to be edited, it's a good idea to double-space your lines and leave wide margins on the page. Then, when you begin revising, you'll have plenty of room for notes, additions, and corrections.

Jump In

Don't stop to agonize over the perfect word. Don't spend time worrying about style or spelling or punctuation. Don't get upset if you find you're not following your outline. Just write. Write as though you're telling a friend a story—you don't stop to correct your wording when you do that, right?

Drafting is hard work! Many authors advise getting through it as quickly as possible, but remember while you're slaving away to give yourself a few breaks. Get up and walk around. Stop for something to drink. Play with the dog. It will clear your head and renew your energy.

Tell your story as completely and as interestingly as you can, but concentrate only on giving yourself raw material to work with. It can be full of holes, bad grammar, and crazy ideas, but who cares? Unless you decide otherwise, no one is going to read it but you.

Let Your Imagination Loose

Drafting is part of the creative process—so be creative! Write down anything that comes into your mind. Be open. Loosen up. You may think, "What possessed me to write that?" when you start editing, but all you have to do then is cross it out. And who knows? A crazy thought that comes out of the blue at this stage may turn out to be a smashing idea that sends your story in an exciting new direction. Many authors say that their first draft is almost nothing like the final version.

Starting at the Beginning

An effective opening is a necessary ingredient of a winning piece of writing. Right off the bat, you want to capture your reader's attention, set the tone and mood, and get the story moving. Your lead can be subtle or sensational, but it should definitely be significant.

ALERT

"The sensation of writing a book is the sensation of spinning, blinded by love and daring. It is the sensation of rearing and peering from the bent tip of a grassblade, looking for a route."
—Janet Burroway, author and educator

Take out your outline (aren't you glad you made one?) and see how you thought the story might start. You can begin a story at any point: at the beginning, in the middle, or at the end—at any spot that you think will carry the reader right into the story. Wherever you choose to start, it's a good idea not to dawdle. You may have only a few paragraphs to pique readers' interest, and though you don't have to open with a hugely dramatic moment, you want to quickly give readers a sense of the engaging story to come.

Write a Lead Sentence

If nothing comes to mind, keep thinking about your idea and let your imagination loose. Remember, it doesn't have to be perfect, it only has to get you going. If nothing continues to come, try freewriting—write anything at all that comes into your head: description, dialogue, phrases, gibberish. Somewhere in the stream of words that pours out will be one that gives you an idea and gets the first sentence on the page. Then you have something to hook the next sentence to.

QUESTIONS?

What makes for a strong start?
A compelling lead that:

- Grabs the reader's attention.
- Establishes the tone and the mood.
- Sets the conflict or main idea in motion.

As you get going, you'll discover that one idea leads to another, one word to another, and one sentence to another. It's a matter of connecting the bits and pieces, using your outline as a framework, and seeing what develops.

Here are some devices you can use to start your story:

- A piece of dialogue
- Showing a main character involved in some action
- Description of a character or setting
- A quotation
- A question
- An unusual fact
- A command or words directed to the reader
- A summary of the main idea
- An invitation
- A definition
- Historical background

For inspiration, here are a variety of intriguing openings:

"It was inevitable: the scent of bitter almonds always reminded him of the fate of unrequited love." (from Gabriel Garcia Marquez's *Love in the Time of Cholera*)

"The weather door of the smoking-room had been left open to the North Atlantic fog, as the big liner rolled and lifted, whistling to warn the fishing-fleet." (from Rudyard Kipling's *Captains Courageous*)

"They're out there." (from Ken Kesey's *One Flew Over the Cuckoo's Nest*)

"We were married in secret on September 22, 1981." (from Susanne Pari's *The Fortune Catcher*)

"'What color is your diet?' That's one of the first questions I ask a patient." (from "The New Eat-by-Color Diet" by Dr. David Heber, in the June 2001 issue of *Self* magazine)

"Through the doorway that led to her receptionist-secretary's office into her own, Catherine Morris Perry instantly noticed the box on her desk." (from Tony Hillerman's *Talking God*)

"When I started my first company in Boston twenty years ago, I had little interest in business." (from Paul Hawken's *Growing a Business*)

ALERT

"An action movie usually starts with a fast sequence, something to grab the audience's attention away from their popcorn and soft drinks and propel them into the story. I'm not saying that all books should be written like Hollywood films, but there is merit in studying how they are constructed."

—Chris Niles, mystery writer

"Once upon a time, there was a woman who discovered she had turned into the wrong person." (from Anne Tyler's *Back When We Were Grownups*)

"Harmony is driving home, eastward out of Las Vegas, her spirits high, her head a clutter of memories." (from Larry McMurtry's *The Desert Rose*)

"For forty years my act consisted of one joke. And then she died." (from George Burns's *Gracie: A Love Story*)

"Call me Ishmael." (from Herman Melville's *Moby Dick*)

"The Latin term *pro bono,* as most attorneys will attest, roughly translated means *for boneheads* and applies to work done without charge." (from Sue Grafton's *'O' Is for Outlaw*)

"I spent several days and nights in mid-September with an ailing pig and I feel driven to account for this stretch of time, more particularly since the pig died at last, and I lived, and things might easily have gone the other way round and none left to do the accounting." (from "Death of a Pig," in E. B. White's Essays of E. B. White)

"'I should feel sorrier,' Raymond Horgan says. I wonder at first if he is talking about the eulogy he is going to deliver." (from Scott Turow's *Presumed Innocent*)

"For a long time, Molly Bonner's strongest reaction to doctors was a fear that they would bore her to death." (from Alice Adams's *Medicine Men*)

"It was breakfast time and everyone was at the table. Father was eating his egg. Mother was eating her egg. Gloria was sitting in a high chair, and eating her egg too. Frances was eating bread and jam." (from Russell Hoban's *Bread and Jam for Frances*)

"Murderers do not usually give their victims notice." (from P. D. James's *A Certain Justice*)

Traveling to the Middle

Great job: You're under way! Now it's time to tell your story—the story you've been wanting to write. The middle is where the main point is developed and the conflict or issues are brought to a head. Continue following your outline, fleshing it out with character development, dialogue, description, information, and action. But remember, the outline is just a guide—be open to any new roads that look promising.

> It's like making a movie: All sorts of accidental things will happen after you've set up the camera. So you get lucky. Something will happen at the edge of the set and perhaps you start to go with that; you get some footage of that. You come into it accidentally. You set the story in motion, and as you're watching this thing begins, all these opportunities will show up.
>
> —Kurt Vonnegut, novelist

Start with the first scene or your first point and try to link it to your opening. If your opening set your travel article in San Diego, and your first stop is the San Diego Zoo, try to visualize the zoo (you made many notes when you were there, took photos, and talked to several visitors, keepers, and monkeys, so you've got lots of information to help you), and write about what was so wonderful about being there. Describe the place in vivid, image-making terms, but don't worry about perfection, just get the gist of it going. Then decide if this is a good time to include the funny conversation you had with a little boy who was spellbound by the giraffes. Try it. You can always move it—or delete it—later. If you've already described one of the baby animals cozied up with its parent, you could try moving into the conversation by describing how the boy came up to the giraffe area perched on his father's shoulders. If you get a good idea but it doesn't work just where you are, jot it down and see if it fits in later.

"A story is like a good party, the opening has much to do with how to get to the location where it's going on. You first need to know where it is, what part of town."
—Josip Novakovich, author and educator

Make connections between your points. Expand on the previous details. If you asked a question, the next step is probably to answer it. Think of all the possibilities. Brainstorm the best way to move ahead (flashing back can be a good way to take the story forward). Keep referring to your outline and think about your main idea. Read over what you've written every now and then (don't fix anything, just read) to aid transitions. Dramatize. Visualize.

Follow your instincts. Compare and contrast. Remember to show rather than tell. And keep going even if you don't know where to go. In fact, many authors advise that you keep going quickly, to get the whole story down in one sitting so you have it all to work with later. If nothing comes to mind in some spots, try coming at them from a different angle, or just write gibberish until something develops. You can always come back and fill in a missing piece. The idea now is to get the bulk of the work—rough though it may be—on paper. The time to make it pretty comes later.

I write on yellow-lined legal pads. I write diagonally against the lines. . . . My first draft is formless, creative, unconfined by someone else's rules of how a line should look or where on the page the letters must be spaced.

—Sophy Burnham, novelist

As you write, try to remember that you're building toward a climax and a conclusion. If you're writing fiction, you want conflict to increase. If you're writing nonfiction, you also want to aim toward resolving or exploring completely the issue you're discussing. Construct your piece with events or information that are engaging and that join together to advance and build the story.

Try It Yourself

To practice filling in the middle of a story, try sketching out a middle for these beginning/ending combinations:

- Three women set out in a rowboat to do some early morning fishing. When they return, one is huddling in a blanket, her clothing soaked and her eyes blank.
- Two elderly neighbors haven't spoken in years. At the end of the story, they're having iced tea together in one of the men's backyards.

Reaching the End

When a lot of authors start writing, they have no idea how their story is going to end—it becomes clear as the story takes shape. Other writers know only how their story will be resolved—they have to develop the beginning and middle in order to reach the end. (Mystery writer extraordinaire Agatha Christie was one of those. She always wrote the last chapter first so she would know "who done it.") Whether you start with the end or end with it, the finale of your work should be a satisfying culmination of everything that has preceded it.

For the most part, and especially in fiction, the ending isn't a summary—it's a resolution. The conflict comes to a head and is then resolved in some way. All endings aren't happy. Many are very unhappy, and some leave it up to the reader to decide what the outcome really is—a step is taken, but it may or may not lead to happiness. But all strong endings are appropriate and fulfilling. And they're believable.

What Makes a Well-Crafted Ending?

The well-crafted ending reflects or highlights the main point or problem that is noted at the beginning. In an article about the headaches of doing laundry on a long trip in a foreign country, you would conclude with how you solved the problem—or tried but failed. In a short story about robots who came to Earth by mistake, you might end with an ingenious way of returning them home, or a scene that solves their problem in one way or another (they might need to remain on Earth disguised as politicians until another robot comes for them). All situations that you've introduced during the course of the story need to be addressed at the end.

ESSENTIALS

To practice writing endings, try picking a favorite book or a classic children's story and writing a new ending. For example, the glass slipper fits Cinderella's foot, but all the years of mistreatment at the hands of her family have made her afraid to trust the prince.

Like beginnings, endings can be subtle or sensational, but they need to be effective. They need to feel like an ending, bringing closure, yet leave the reader thinking about what he or she just read and learned. They also should be compact—sometimes it's hard to know exactly where to end, so you go on a little longer. Luckily, wandering endings can be dealt with when you revise.

Writers use several different methods to bring their stories to a close, including:

- **Simple resolution:** A little boy is lost and his dog leads rescuers to him.
- **Awareness or understanding:** A sister realizes that her brother's drug habit comes from a fear of being alone.
- **A surprise:** The best coffee in town can be found at Michael's Diner, not The Coffee Place.

Because the ending is the last thing the reader reads, you'll want to pay careful attention to the wording of the final few sentences and paragraphs. Again, this is something that you can perfect when you revise, but keep in mind image and mood as well as the meaning you're trying to convey. Saying your closing sentences out loud can give you a sense of their impact.

Example of a Successful Ending

Here's an example of an ending that resolves a problem, brings understanding, and does it with a surprise. In Elizabeth Berg's *Range of Motion,* Elaine's husband, Jay, has been in a coma, the result of a freak winter accident, for the length of the novel. After steadfastly refusing to consider he might never wake up, and painfully reminding herself of how great their life had been, Elaine begins to understand that she will have to go on without him. Then he wakes up. Here is the ending of the book, narrated by Elaine:

> Sometimes when I'm alone in the house I kind of ask for Evie [a ghost Elaine believes spoke to her while Jay was in the hospital] to come back . . . I want to tell her about the day Jay came home, what it was like when he opened the door to his house and walked back in. . . . There was just the slow lifting of his hand to the familiar banister at the foot of the stairs, the glint of the wedding ring that has never left his finger since the day I put it there. I want to say that I understood something at that moment, which was this: the gift is not that I got to bring Jay back. The gift is that I know what I brought him back to, and so does he. . . .

CHAPTER 15
Editing

Your first draft is finally done, but it's not yet time to relax and enjoy your work. The writing process is only halfway over. It's time for some serious rewriting. This chapter will get you on your way to a final draft that you had in mind.

Rewriting Is Important

Editing your work can be fun, because here is where you take your raw material and turn it into an exciting, polished piece, the one that you've been envisioning and working toward. Editing gives you the opportunity to make all the changes needed to make your writing the best it can be.

Nonfiction author and screenwriter Murray Suid likens editing to checking yourself in the mirror before you leave the house. After you get dressed, you see how you look. Uh, oh, your shirt doesn't work with your pants. You choose another shirt. Is a button missing? You look for a new button and sew it on. Do you look washed out in the outfit? You try on a more colorful ensemble that suits you better. Would adding a little something pull it all together? You put on a necklace or add a power tie.

With editing, you search out all of your writing's imperfections. And if you've heeded many authors' advice, you'll find plenty of areas to work on, because you weren't aiming for perfection in your first draft. Don't be intimidated. Think of editing as a kind of treasure hunt for problems where the prize is a big one—a greatly improved piece of writing.

How to Start

The best way to start editing is . . . to do nothing. (See, this isn't so hard!) Most likely you've just spent a lot of time and energy getting that first draft down on paper, and you've done such a good job that you deserve a break. So take one. Put the article or poem or press release away for a while. You'll probably keep thinking about it, but try not to work on it. By stepping away for a bit, you'll come back to your piece with a fresh eye and the energy you need to revise. In fact, you may have promised yourself—and can now get—a big, revitalizing reward for getting your first draft completed: lunch with a friend, a walk in the park or at the beach, a day without any household responsibilities. Give yourself—and your writing—a good rest.

What to Look For

When you're ready to jump back in, it's a good idea to begin by reading your draft from start to finish. You may want to make notes or flag areas to work on, but try to look at the piece as a whole, rather than as sections or chapters or stanzas. Read slowly and think about your central idea and what you planned to say. Keep reminding yourself of your original intention. It's also a good idea to approach the piece as an uninvolved reader might, someone who isn't familiar with the material and will come to it looking to be informed or entertained in a clear, understandable, and engaging way.

FACTS

"A friend of mine says the first draft is the down draft—you just get it down. The second draft is the up draft—you fix it up. . . . The third draft is the dental draft, where you check every tooth."
—Anne Lamott, novelist and memoirist

After a thorough reading, some authors like to start their next draft from the beginning—a complete rewrite. They uncover a great deal of information through careful review and decide to deal with that information by starting over. Many authors, though, work from their draft section by section, improving the original material in more of a step-by-step fashion. Still others rework by concentrating on one element at a time; for example, description, grammar, plot or steps, characters, spelling, and so on. Whichever way feels most comfortable, during the revision process you should be looking for a number of things. It's often helpful to start with the larger, more general concerns and then work on the details.

At the Macro Level

Think about your work by taking in "the big picture." Read for:

- **Meaning:** Do you know what the novel/poem/article is about? Does it say what you want it to say?
- **Ideas:** Do they make sense? Are they logical? Do they support your meaning? Are facts identifiable as facts and opinions as opinions?

- **Clarity:** Are your points clear and focused? Could anything be misunderstood? Are the *who, what, when, where,* and *why* readily apparent? Are your sentences so long that they're confusing?
- **Consistency:** Does the point of view remain the same throughout? Is the style consistent? Have you followed your organizational pattern; for example, are all the key points presented in chronological order? Are your characters always recognizable? Did you start writing in the present tense and then switch to the past?
- **Conciseness:** Have you used too many words when a few, more precise ones would make the work stronger? Do you cover the intended story and no more? Does the beginning actually begin the story, or do you have to read on a ways to get to the start? Does the ending continue on too long, adding nothing but extra words?
- **Completeness:** Have you given the reader everything he or she needs to know to understand the story? Did you tell it all, or has something been left out? Have you fleshed out areas that you only sketched in in your first draft? Have you resolved the main problem or addressed the main point?

At the Micro Level

Take a look at your writing with an eye to details. Pay attention to:

- **Wording:** Is your language vivid and imaginative? Is there a section that's boring? Is the dialogue realistic? Do you trip over a word or phrase? If you do, your reader will too. Is the wording precise? For example, would it give your reader a better idea about your character Phil if he snorts or giggles instead of just laughs? Do you show rather than tell? Do you employ rhetorical devices (see Chapter 17) to bring your characters and scenes and information to life? Have you used any sexist or other offensive language? Are there any clichés? Have you used a variety of words, or do you use *big* every time instead of *enormous, vast,* or *extensive?*
- **Flow:** Does one paragraph lead smoothly and clearly to the next? Is the sequencing logical? Do you need additional bridge material? Is all the interesting stuff in the middle, making the end and the beginning

seem tacked on? Does the conflict build? Does every sentence keep the story moving forward? For shorter works, it may help to read the piece out loud to see if you hear the music.

Which word conjures up a better image?

- "broken" or "splintered"
- "small" or "pebble-sized"
- "loud" or "thunderous"
- "plant" or "bougainvillea"

- **Mechanics:** Are all the words spelled correctly? Should *there* be *their*? Is your grammar solid? How about punctuation? Have you capitalized all the proper nouns? Do your sentences run on? Do your paragraphs run on? Do you use quotation marks around quoted material and dialogue? Use your dictionary and a style guide such as *The Chicago Manual of Style* for help—the spell checker can only do so much. If you're not confident of your skills here, you can have a professional copy editor or proofreader give your final draft a once-over.

Do a Character Check

Check to see that your characters act in a consistent way. This is especially important in lengthier writing, such as a novel or a screenplay. If you decide a character doesn't like dogs, that character needs to shy away from any dog that trots through your story. If another character is portrayed as supremely moral for three-quarters of the novel, she can't run off with the milkman for a shocking ending (unless some major event has completely transformed her lifelong way of thinking).

In an early novel written by one of my favorite authors (I don't want to name names here because I'm crazy about almost everything she's ever written), a male character has a sudden affair with his new stepmother-in-law after showing nothing but animosity toward her for nearly all of the book. There were no signs leading up to his change toward her—it just suddenly happened, and it made no sense. In fact, it made me angry. It was a plot device that changed the course of the story, but it wasn't true to either character. I wanted to write a letter to the author and say, "What were you thinking?" (I didn't, but she must have known what I thought because she never made that mistake again.)

ESSENTIALS

"I begin with . . . the main characters and draw a line from the beginning to the end of the screenplay to see what has occurred with each. . . . Once you see the progression, you can pinch here and tuck there."

—Christopher Keane, screenwriter and teacher

To review, characters should be:

- Believable
- Intriguing
- Out of the ordinary
- Consistent
- Not stereotypes
- Not overdone
- Three-dimensional

Make Your Changes

A careful reading of your material has probably produced a number of areas that can use some work. This is a good thing! Now, using the notes you made, start revising. Keep thinking like a reader, making changes that will provide even more clarity, appeal, and punch. Shorten. Expand. Add detail.

Find the precise word. Reroute the plot. Correct the spelling. Use a different organizational pattern. Don't be afraid to change things—trust yourself when you decide that your story really should be told by Nate rather than Matt. Often, a second draft is almost nothing like the first draft. Be fearless. Be creative.

Be Ruthless

A big problem for many writers is that they fall in love with a certain sentence or paragraph or character or format, and during editing realize that it just doesn't work for the story. But they can't bring themselves to cross it out. It's too perfect. It took so long to craft.

If you make major changes during editing or begin again, be certain to save all your original work. Just because you're not using it now doesn't mean you won't use all or some of it later on. Words, phrases, or ideas may come in handy at another time. Save everything!

Sorry—you've got to start deleting. As wonderful as it might be, if it doesn't work with the story, it simply can't be there. Summon up your courage. Besides, you don't have to throw those words in the trash. Save them for another article or story—if they're that important to you, you might even build a story around them. And until you get to that next project, why not pin the lines up where you can see them? They'll remind you of how creative and excellent a writer you can be.

Now, Do It Again

At this point, you've improved your writing enormously. Reward yourself with another break. Then, read the material again, still thinking like a new-to-it reader, still looking for "treasure" at both the macro and micro levels. Most likely, you'll come up with several issues you feel still aren't quite right. Note them, think about how to resolve them, and work on them. And keep on reading and revising until you're satisfied that what you've created is the best it can be. This can take a while, so try not to be discouraged: It's said that author Raymond Carver revised his drafts twenty to thirty times, and that Dylan Thomas rewrote one of his poems seventy-one times.

Which brings up one more point: Seventy-one revisions may have been right for Dylan Thomas, but four may be right for you. It is possible to get so caught up in revising that you forget you need to stop at some point and say it's finished. Edit until you're happy with what you've done—until you think you've made real the vision you started out with. Then save your work, print it out, and turn off the computer.

FACTS

When asked if he did a lot of rewriting, Ernest Hemingway said, "It depends. I rewrote the ending to *Farewell to Arms,* the last page of it, thirty-nine times before I was satisfied."

CHAPTER 16
Evaluating

Well, you did it. You came up with a great idea, you developed it, and you polished it. You created a written work that expresses your ideas and your feelings in a way that only you could do. You saw it through, even when you thought you couldn't. So, what's the next step?

Assess Your Achievement

I know, I know—you're probably thinking, "What else could there be to do?" You've completed your project. You've successfully written your memoir or travel article or poem. But there is another step.

Whether or not you decide to have your work published, it's a good idea to get some feedback. Having your work evaluated—by yourself and others—may seem an unnecessary part of the writing process. But investing time in this step will reward you with valuable insights, encouragement, and direction.

Send Your Baby out into the World

Now that your work is more or less polished, you should be ready for another pair of eyes to read your story. Seeking the comments of a caring, impartial critic whose opinion you respect can help to improve it.

Choose one person or a few people whose opinion you respect, and who will be honest. Or choose a professional editor who will be completely objective. Ask for feedback. This can be scary—someone is going to be assessing your darling—but try to remember that it will add to your knowledge, and if it can improve your writing, then it's a good thing.

It can hurt—deeply—when someone finds fault with your writing. But the purpose of getting feedback is to help you produce the best work possible, and a momentary pain can lead to a long-lasting feeling of achievement.

When receiving feedback, it's crucial to remember that your *work*—and not your personality or self—is being evaluated. It's also important not to get defensive; if you're always defending your work, you won't hear the criticism that's being offered, and that means you can't benefit from it. If you've chosen the right people to ask for comments, the criticism you hear will be intended to help, not hurt.

And while you should certainly take the reviewers' comments seriously, keep in mind that you don't have to act on the feedback you get if you don't agree with it. This is still your work, and your opinion is the key one. However, if you have several readers review your work and they all say there's a problem with the plot or that a flashback is confusing or that your argument just doesn't prove your thesis, then you should probably take their criticism to heart.

FACTS

Screenwriters have a special way of getting feedback. Because screenplays are meant to be read by actors, screenwriters organize a group of friends or colleagues to read the different parts aloud at a table reading. Such a "performance" is critical to polishing a script.

If you want, you can ask your reviewers to check out the kinds of things you looked for when you were editing: spelling, flow, typos, grammar. Mostly, you want to know their answers to the big-picture questions. Jotting down these questions ahead of time will help you get answers to the main issues you're interested in. For example:

- Does the story make sense?
- Is the message they got the one you intended?
- Did the sequencing make sense?
- Did they learn something or enjoy the story? Was it interesting? Believable?
- Are there any weak spots?
- Is the writing clear?
- Is it ready to send to a publisher or to be self-published?

If you have particular concerns, it's probably a good idea to write them down or discuss them so your reader can be on the lookout for them. Specific questions might look something like these:

- Does the metaphor on page 6 sound overly dramatic?
- Does the character Seth sound believable in the dialogue on page 35?
- Does the car accident on page 40 work as an effective and sufficiently dramatic plot point?

You can put together an informal questionnaire to guide readers in their review, or get together to discuss their thoughts after they've completed the reading. The more specific you are, the better your reader will understand what you're looking for. In addition to reading a story, some reviewers enjoy assessing a piece of writing by hearing it read aloud. Hearing the words can add to reviewers' overall sense of the piece and better enable them to assess its rhythm, tone, and clarity.

Ask anyone who reviews your work for as much information as he or she can give you: reactions, concerns, general and specific suggestions, strengths and weaknesses, what could use some work, and what they enjoyed (positive feedback is valuable, too!). Assure your reader that you're looking for explicit comments, both pro and con, and not to be afraid to be honest. Learning about weak spots will enable you to improve them.

QUESTIONS?

What should you do if you agree with a negative evaluation? Use what you find out to revise, or put the work away and start in on something new. Just don't beat yourself up: Everything you learn will increase your chances for success the next time around.

Once you have these answers, sit down and really study them. Try not to get defensive, just concentrate on deciding if they'll improve your work. If they will, turn the computer back on and start revising. If you truly feel they won't, put them away and stay with your final version.

Look Back in Order to Look Ahead

In addition to evaluating the written work you've created and having others review it, it's also helpful if you sit back and evaluate the entire process you've just been through. You've put time, energy, imagination, and emotion into a deeply involving and possibly a brand-new experience, and giving yourself a chance to think about it can tell you a lot.

You can evaluate your experience in several ways. One is to think about the writing process.

- Did you enjoy it? Are you looking forward to doing it again?
- Would you follow the exact same route for your next project? Would you spend more time in some areas, for example, research?
- Would you be sure you had the ending to your mystery firmly in your mind before you started writing another one?
- Would you make a detailed outline by grouping together index cards, instead of just making sketchy notes?
- Did the project make you realize you need to brush up on your grammar and punctuation skills?
- Was interviewing people surprisingly enjoyable?
- Would you be able to exercise your writing muscles more by writing for a young-adult rather than an early-reader audience?
- What were the best parts of the process? The hardest?
- What would you never do again during the development of other stories?

Another thing to think about is genre.

- Are you happy with the type of work you produced?
- Is the poem you penned wonderfully satisfying, even though its core idea could have been explored more fully in a short story?
- Do you feel you've gotten to understand the way a strong memoir is put together, and are you now ready to try something completely different, say, a screenplay?
- Did doing all that exciting research interest you in writing a nonfiction article next rather than another fiction piece?

Perhaps you'll also want to step up the length of your next piece. Author Susan Fry (see the interview with her on pages 24–28) began writing newspaper and magazine articles, then moved to short fiction, and is now working on a novel.

What Are Your Goals?

The goal for many authors is to complete a piece of writing—one that expresses something important to them and does it in a satisfying way. They write for themselves, not an audience. They may share their work with a writers' group or with close friends or family members, but basically they write to fulfill a personal need.

Other authors write with the goal of having their work published. They create works of fiction or nonfiction from a deep desire to do so, but they believe that the final step of the writing process is to share their words with others, and that these words don't reach their full potential until they are out in the world.

Consider Publishing

Reflect on the following questions:

- Have you written your piece to satisfy a personal need or interest, and are you content just knowing that you completed it?
- Or, after thinking about all the creative effort you put into it, and your excellent results, do you think you want to share your thoughts and words with others?
- If you do want to publish, are you ready to begin the process of looking for a publisher or self-publishing your work?
- If you're going to self-publish, do you need to learn about page design, typesetting, and marketing?

ESSENTIALS If you decide you want to publish your work, be sure your manuscript is in top-notch shape. That means neatly typed, double-spaced, no typos or spelling or punctuation mistakes, no coffee stains, and numbered pages. Make a backup copy and keep it in a safe place.

If you think it might be difficult to hire an agent or find a publisher, or you'd rather keep complete control of your work rather than put it into the hands of someone who may not do everything to your liking, self-publishing may be your route to a wide audience. Self-publishing, or independent publishing, keeps the author in the driver's seat. When you publish your own work, you decide on the design, the content, the art, the cover, the paper, the size, the amount of money that goes into it. You also keep all the money from sales, rather than just the royalties. And all rights to the book belong to you.

FACTS

Self-publishing is not the same thing as vanity press publishing. A vanity press will charge you to publish your book, an unnecessary expense now that technology has made it so much easier and less costly to publish your own work.

The down side? While you keep all the money the book brings in, you also pay all the expenses for producing it. And, just as important, self-publishing takes an enormous amount of work. Independent publisher Ken Rudin thinks of independent publishing as a cottage industry—nearly a full-time business. Self-publishers are in charge of everything—the design, editing, proofreading, layout, artwork, printing, binding, warehousing, distribution, advertising, and promotion of their book.

Moving Forward

By reflecting on all the aspects of the writing process, you'll learn a lot about what you've experienced and also about what you want to do next. Because, very likely, you're going to want to do this again. Maybe not in the exact same way, and maybe not in the same genre, but I'm willing to bet that now that you've successfully completed a creative work, the urge to keep writing is not going to go away.

FACTS

Some authors evaluate again after their work has been published—and then revise their story. Author Tim O'Brien revised his published short story "Ghost Soldiers" into a chapter in a later work, *The Things They Carried.* He realized that the story could work in a different way—and changed it.

So think about the process you've been through, and use what you've learned to move ahead. Looking back and evaluating will help prevent you from repeating missteps, guide you to new and more enjoyable ways of working, and strengthen your writing skills. And most importantly, you'll gain the confidence to go forward—just look at what you've accomplished!

CHAPTER 17
Rhetorical Devices

C reative writers do not merely provide their readers with information—
information must be presented
effectively and with style. To write in a fresh
and interesting way, writers employ rhetorical devices.

Words at Your Disposal

One way to paint vivid word pictures is to use powerful adjectives and other parts of speech that help readers visualize the message. Precise and expressive words let readers see in their minds just what the writer sees in his or her mind, enriching understanding and the communication process.

Writers also have at their disposal a number of language devices that they use to provide visual help to the reader and to draw attention to and layer meaning. Rhetorical devices work not only to create an image, but also to help readers see the familiar in fresh ways and to add interest and excitement to reading. They also evoke strong feelings. By employing a variety of figurative language and writing devices, you can enliven your prose and provide increased reading pleasure.

Employing Rhetorical Devices in Your Writing

Using rhetorical devices will probably come naturally. That's because all of us use these constructs in our daily lives—without even thinking about them. How often have you said you've read zillions of books on a subject? Or that traffic was moving at a snail's pace? Or that your kid's room looks like a bomb went off in it? We all use figures of speech every day to make a point, communicate a feeling, or draw attention to a fact— it's a very human way of expressing ourselves. Comparing, exaggerating, understating, personifying, and using humor and sounds to get across a message can also be a lot of fun.

FACTS

Rhetoric is the art of effectively using language for persuasion in speaking or in writing; a rhetorical device is an artful arrangement of words to achieve a particular emphasis or effect.

That's not to say that you should immediately start to pepper your prose with a shakerful of figurative devices (if I had said, "That's not to say that you should don your toque and pepper your prose with a shakerful of figurative devices," that would definitely be overdoing it). The judicious use of image makers will add much to your work—their overuse will ruin it.

When you use language to build images, try to incorporate all five senses. A description of a trip to the beach could include what you see: stork-legged children burning off the pall of winter; what you hear: radios bleating; what you smell: the summer scent of hot dogs and sunscreen; what you taste: once-cold lemonade that's lost its snap; what you feel: sunburned skin as parched as paper. Sensory wording will help you show, rather than tell, and give readers many ways to paint pictures of their own. Studying poetry may help you see how important and effective this type of wording can be.

Coming up with inventive, memorable language will take time and practice, but it's definitely worth the effort you put into it. Using figurative language will add depth and power to your words. And lucky you—the English language is one of the richest and the largest in the world, with hundreds of thousands of words to choose from. Just think of the possibilities!

Alliteration

Alliteration is the repetition of a beginning sound, usually a consonant, in two or more words in a phrase. Often found in poetry, this figure of speech can also be effective in prose. Alliteration is a very old rhetorical device in English verse, and was an essential part of a poem's metric scheme until the late Middle Ages. In the late nineteenth century, the poet Gerard Manley Hopkins revived the use of alliteration for achieving special effects. In his poem "Spring," he wrote:

Nothing is so beautiful as spring—
When weeds, in wheels, shoot long and lovely and lush . . .

The poet W. H. Auden also experimented with alliterative verse, as in these lines from *The Age of Anxiety:*

For the others, like me, there is only the flash
Of negative knowledge, the night when, drunk, one
Staggers to the bathroom and stares in the glass . . .

Today, alliteration still can be found in poetry, as well as in slogans, jingles, book and song titles, fiction and nonfiction, even product names—think of Beanie Babies and Silly String. The repetition of sound draws attention to the words whose consonants make that sound, asking readers or listeners to pause to reflect on them and "see" an image. Alliteration can also set up a cadence or rhythm, adding a musical quality to your words. In fact, you might want to study song lyrics, particularly standards, for alliteration inspiration.

Allusion

An allusion is a phrase or passage that refers to another work of literature or art, or to a fact or a person or an event or a thing. In *Moby Dick,* Herman Melville calls a beggar a "Lazarus," referring to a beggar in the Bible in the parable about the rich man and the poor man. Melville also calls a character a "Job," making another biblical reference to a good man who was severely tested but stayed true to his beliefs.

ESSENTIALS

The idea in making an allusion is to enrich and give depth to a concept by associating it with something else the reader has experienced or knows. For an allusion to be successful, then, it's necessary for the reader to be able to pick up on it and understand the reference.

Keep your audience in mind when making allusions in your writing. Allusions work only if readers are familiar with what you are referring to. Think of cultural icons or ideas that are common knowledge—baseball games, a child's habits, Christmas celebrations, or a character in a Dr. Seuss book. An allusion to any one of these could enhance the meaning of your writing because these are things that most people are familiar with. Using targeted, inventive allusions can add greatly to readers' understanding.

Allusions in Everyday Speech

Adding allusions to your writing may seem like a difficult undertaking, but you most likely already make them unconsciously in conversation or come across them in daily life. For instance, when your husband suggests taking away your errant teenager's driving privileges for three weeks, you may say, "That seems a bit Draconian." You're alluding to Draco, the seventh-century Athenian lawmaker known for establishing a severe code of laws. With a little bit of effort, it's likely that you can come up with allusions that will enlighten, expand, or add playfulness to your prose.

Analogy

An analogy is an extended comparison between two different things. In an analogy, you point out several things that are alike about what you're comparing, even though the items or events are completely different. This kind of comparison can help a reader understand a difficult or complicated idea, and it allows the writer to get very creative.

FACTS

"All mentality begins in analogy; in the act of recognizing the essential likenesses and essential differences, and of discovering how such likenesses and differences illuminate the interrelation of things."
—John Ciardi, critic and poet

For Example

In a letter to the editor, you might want to urge other community members to join you in protesting the closing of your local library branch. When you talk about the importance of books, you could say, "Books are like food. Some are meat and potatoes, and fuel our daily lives. Some are candy, and treat us with their sweet flavor. Some are hard to chew, and must be consumed slowly and carefully. Books sustain us and help us grow in so many ways."

In her book of essays entitled *High Tide in Tucson,* Barbara Kingsolver continues an analogy from the first essay through to the last—an analogy between herself and a crab she unknowingly brought home in a shell from a vacation in the Bahamas. Kingsolver begins her book with "A hermit crab lives in my house." She then relates, through many stories, how, like Kingsolver herself, the crab is hiding out, tries on and casts off different homes (seashells), began life with soft skin that hardened over time, and has become larger since it molted from its soft shell. Kingsolver ends the book by saying, "And so I have molted now, crawled out of my old empty banged-up skin with a fresh new life. . . . Right now, this minute, time to move out into the grief and glory. High tide." Analogies come in all sizes and can be an excellent way to paint pictures and make connections.

Metaphor and Simile

The metaphor, and its close friend the simile (see below), are commonly used figures of speech. The term *metaphor* came from the Greek word *metaphora,* which means "carrying from one place to another." So in a metaphor, the meaning is carried over from one term to another—that is, something is described in terms of something else. For example, "the beach is a cream-colored scarf." A simile, on the other hand, is like a very brief analogy, where the two terms are compared, instead of the one term's meaning being carried over to the other. For example, "the beach is like a cream-colored scarf." You can easily recognize a simile because each one uses *like* or *as* to make the comparison.

Metaphors Illuminate Meaning

Metaphors paint particularly vivid pictures because they indirectly compare two very dissimilar things. By using effective and unusual metaphors, writers can intensify as well as stretch their images and ask readers to think about their ideas in new ways. Well-crafted metaphors can also add zing to your writing.

Metaphors are used to describe people, places, things, and actions. You might say the taxi driver in front of the airport bulldozed his way through the crowd to claim you as a passenger. The image of a powerful, ground-chomping bulldozer intensifies the picture of a man forcing his way through a crowd. To describe a bad guy who's extorting a victim in your mystery, you might refer to him as a scraggly-haired python. Pythons, of course, don't have hair, but by describing a scruffy-looking mobster as a snake that squeezes and crushes its prey, you give readers another way of thinking about your villain. Using metaphors, you can call your childhood home an altar to the saint of political correctness, or M&M's a rainbow for your mouth. Metaphors can be constructed with incredibly dissimilar objects, as long as one gives deeper meaning to the other.

Get to the Point with a Metaphor

Metaphors can also help you to eliminate unnecessary or unwanted words from your writing. You could take paragraphs of valuable space describing a setting: well-dressed people sitting along the shore of a river, the trees a swirl of bright green, the sunny, relaxed mood of the moment. Or just use a metaphor—"it was a Seurat painting come to the shores of the Allegheny." With a metaphor, you paint a vivid picture with just a few words.

SSENTIALS

Exercise your imagination by creating some unusual metaphors. Make two lists of very different things, then compare something in one list to something in the other. Be open and playful, and try to look at the items, actions, people—whatever you're comparing—in new ways.

When you're writing, be it fiction, nonfiction, or poetry, effective metaphors will probably just come to mind. Don't try to force them— though powerful metaphors do enrich writing, you don't need a huge number of them in every piece you write. Forced metaphors will probably come off as forced, and will distract more than they enlighten. Better to be open to compelling metaphors, but let them develop naturally and only when appropriate.

Warning!

Don't use what author Janet Burroway calls "dead metaphors"— comparisons that have been used so often that they no longer have any effect. "My love is a rose," "the eyes are the windows of the soul," and "the world is a stage" have been heard so often that we don't even notice the metaphor, let alone gain insight from it. Tired, stale metaphors will add nothing to your work, but lively, fresh ones will add a great deal.

When constructing similes and metaphors for children's books, be sure to make comparisons that children will understand. Well-crafted comparisons will help make abstract concepts concrete and develop children's ability to analyze and associate. Freshly worded comparisons will also encourage children's love of language.

Still another "don't": Don't mix your metaphors. That means don't compare one thing to two or more different things. For example, "The cinder blocks of his hate became a tornado of rage" is a badly mixed metaphor. Cinder blocks describe hate as a heavy, powerful, building force; also calling hate a tornado confuses the image and sends it in a different direction. The best metaphors communicate an idea simply and clearly and create one strong image at a time.

Simile Is Like a Metaphor

Like metaphors, similes clarify and enhance images by comparing one thing or action or idea to another, dissimilar one. Similes can also heighten and intensify readers' understanding of what the author is trying to accomplish by asking them to slow down and make connections. Like metaphors, similes can paint a concrete image of an abstract idea.

In order to be effective, similes should not only enlighten but surprise. Tired, overused similes—sweating like a pig, as white as a ghost, as cold as ice, night fell like a curtain—do little to add color or clarity to a word painting. When you create similes, be sure to construct them in fresh, imaginative terms.

Like powerful metaphors, powerful similes work their magic by creating images with details of sound, sight, taste, smell, and touch. Shakespeare was the master of the simile, but modern pros know how to use this figure of speech to achieve powerful results as well. Pulitzer Prize–winning author Michael Chabon constructs brilliant, sensory similes in his 1995 novel *Wonder Boys*, such as this one: "The whiskey tasted like bear steaks and river mud and the flesh of an oak tree." You've probably never tasted any of these three things, but you immediately know what Chabon is saying: There was an intense smokiness and earthiness—life—in that swallow.

QUESTIONS?

When should you use a simile?
There are no rules to follow, but you may want to consider inserting similes if your writing seems a little plain or unexciting. Similes can add vigor to your words while they give insight to your readers.

Another of his compelling similes paints a picture with both sight and sound: "The top [of the car] was down and I listened to the hiss of the wheels against the street, the flow of wind over the car, the sound of Stan Getz blowing faintly from the speakers and trailing out into the air behind us like a pearly strand of bubbles from a pipe." The language isn't flowery, it's simple and straightforward, and we connect with the image quickly and hear the music floating by.

Conceit

A simile (and a metaphor) can be constructed in the form of a conceit. This term began life centuries ago as a synonym for *thought* or *concept*, and now has come to mean an extended figurative device meant to delight or inform through its witty or unusual comparison. The understanding and pleasure readers receive from a conceit is more intellectual than sensory, because the two things that are compared are wildly different. It's usually not easy for the reader to make the connection, and so the author must explain it in order for the conceit to make its point; when the connection is made, a little light bulb clicks on.

Conceits are often used in poetry, but they can add wit or offer a very fresh way of looking at things in fiction and nonfiction as well. The poet John Donne used them often in his work; in a "verse letter" to a beloved friend, he compared receiving a letter from the friend to alms, to show the importance of his friend's affection:

> And now thy Almes is given, thy letter is read,
> The body risen againe, the which was dead,
> And thy poore starveling bountifully fed.

Centuries later, novelist Tom Robbins used the conceit in a more humorous way: He compared juggling to writing on a typewriter, to emphasize the difficulty and precariousness of being an author:

> My old typewriter was named Olivetti. I know an extraordinary juggler named Olivetti. No relation. There is, however, a similarity between juggling and composing on my typewriter. The trick is, when you spill something, make it look like part of the act.

Creating a conceit can give you a chance to come up with truly inventive comparisons to enrich your writing: love and a porch (both are home to human interaction, both are a place where most people would like to spend time, both can be walked all over); time and a termite (time eats away at life, a termite eats away at your home); whatever your creativity cooks up.

Onomatopoeia

Onomatopoeia, sometimes called "imitative harmony," is the forming of words that imitate a sound and that are associated with the object or action making the sound. The term is derived from the Greek word *onomatopoeia,* which means "the making of words."

For example, in "clanging of the bells," *clanging* is a word that sounds very much like the sound a bell makes when it's rung. The word *crackle* sounds like the sound a fire makes, or the rough noise we hear when something stiff is folded or broken. *Whoosh* sounds like the noise we hear when something speeds by. *Meow* is just like the cry a cat makes. All of these are pretty familiar forms of onomatopoeia, but poets and prose writers alike use inventive forms of this tool to add a further dimension to their work. In fact, you may want to create some onomatopoeic words of your own—try reading Lewis Carroll's poem "Jabberwocky" for inspiration.

SSENTIALS

Consider using words like *gush, mumbling, whirr,* and *plunk.* These onomatopoetic terms will add sensory detail as well as provide readers with more complete understanding.

Phanopoeia

Poets have also used a form of onomatopoeia to reflect sense, rather than its sound. This is called *phanopoeia*, from the Greek word meaning "making something visible." An example of phanopoeia is found in D. H. Lawrence's poem "Snake":

> He reached down from a fissure in the earth-wall in the gloom
> And trailed his yellow-brown slackness soft-bellied down, over
> the edge of the stone trough
> And rested his throat upon the stone bottom,
> And where the water had dripped from the tap, in a small
> clearness
> He sipped with his straight mouth, . . .

The rhythm, pace, and longer length of the lines create the image of a snake's slow and winding motion.

Personification

To personify an inanimate object or an idea means that you give it human attributes. Personification provides another way to make a comparison and to give deeper meaning to a concept. Personification is an effective writing tool because readers intuitively understand human traits and qualities and so can easily grasp the concept the writer is conveying.

Personification is found in both poetry and prose—even in jingles, advertising, and cartoons. In poetry, personification has been used for centuries. Here are some examples:

- "Their frail deeds might have danced in a green bay . . ."
    —Dylan Thomas, from "Do Not Go Gentle into That Good Night"
- "The moon . . . drags the sea after it like a dark crime"
    —Sylvia Plath, from "The Moon and the Yew Tree"
- "So the loud laugh of scorn, . . . / From the deep drinking-horn / Blew the foam lightly."
    —Henry Wadsworth Longfellow, from *Ballads*

Personification, when used sparingly and well, can be an excellent tool for helping readers connect to your images and ideas.

Personification also has a long history of prose usage. In his 1935 classic *Tortilla Flat,* John Steinbeck described nature in human terms when he wrote, "every tree crept stealthily along . . ." and the "tree-tops in the wind talked huskily, told fortunes and foretold deaths."

In his powerful 1963 novel *Sometimes a Great Notion,* Ken Kesey described the onset of unwanted winter as heralded by the arrival of flocks of geese. He wrote: "All the little coast towns listened, and all despised the geese in those first dingy November days."

Repetition

When you saw repetition listed here as a rhetorical device, you might have wondered why. Probably you've noticed that the repetition of words can make writing boring or produce sentences that have no rhythm or are just badly constructed. You wouldn't want to write: "It was a great day when we went to visit our Aunt Roberta, because she was a great pianist and we had a great time when we went to see her."

But repetition, when used well, can actually emphasize a point, heighten drama, and tie elements together. Words, sounds, phrases, syllables, allusions, stanzas, metrical patterns, and ideas can all be repeated in poetry and prose. But repeating words or elements should be added carefully to your writing and for a specific purpose.

Repetition can be used to great effect in song lyrics. The repeated sounds or words can set up a rhythm that adds to the language's musical quality, focuses the message, and supports or draws attention to the melody. One excellent example is found in Richard Rodgers and Lorenz Hart's "Blue Room," from the 1926 musical *The Girl Friend*. The word *room* is repeatedly used: "We'll have a blue room, / A new room, / For two room . . . ," setting up a rhythm that works with the melody. According to Rodgers, "All the rhymes and inner rhymes occur on the same note, C. Every time you are going to hear the half note which is the center of the melody, it is preceded by the repetition of C and the rhyme. And this half note is always the note which carries . . . the word *room*, the most important word in the song . . . both words and music are used to underscore the note which gives the song its individuality."

Repeating words in speeches can add great dramatic intensity. A famous and brilliant use of repetition is found in a speech Winston Churchill delivered in 1940, when Nazi Germany was threatening to conquer England: "We shall go on to the end. We shall fight in France, we shall fight on the seas and oceans, we shall fight with growing confidence . . . we shall defend our island. . . . We shall fight on the beaches, we shall fight on the landing grounds, we shall fight in the fields . . . we shall fight in the hills . . . We shall never surrender."

Churchill's repeated use of the phrase "we shall fight" gave both rhythm and power to his words. Using the phrase he describes how Britain will fight in every place and in every way, and will never give up. The phrase also worked as a rallying call to Churchill's countrymen to take up the fight and to join him in his determination never to surrender.

Dramatize and Emphasize

In poetry, many writers, past and present, have used repetition to good effect. For instance, in his poem "The Bells," Edgar Allan Poe repeats the subject word several times in each stanza. The repetition of the word unifies the stanzas while drawing attention to the different emotions bells invoke. Poe speaks of silver bells, mellow wedding bells, loud alarum bells, the anger of the bells, the throbbing of the bells, the moaning and the groaning of the bells. The poem gains momentum and strength through the continuing and strategic use of the word *bells*. Other poems by Poe, including "Annabel Lee" and "The Raven," also exhibit moving use of repetition.

FACTS

Repeated nonsense words and simple words also beguile children and encourage a love of language. Just think of the Dr. Seuss classics, Margaret Wise Brown's *Good Night Moon*, Russell Hoban's *Bread and Jam for Frances*, and Robert Munsch's *Love You Forever*.

Repetition can also be used to great effect in children's books. Recurring words, phrases, and sounds can keep children fascinated and encourage prereaders to participate in story time. In *Pierre: A Cautionary Tale in Five Chapters and a Prologue*, Maurice Sendak writes of "a boy named Pierre who would only say, 'I don't care!'" Pierre says "I don't care" again and again, and nearly every child who listens to this story will soon be saying it right along with him.

Understatement

Understatement is a figure of speech that makes a point through subtlety and humor. When you understate a point, you couch it in terms less strong than the facts indicate—you make your point lightly rather than with drama. Instead of writing that a nuclear bomb is the most terrifying weapon of mass destruction, you could write that a nuclear bomb would inconvenience an awful lot of people. The reader would think,

"Inconvenience! A nuclear bomb could wipe out an entire country!"—and immediately get your point. Using understatement allows writers to make the point by showing it to readers from a completely different angle.

Understatement of the Point

Many authors employ understatement in the short story and novel, but it is also a value tool in the screenwriter's and nonfiction writer's toolbox. In film, understatement can get a point across in few words, instead of taking valuable time for explanations. A classic example is found at the end of *Casablanca*, after the French police captain Louis Renault decides to conspire with bar owner Rick Blaine to let the woman he loves escape danger. Louis does something that wins him to Rick forever, and all Rick says is, "Louis, I think this is the beginning of a beautiful friendship."

ESSENTIALS

Understatement prevents writing from becoming melodramatic or overwrought. For example, a long diatribe on the evils of nuclear weapons might actually turn readers off, since they already know the horrific destruction these weapons cause.

Columnists and reviewers also use clever understatement to get a good laugh from readers. Miss Manners, a champion of witty remarks, uses understatement often. Responding to a single woman who wondered if it would be a good idea to ask a man out for coffee so she could find out if he was married, Miss Manners wrote, "it will take a few sips of coffee—not many—to find out whether he lives with someone, or if he believes that any lady he takes up with should make it up to him for the rotten way his ex-wife treated him. Miss Manners would think you would consider that worth knowing." Well, *of course* she would! Using subtlety and wit, the point is made lightly, rather than through a long, serious explanation.

Another master of witty understatement, *New Yorker* movie critic Anthony Lane, enhances readers' understanding of his reviews—and their reading pleasure—by making low-key movie and TV references. In his review of the movie *Sexy Beast,* Lane details how the main characters, ex-crook Gal and his wife Deedee, get back into the game. He sums up his review by saying that he knows the ideal neighbors for Gal and Deedee: "a loving couple from New Jersey, dreaming of decency and contentment with a few old habits to kick. A Mr. and Mrs. Soprano."

FACTS

In praising an understated scene in Jane Austen's *Emma,* editor and author Patricia O'Connor notes that she admires it for "what's left out. Without realizing it, we provide the missing pieces as we read. We use our imagination. And . . . we remember that scene as being more impassioned than it actually is."

Children's book authors can also use understatement to good effect. While exaggeration is a favorite of youngsters, understatement can also make a big hit, and encourage children to think about things in new ways. Understated remarks can work especially well in picture books, emphasizing a point in the illustration by coming at it from a different angle. In Steven Kellogg's *Can I Keep Him?* a boy who's been asking his mother if he can keep a number of animals—from a lost kitten to a fawn to a python—asks if he can keep "a bear that fell off a circus train." The drawing shows an enormous, scruffy bear destroying the family's living room, surrounded by several people holding their nose and looking like they're about to be sick. Kellogg uses charming understatement when he has the mother say, "No, dear. Bears have a disagreeable odor."

On the flip side of understatement is hyperbole, which is exaggeration or overstatement. Hyperbole can sometimes get your point across more quickly and more easily than a serious presentation—but watch out for tired forms: "As big as the ocean" is "as old as the hills."

CHAPTER 18

Word Usage Pitfalls

Writing creatively is hard work. You have to search for the right story, the right words, the right style. It's a continuing process of experimentation and examination, of insight and rewrite. You need to be open to inspiration, yet guard against the writing pitfalls that can infiltrate your work.

Part of the Rewriting Process

When you first draft your story, you should concentrate only on getting it down, using any words that come to mind. Then, during editing and evaluating, you can spend more time selecting the precise words and structure that will make your story rocket off the page. While you're looking for those perfect words, you should also look for—and eliminate—any imperfect constructions that keep your work from soaring.

The words you tie together need to evoke an image. They won't be able to do that unless they're strong and colorful. Your story may be filled with compelling information or fascinating characters or moving ideas, but readers won't bother reading it unless your language is rich and exciting.

Make the effort to put together sentences that will grab your readers' attention and inject life into your story. Check each one carefully to see if it sends the message or image you have in your mind. Then replace any word that's not doing its job. You may have to scour your journal, or spend time with your friend the thesaurus, but when you come up with that perfect word, you—and your readers—will be very happy you did.

Clichés

Clichés are old hat. They're over the hill. They have one foot in the grave (actually, two). They're dry as dust. They're dead as a doornail. They don't have a leg to stand on. Get it? Noteworthy creative writing is fresh, inventive, and sparkling—the exact opposite of the cliché.

QUESTIONS?

Did you know that some clichés really *are* as old as the hills? Plutarch is said to have coined "one foot in the grave" in A.D. 95. "Rome was not built in one day" was included in John Heywood's 1546 collection of English colloquial sayings called *Proverbs.*

Clichés are overused words and phrases. When they were first created, they were considered fresh and inventive and did what creative phrases are supposed to do—convey an idea or an image in imaginative terms. Think of the cliché "as easy as pie." It probably added a sparkle to stories and conversation, linking the concept of simplicity to making (and, with luck, eating) a favorite dessert. (This cliché would not exist, however, if I had come up with the concept—it would be "as difficult as pie," or maybe "as easy as buying a pie.") The expressions we now think of as clichés grew to be so well loved that they were repeated everywhere, and became so commonplace that they lost their spark.

Not all clichés are old. Watch out for current overused phrases or trendy wording, for example, "Make my day," that have caught on from popular movies, TV shows, song lyrics, and advertising.

Now, when we read or hear a cliché, we don't even think about the message or the image it was meant to send. Worse, if we read a story or an article that's full of clichés, we think it's boring, and that the writer hasn't put much effort into the piece. Searching out and removing as many trite offenders as possible from your work will keep your readers from beating a hasty retreat. (Did you catch that one?)

When someone starts to say "Accidents will . . . ," do you fill in the word *happen* before the person says it? If you can finish an expression after hearing or reading the first few words, you're dealing with a cliché. To help banish clichés from your repertoire, practice rewriting the following tired expressions in lively, forceful language:

- As free as the breeze
- Easier said than done
- Get to the heart of it
- Hit the nail on the head
- As slow as molasses

Keep in mind that expressive terminology needs to be framed with fresh appeal. Then, whenever you want to use an expressive phrase and come up with a cliché, remember that the thought may be a good one, but the wording and the approach need to change.

Weak Nouns, Verbs, Adjectives, and Adverbs

To write we need words—and luckily there are so many to choose from! That means you don't have to settle for any word that's ordinary or inexact or lifeless—you can hunt down the very one that will convey your image exactly. Take the time to choose strong, expressive, specific words that will make your writing soar.

QUESTIONS?

How can you add to your storehouse of powerful parts of speech? Make good friends with your thesaurus, for one. Also be on the lookout for exciting language in newspapers and magazines and on TV or the radio. Jot down every word that catches your fancy in your always-handy notebook.

Nouns

Sometimes there won't be any question about the right noun to use—it will be the name of a character or a city or an event, a proper noun. But if you're writing about general things, using common nouns—for example, *children*—you'll want to avoid using the word over and over again and come up with colorful synonyms that keep your writing from being dull. Instead of *children,* you could use *young ones,* or *preteens* (if that's the age group you're writing about), or *diaper denizens* (if you're writing about very young children), or *the knee-high crowd,* or *the stroller set,* or *toddlers,* or *those in the "no."*

Use your imagination to develop nouns or noun phrases that keep your writing fresh and engaging. Think in terms of sight, smell, sound, touch, and taste. While you may think that vivid description comes about through the use of adjectives, it is actually nouns that do most of the showing.

To see this for yourself, write a few sentences that don't contain any adjectives. If you choose hard-working nouns, you may be pleasantly surprised with the images you create.

Verbs

The word *verb* comes from the Latin word *verbum,* which means "word." This fact should give you an idea of how important verbs are in the construction of strong, image-making sentences.

Verbs describe action, so make them action packed. If you want a character to run across a field, think about the precise verb that would show the way you see him running: The character could race, or flee, or stagger, or stumble, or reel, or speed, or jog, or dart, or scurry, or rush. Any of these verbs would give readers a much better idea than *run* would of just how your character is making his way across the field.

FACTS

You can set your sentences in motion by showing people, objects, and events in motion. Even normally motionless objects can have life: doors can groan, TV sets can blare, statues can be hulking, festivals can invite.

Specific, well-chosen verbs can help readers visualize your words without the need for an armful of adverbs. They're also a great way to energize your writing and make your readers say "Ah!" For example, instead of writing, "Judy drew back when the horse tried to bite her," you could say, more vividly and more forcefully, "Judy flinched when the horse snapped at her fingers."

Adjectives

The right adjective can tell readers in a word what might otherwise take a paragraph to describe. They modify nouns, providing more information about them. An adjective tells readers if they should be picturing a russet-colored dog or a wolflike dog or a purse-sized dog or a raincoat-wearing dog.

Exercise your adjectives. Think of five ordinary adjectives—for example: pretty, fat, happy, small, and red—and include each in a sentence. Then come up with five image-making synonyms for each, and see how much more vivid your sentences become.

ALERT

When you edit your work, it's always a good idea to check for—and remove—unnecessary adjectives that overload your sentences or add only fluff, not meaning.

While adjectives add color and meaning, it's easy to get carried away and use too many of them. When you're composing your sentences, be sure to use only those adjectives that provide needed detail or nuance and pep up your language; if you use good, strong nouns, you will not need to modify each of them with an adjective.

Adverbs

What adjectives do for nouns, adverbs do for verbs, as well as for adjectives and other adverbs. Adverbs clarify, telling how, when, where, and to what extent, giving readers valuable information for picture making.

Like adjectives, adverbs can be overused when writers rely on them for detail instead of using a strong verb. But when used sparingly, they can liven up sleepy sentences and layer meaning. For example, if you wrote, "It was precisely 8:30 when Aiko opened the door to the small man carrying a rain-soaked briefcase," the adverb *precisely* makes *was* more interesting and more specific, and also adds a particular tone to the sentence: We think of the scene as being carefully arranged, and Aiko as a precise and measured person. If you wrote, "It was early morning when Aiko opened the door to the small man carrying a rain-soaked briefcase," you would establish a different tone and set a slightly different scene. Precise, vivid wording makes all the difference in your writing.

Unnecessary Words

It's easy to overwrite. We're so busy searching for that perfect word, that when we come up with one, we want to use it—and another and another. All of a sudden, every noun is clarified by an adjective; every verb has a trailing adverb. We describe things down to the tiniest detail—and wind up writing stories that overload readers with unnecessary verbiage. We pile on the similes and make sure every sentence contains a metaphor. If one descriptor is good, then two must be better.

"A sentence should contain no unnecessary words, a paragraph no unnecessary sentences, for the same reason that a drawing should have no unnecessary lines and a machine no unnecessary parts."
—E. B. White and William Strunk, from *The Elements of Style*

When editing your work, remember the saying "less is more." Using powerful language will eliminate the need to load on the adjectives. And checking carefully to see that every word imparts some information, or is necessary to a phrase or description, will keep your writing moving. If you're describing a mountainous area as part of a travel article, saying that the rocks are light gray is unnecessary—many rocks are a grayish color, and readers know this without your telling them. If, on the other hand, the rocks are covered with pictographs, that's news and needs to be included.

Providing every detail also gives your readers less of a chance to use their imagination. If you write that a scruffy cat suddenly appears in a little boy's yard, readers can decide if it's a marmalade-colored cat or a skin-and-bones cat or a playful cat. With just the right amount of guidance, readers can make their own associations.

Short stories, screenplays, children's books, and poems are good models of tight writing because their formats put every word at a premium. Studying these works will help you whittle your words down to the bare essentials for telling the tale.

Process of Elimination

To practice editing wordy text, try eliminating the unnecessary words in the following sentence:

As the bloodred dawn broke widely across the gray blue hills and the dark green lake, four men dressed in hip boots, tan vests, and heavy, large overcoats stood drinking small cups of steaming coffee as they waited for the noisy approaching boat.

Redundancy

Also watch out for redundant words and phrases. You don't need to write the "month of June"—readers know that June is a month. Likewise it's unnecessary to write "the bag was completely full"—*full* means *completely filled,* and adding *completely* is redundant. And never say "very unique." Unique is unique.

Unclear, Unvaried, and Run-on Sentences

Compelling fiction and nonfiction are created one sentence at a time. That means when you edit your work, you need to check each sentence for clarity and strength. Sentences can be informational, questioning, or commanding, but all need to have a subject and a predicate (except sentence fragments) and read smoothly, clearly, and engagingly. Fuzzy, same-sized, and marathon-length sentences prevent your writing from being its best. They also confuse and upset readers.

FACTS

Simple sentences have one subject and one predicate. *Compound sentences* contain two or more independent clauses, often joined by a conjunction such as *but* or *and. Complex sentences* have one independent clause and one dependent, or incomplete, clause. *Sentence fragments* lack either a subject or a predicate.

Unclear Sentences

"Hsun said that many of his flowers wilted on Tuesday." Here is a prime example of an unclear sentence—it could mean just what it says, that Hsun's flowers succumbed to a heat wave on Tuesday, or it could mean that Hsun said on Tuesday that his flowers had wilted. Sentences should be constructed so readers have no doubt about the meaning (unless the ambiguity is intentional). The message in the example sentence would not be in doubt if the sentence were rewritten: "On Tuesday, Hsun said his flowers had wilted."

Sometimes, in revising, an author is too close to his or her material to see pronoun problems. It's always a good idea to have an outside reader check to see if your references are clear. Reading sentences aloud will also help.

Muddy sentences also occur when the subject and predicate are too far apart. Here's an example: "When Nancy, who had just finished her aerobics class and was incredibly hot and thirsty and looking for a place to stop to rest, finally sat down, she dropped heavily into the chair." This sentence is much too long and awkward, and as we read it we keep searching for the action—what did Nancy do? The structure is confusing and slows the reader down. Better to write, "After finishing her aerobics class, Nancy was incredibly hot and thirsty. She dropped heavily into a chair as soon as she found one." Breaking the long sentence into two shorter ones helps enormously, but so does moving each predicate close to each subject.

Unclearly referenced pronouns also contribute to muddy sentences. In the sentence "Arlen told Eduardo that he needed to see a doctor," it's unclear *who* needs to see the doctor—Arlen or Eduardo. Meaning is made clear when a pronoun is placed close to its antecedent, but sometimes you will need to restructure or break up a confusing sentence. For example, the message in the example sentence would be clear if it were rewritten: "Arlen said to Eduardo, 'I need to see the doctor,'" or "Arlen needed to see a doctor. He told this to Eduardo."

Unvaried Sentence Length

It's possible to write a piece of fiction or nonfiction with sentences that are pretty much the same length. But that's not a good idea. Consider this paragraph:

> Latoya was tired of waiting. She tapped her foot. She looked around. Millie was still not in sight. Latoya's mouth turned down. She could feel her breathing quickening. Her heart beat fast.

Monotonous, right? Varying sentence length will provide interest and also give your writing rhythm. A short sentence following several longer ones can emphasize a point. A longer sentence can provide a sense of flow, or enrich or extend an image. In dialogue, sentences of varied length make the conversation more real—you will probably want to include sentence fragments there, too, because people use them often in real life.

If you're writing an informational piece, keep sentences on the shorter side. Many news writers restrict their sentences to twenty or fewer words, with only the occasional longer sentence cropping up.

Sentence length can do much to establish tone. If you're writing a chase scene or developing intercharacter tension or reporting news in the making, short sentences can deliver a sense of urgency. If you're describing a country scene or want to establish a feeling of elegance or laziness, longer sentences can help convey a message of ease and tranquility. Often writers find that they have a natural feel for how to vary their sentences, but you may find it necessary to work at mixing them up.

Run-on Sentences

Just as it's easy to get carried away with adjectives and adverbs, it's also easy for writers to get carried away with an idea. Once you get going, it can be hard to stop. You describe and you point out and you show and you explain and all of a sudden your sentence takes up an entire page. And no one can understand it!

During editing, look carefully not only at the variety of your sentences but also at how long they are. If they roll on and on with nary a period in sight, some cutting or dividing needs to be done. Compound and complex sentences are great, but you don't want to wear readers out or bamboozle them. A sentence should be long enough to express one idea—and no more. You can achieve a pleasing flow and give readers a chance to catch your meaning by smoothly linking shorter sentences.

Within the Sentence

In addition to varying sentence length, vary sentence function and form, too. Begin some sentences with the subject and some with an introductory phrase. Be sure every sentence doesn't start with "The." Mix compound and complex sentences with simple sentences. Make some sentences questions and some commands.

A good way to emphasize a point is to put the most important words at the end of the sentence. These are the words that will remain in the reader's mind. Similarly, it's effective to put the most important sentences at the end of a paragraph.

SSENTIALS

"We like that a sentence should read as if its author, had he held a plough instead of a pen, could have drawn a furrow deep and straight to the end."

—Henry David Thoreau

Also, to get across the core idea in a complex sentence, put the key words in the independent, or main, clause. Put the supporting details in the dependent, or incomplete, clause.

Inconsistent or Inappropriate Tone

Tone can be tricky. It lets readers know the type of writing at hand—straightforward, humorous, angry, or scary. But not only must every word support the chosen tone, but the tone itself must remain consistent in order to pull off the desired effect.

You can think of tone in writing in the same way you think of it in speech. For example, if you're telling a friend about the rude way someone treated you, every word you use, and the way you string your words together, is going to relay your unhappiness over the encounter. Plus, your entire diatribe is going to pour out in the same way—you're upset, and you stay upset for the length of your rant. If you start out emotionally, spitting out your words, and then continue by speaking calmly and softly, the impact of your words will be lost and your friend will be very confused.

It's the same way with writing. You choose a tone, and then you stick with it to make your intent clear. But sometimes tone can slip away from you, and what started out as a serious account is suddenly mocking or accusatory. If you're happy with the wording, you can miss the fact that the tone has changed and no longer suits the story. For example, it's not a good idea for a marketing piece, no matter how clever, to make fun of a product instead of touting it.

 **SSENTIALS**   Read a press release or a letter to the editor. What is the overall tone? Once you determine it, read the piece again and pick out the specific words that put the tone across. Are they consistent?

You can check for tone consistency by checking your wording. Keep in mind the tone you intend as you review and revise. In fact, it's helpful to write down the intended tone and refer to it as you work. If your tone is meant to be funny, check to see that the words you used are light and sarcastic, not academic or cruel. Or if your intent is to persuade people to take up a cause, make sure your language is coaxing and encouraging throughout, not threatening or abusive. Precise wording is key to keeping tone consistent and reflecting the mood and emotional level you have in mind. It's also the way to convey your message to readers.

Inappropriate Language

Once you know the tone of your piece, keep it consistent by editing out unsuitable wording. Inappropriate language comes in several varieties.

Sometimes words that have a perfectly innocent meaning in English have a not-so-innocent, or a downright offensive, meaning in another language. If you're writing a speech or preparing copy for other than native English speakers, check with experts for culturally inappropriate expressions.

- If you're writing a book for young children, you need to use words that are appropriate to their understanding and their age. Stretching their vocabulary is great, but you don't want them to struggle so much that they give up in despair.
- If you're writing for a general audience but covering an esoteric subject, you need to make sure that the language you use has meaning for the reader, or else provide definitions for any jargon you include.
- If you're writing for an academic audience, you probably won't want to include slang, and for a hip-hop crowd you'll write more casually.
- Whatever age or audience you're writing for, don't talk down to your readers or insult their intelligence. Always assume you're writing for bright, with-it readers—they're reading your material, after all!
- For all forms of writing, beware of alienating your audience by using sexist, ageist, racist, or culturally offensive words. When you check your work for appropriateness, though, you don't need to call in the politically correct police. Just use your common sense.

Excessive Use of Passive Voice

Which sentence is more powerful?

1. Basset hounds are little known by most people.
2. Most people don't know a thing about basset hounds.

Did you pick sentence #2? If you did, you know that framing your words in the active voice produces much more direct, vigorous writing.

A sentence in the active voice puts the subject in the power seat: "Portia entered the kitchen." A sentence using the passive voice makes the object of the verb the subject: "The kitchen was entered by Portia." The passive voice creates an indirect, weak construction, reducing punch and adding words. Subjects are acted upon instead of doing the acting, and readers generally find this dull or misleading. The passive voice can also slow down readers because they expect sentences to unfold in subject-follows-predicate order.

To engage your readers in what they're reading, and to make your writing more emphatic, choose the active construction. Scour your sentences for passive wording that drags your writing down. The inclusion of a linking verb such as a form of *be, appear, look,* or *seem* can indicate passive wording. The following sentences are written in the passive voice: "My son was laid low by the week-long heat wave" and "The snake was looked at by everyone as it made its slow way across the riverbank."

QUESTIONS?

Can you reword these sentences so they have more punch?

- Sunny found himself blushing.
- There was a sudden hush that came over the party.
- A solitary backfire was heard.

Even sentences that show little action are best when couched in active terms. "Keiko focused on the coming day" is stronger than "The coming day was focused on by Keiko." "Two spotted cows munched on the grass" is more compelling than "There were two spotted cows munching on the grass." When you revise, if you find any sentences that you unintentionally wrote in the passive voice, refocus them for action.

Exceptions to the Rule

Is there ever a good reason to use the passive voice? There are occasions when the passive voice is useful. For one, the passive voice can put the focus on the object or person being acted upon, if that's your intent. Using the passive voice, you can say, "The letter was written by Irena," when the letter is what's key. Or you can say, "Jerry was strangled with his dog's leash," cluing readers in to how Jerry was murdered—they already know that he's dead.

You can also use the passive voice if you either don't know or don't want to say who is responsible for an action. For example, journalists who aren't free to quote a source often say, "It has been reported that . . ." If many people and many travel books tell you that the Tetons are a great vacation spot, you might say, "The Tetons are said to be . . ." Such constructions get your message across, but they do it weakly, without punch.

CHAPTER 19

Overcoming Writer's Block

As with anything important you work at—your nine-to-five job, sports, parenting, relationships, caring for your garden and your home— you're going to have good writing days and bad writing days. This chapter will help you deal with the bad days each writer faces sooner or later.

When Your Creative Juices Aren't Flowing

Some days there will be so many ideas bubbling in your brain that it will be all you can do to make it to your writing time and get them down on paper. The words will pour out like French champagne into crystal. You'll be humming and smiling—creative writing is the best!

On other days, it won't be as easy. Still, the energy is there, and though you sigh a bit and pace a bit, the words come. You get something good down, or maybe you spend time revising and are pleased with the pages you put a shine on. You're productive, and you're satisfied. This writing life is okay.

FACTS

"In the creative state a man is taken out of himself. He lets down as it were a bucket into his subconscious, and draws up something which is beyond his reach. He mixes this thing with his normal experiences, and out of the mixture he makes a work of art."

—E. M. Forster

But sooner or later a day arrives when nothing comes, and you find yourself sitting there staring at your fingers, wondering what you've done wrong or thinking you really should be cleaning the litter box. The blank computer screen waits expectantly, but you have nothing to tell it. Not a word. Or a horrible word that you immediately erase.

It's writer's block, and it's got you in its grasp. It can last a short time or be interminable—some writers never recover from it, and give up and find a new activity. But that's not going to happen to you. Almost all authors have at some time gone through a period of being blocked, and most have found techniques that let them break through the wall.

Causes of Writer's Block

Whenever you get stuck, try to determine what's really blocking you. The causes might be emotional, physical, or literary. Once you diagnose the problem, you can figure out how to overcome it.

Fear of failure. Just about every writer suffers at some point from a bad case of nerves. I'm not good enough, you think. I can't possibly do this well. Who am I to think I have anything important to say? Even while you're loving what you're doing, and occasionally seem to put a few decent words together, you're certain that you can't possibly measure up to your own or to others' expectations. You think, why bother to write anything when it will never make the grade?

Fear of success. The flip side of fear of failure is fear of success. Things are rolling along, and you're feeling pretty good about your writing. But what happens when you finish your play or your poem? You're going to have to send it out into the world—and editors and readers might enjoy it! Then you'll have to write something else. There will be new decisions to make, new commitments, new challenges. If your work does very well, you might even have to give an interview or speak in front of an audience. It all makes you wonder if you shouldn't just stop right now and avoid all those new problems.

Lack of concentration. The dog just threw up. You have to leave in twenty minutes to take your kid to the orthodontist. Your mother-in-law is arriving this weekend for an indeterminate stay. Your boss has been looking at you funny for a few weeks. Another of your tech stocks just tanked. You have a big exam coming up. The world is too much with you, but you promised yourself you were going to write every day. So you close the door and sit down—and can't think of a word to write.

"Sometimes . . . agony visits the head of a writer. At these moments, I stop writing and relax with a coffee at my favorite restaurant, knowing that words can be changed, rethought, fiddled with, and, of course, ultimately denied."

—Steve Martin, author and comedian

Lack of energy. Like all the things that can distract you, feeling less than your best can contribute to writer's block. Maybe you're coming down with the flu, or you've just gotten over a cold. Maybe you're worried about . . . well, any number of things, and you were up all night. Maybe it's crunch time at school or the office, and you've been putting in many more hours than usual. You hurt your knee skiing. You're depressed about losing out on a promotion, or shaken from a run-in with a driver with road rage. You've been revising your article all day. Just about any physical or mental stressor can block the creative flow, for a few hours or much longer.

Lack of down time. Everything's been going well. You came up with a great idea, you did your research, you wrote a rough but decent first draft. Then, without taking a break, you jumped right in to start shaping and polishing—and you're stumped. You can't imagine where all your excitement went, all your energy. You begin to doubt everything you've done. What in the world were you thinking?

Lack of material. The idea came so easily, and you know it's a topic that will appeal to a broad range of readers. You were pretty familiar with the subject, so you didn't spend much time on research. Now it seems the idea wasn't so great after all—there's really not much to write about. You've sketched out a couple of pages, but nothing more comes.

To help prevent writer's block, end each day's writing in the middle of something that's working well. When you start up again, you can continue with that section and have its momentum keep you rolling. If you complete a section, make yourself a note about what comes next.

A problem with the story. You know where you're going but you can't seem to get there. The conflict isn't developing properly. Your character seems one-dimensional. The drama just isn't there. When you first came up with the idea, you saw the story very clearly. There really wasn't a need to do any planning or make an outline, because it was obvious what should happen. Now that you're in it, though, you can't make anything work. The whole project has bogged down.

You're trying to fix the wrong problem. You can't understand it. You developed your story point by point, and now you can't write the ending. Everything should have led up to a dynamite conclusion, but you're stymied. Is it possible you took a wrong step earlier? No, it's just that you're tired or having a bad day—isn't it?

Dealing with the Problem

The first thing to remember when coping with writer's block is: Don't make yourself crazy. The second thing is: Trust that this is not a permanent condition. Something is going to get you writing again— unless deep down you have decided that you never want to write again.

QUESTIONS?

Does the story you're blocked on still interest you?
Your inability to write might be due to the simple fact that you no longer want to write this particular piece. For whatever reason, the topic no longer excites you—and without passion, there's nothing to drive you.

When you first realize that every word count is producing the same number, don't panic. It may be just a short-lived thing, and getting up and stretching or getting something cold to drink will get you back in the groove. But if you've done ten sets of exercises and drunk ten glasses of water without effect, it may be time for some stronger measures.

If You Are Stuck

Reread from the start and find the last paragraph that you think is a good one. Start again there (don't delete everything from that point forward, just move it out of the way—you may want to rework it at a later point). Build your story by hooking on to something promising.

> Unlike many people, I have no fear of writing, I have a facility for putting words on paper. Not writing scares me more! But if I find myself stuck on a project, I jump to something else. I always have several activities going at once. Also, the thesaurus is one of my favorite tools. I'll write something simply, and then jazz it up in a later draft.
> —Annalisa McMorrow, business writer and novelist

Or try adding a new scene, a new character, a new point. If you're stuck on what you've got, creating a new element may be the way to get the whole thing rolling again. The energy of the new feature may send your work in a different direction, and carry you along with it.

Take a whole new tack with the project. Change voice, point of view, tense, even genre. Or narrow or widen the focus. Maybe the idea is right but the approach is wrong. Experiment and see what works.

FACTS

When author Tom Wolfe tried to write a magazine article about custom cars, he was blocked. The editor suggested Wolfe type up his notes for someone else to write. While typing, "something [began] to happen," and his notes turned into a 49-page story that became *The Kandy-Kolored Tangerine-Flake Streamlined Baby.*

If none of these strategies work, show your work to an outside reader. Explain that you're bogged down, and ask for help in pinpointing the problem. Is the story making sense? Is it interesting? What can be done to add drama? What would be a logical next step? Brainstorm possibilities. Even if you don't think any of the suggestions are helpful, just talking about the piece may make it more real in your mind, and you'll come up with an idea that breaks the block. Remember, you don't have to go this alone.

If You Lost the Energy

Take a major break. Shut off the computer, or put your pen back in the drawer. Get up and walk away—for the rest of the day, for a few days, or even longer. Try taking a complete vacation from what you're working on. You may be so wrapped up in it, or so tired from all the hours you've put into it, that you're simply overloaded. Giving yourself a rest, and coming back fresh, may be all that's needed to restart your engine.

If you are reluctant to take a break, at least take a break from writing and instead work on another part of the project. Edit what you've written so far, or look up additional material—lack of enough to work with may be holding you back. Or go out and do the interview you've been putting off. You'll be giving yourself a break from word production, but still moving ahead.

If You Are Stressed

If you are pressed for time, try to concentrate on how much you've already accomplished. Reread what you've got so far, and congratulate yourself on how far you've come. If you've come this far, you can go farther.

A big project can easily overwhelm a writer. Break up your work into sections. If you're writing a 5,000-word short story, work on the project in 1,000-word increments. The thought of having to write 1,000 words is less intimidating than having to write 5,000 words.

FACTS

"When I have trouble writing, I step outside my studio into the garden and pull weeds until my mind clears—I find weeding to be the best therapy there is for writer's block."
—Irving Stone, novelist

Take care of any non-writing-related problems that may be bothering you. If you're worried about a presentation at work, don't try to write until you've made it. If you need to do your taxes by next Friday, sit down with the forms now. Anything that's putting pressure on you can put a halt to the creative flow.

Maybe the lack of deadlines stresses you out. Go ahead and assign yourself a deadline. Tell yourself that you have to finish the piece in three days, or whatever seems reasonable. The pressure of a deadline worked in high school and college—maybe it will work again now.

Doctors recommend exercise to relieve stress, so if you are stressed about writing, get up from your desk and head for the gym or the park. At least a half hour of walking, running, jumping rope, swimming, or whatever you like to do will do you good. Exercise can relieve pent-up anxiety, plus it may tire you out enough to get a good night's sleep, reviving you for a better day's work tomorrow.

A Change of Scenery

Move your writing location, time, or tools. Most of the time you may need to be in your comfortable chair at your familiar computer, dog at your feet, to write well. But shaking up your routine may wake up your creativity. If you always write in the kitchen, try the living room. If you always write from six to eight in the morning, experiment with creating later in the day. Take your laptop or a notebook to the local coffee place. Move outdoors, or to the library or a bookstore. If you always work at the computer, see what writing longhand produces.

ESSENTIALS

Give yourself some visual stimuli. Look at photographs, artwork, magazines, gardens. The colors, textures, and subject matter may be just what's needed to unlock your artistic gates.

If the new scenery can't fire up your creativity, maybe a new project will, so start all over. I know, this sounds awful. But if you try a number of fixes and nothing seems to help, maybe the problem is that the piece is simply unworkable. It happens. But don't look at it as the end of the world. Put the work away, and start looking for a new idea. Comfort yourself by remembering that the time wasn't wasted. Everything you write, even stories that you never complete, adds to your knowledge and exercises your imagination.

Additional Strategies

If nothing else works, try the following strategies. Who knows what might work!

• Write for ten minutes. Even if you can't think of a thing to say, set the timer for ten minutes and write something until the bell rings. Just writing "blah, blah, blah" over and over may put your mind back in writing mode.

"Write to yourself about being blocked. Explain to yourself the feelings of frustration you are feeling, or the anger. . . . Describe to yourself the chapter or scene you are writing. . . . Believe me, it will start to come. . . ."

—Dominick Dunne, novelist

• Eat. Your lack of imagination may be the result of a lack of food. Engines can't run without burning gas. You can't run without breakfast, lunch, and dinner.
• Decide on a way to reward yourself when you complete the project. If the treat is good enough, it will serve as an incentive to get back in gear.
• If you're writing for pay, remind yourself that if you don't finish, you won't get that check. A glance at your bill pile couldn't hurt either.
• Read some writing that really excites you. Reminding yourself how the greats do it may help you to uncover the problems in your own work that are holding you back.
• Talk to other writers. Ask how they solve the problem or for any techniques they know about it. Even if something didn't work for them, it might help you.

Be patient. If one start-up technique doesn't work, give yourself a break and then try something different. If you get a few sentences down and then have more trouble, don't force yourself to keep going, just try again tomorrow. It may take a little while, but keep telling yourself you'll eventually get back to writing. And you will.

Make it a point to learn new words. Words are the ingredients of the dishes you serve up, and the wider your vocabulary, the more scrumptious your meals will be. Read widely. Look up words you don't know in the dictionary. Play word games and solve word puzzles.

Sometimes it can take much longer than a few hours or a few days before you're ready to start back in on a piece that's been blocking you. Some authors have set aside work for years before they found the inspiration to complete it.

CHAPTER 20

Working with Others

Writing can be a lonely occupation. Idea generating and research may take you out into the world, but most of the time it will be just you and your computer. It's important to leave your corner from time to time for the assistance and the camaraderie of other writers.

Collaboration

Playwright and author Moss Hart saw collaboration between writers as a "protest against the unalterable fate of being alone." If you're working on a small project, this may not be practical. But for something larger, especially a piece of writing that involves a good deal of research, it may benefit you to seek out another writer to work with.

FACTS

Collaboration enables writers to pool talents and to share resources, skills, and legwork. It also doubles (or triples) time available for a project and provides an immediate source of feedback and evaluation.

If you collaborate, there are two (or more) heads to address problems and come up with solutions. If you're thinking of ditching for the day, you're more likely to decide to do your share. And by collaborating, there's always someone to complain to, laugh and celebrate with, and count on, and someone who understands your work inside and out. With a writing partner, you're not alone.

Writers collaborate in different ways. Some work together crafting each sentence. Some evenly distribute the responsibilities: One does the research; one does the writing. Or both take part in every phase but work on separate chapters or scenes. Sometimes writers will brainstorm ideas, and then one will write a first draft for the other to revise and refine. Whichever route you choose, try to use each person's talents in the best way possible, and find a system that makes you both happy.

Working together can lighten the load and enrich the writing experience. But trying to collaborate with four or more writers can become unwieldy. It's more likely you'll have a successful "marriage" as a twosome or, at the most, a threesome.

What to Expect

If you've never collaborated before, it may take some getting used to. It will definitely help if the writers have compatible personalities and work habits, and complement each other's skills. It's also important that you respect each other and listen to each other. Before you get under way, set aside some time to map out how the process will work. You can always make changes as needed, but setting up a system can help you determine and agree on your goals.

Here are some issues to take care of first:

- Make a list of all the work involved, and then divvy it up. Include such jobs as library and online research, interviews, word processing, editing, proofreading, keeping track of costs, safeguarding notes and other materials, and submitting work to potential publishers.
- Decide how you will share any profits and expenses.
- Decide how you will settle the inevitable disagreements—find a middle ground or agree not to go forward with something unless both partners are happy with it—and more important, how you'll work to prevent serious problems—with respect, fairness, honesty, and humor.

 **SSENTIALS**

Bestselling collaborators Val Corbett and Joyce Hopkirk, who write as Val Hopkirk and have coauthored six novels, say they've learned to criticize each other's ideas constructively. If they disagree, they don't make vomiting sounds; instead, they say, "Yeess, that's one way forward but . . . what about if we . . ."

- Decide when and where you'll work (collaboration can be done over the Internet, but it's generally better to meet face-to-face).
- Determine if you want a written rather than a verbal agreement that covers all aspects of the collaboration.
- Work out a deadline schedule.
- Decide whether you'll write under both of your names or come up with a different one.

Collaborating with another writer can be a great way to learn and improve your skills. But remember that it can also be a way to lessen isolation and pressure and share your love of writing. Make time to talk about writing and other interests as well as about your project. Take your work to a café or go out to lunch together. Work hard, but work on encouraging and supporting each other, too.

Winning Teams

The following list includes novelists, screenplay writers, and songwriters who succeeded through collaboration. Some, like Charles Dickens, are writers in their own right, while others have established lengthy collaborative efforts that span their writing careers.

- Wilkie Collins, the nineteenth-century author of *The Moonstone* and *The Woman in White,* and renowned writer Charles Dickens, author of *Great Expectations* and *Oliver Twist.* Literary collaborators and traveling companions, they penned *The Lazy Tour of Two Idle Apprentices.*
- Julius Epstein and Philip Epstein. Twin brothers, the Epsteins worked together on the screenplays of several movie classics, including *Arsenic and Old Lace, The Brothers Karamazov,* and *Casablanca.*

FACTS

Charles Nordhoff and James Norman Hall, who cowrote *Mutiny on the Bounty,* used both names but needed to determine which would come first. They decided on "Nordhoff and Hall" because Hall thought it was more effective to end a sentence or anything else with a "short, crisp word."

- Edith Anna Oenone Somerville, a nineteenth-century Irish author, artist, and suffragist, and Violet Florence Martin, Somerville's cousin who wrote under the pseudonym Martin Ross. Together the women collaborated on a series of humorous novels about the rural Irish gentry. Their most important literary achievements were *The Real Charlotte,* in which the two main characters are cousins, and *Some Experiences of an Irish R. M.,* which was adapted for television in 1983.
- Edmond-Louis-Antoine Huot de Goncourt and Jules-Alfred Huot de Goncourt. Known as *les deux Goncourt,* these French brothers authored a number of well-known novels of the naturalist school, including *Mme. Gervaisais* and *Soeur Philomène,* and a study entitled *The Woman of the Eighteenth Century.* After Jules's death, Edmond

continued writing under both names because he felt that he and Jules were still communicating.

- Charles Nordhoff and James Norman Hall, who cowrote *Mutiny on the Bounty*. Nordhoff met Hall in 1916, and the two soon wrote a book about their World War I flying unit, the Lafayette Flying Corps. When they received an advance from *Harper's* to write travel articles, they moved to Tahiti, where they coauthored three very successful novels about the H.M.S. *Bounty*. They later collaborated on six other books.

"When one is at a low point . . . , the very presence in the room of another human being, even though he too may be sunk in the same state of gloom, very often gives that dash of valor to the spirit that allows confidence to return and work to resume."
—Moss Hart, playwright

- Frederic Dannay and Manfred B. Lee. Using the name Ellery Queen, these cousins cowrote a large number of popular mysteries, including *The Hollywood Murders* and *The Tragedy of Errors and Others*. They also developed the idea for *Ellery Queen's Mystery Magazine*, which Dannay edited from 1941 to 1982.
- Lowell Ganz, Babaloo Mandel, and Bruce Jay Friedman. A dynamic collaborative team, these writers developed the screenplay for *Splash*, the highly successful 1984 comedy about a mermaid who falls in love with a New Yorker, starring Tom Hanks and Daryl Hannah.
- Moss Hart and George Kaufman. A prolific and critically acclaimed writing duo, Hart and Kaufman wrote six plays together, including *The Man Who Came to Dinner* and *You Can't Take It with You,* which won the Pulitzer Prize in 1937.
- John Lennon and Paul McCartney. Known the world over, this extraordinary half of the Beatles wrote some of the most well-loved and revolutionary songs of the twentieth century, including "Norwegian Wood." A friend of theirs, Hunter Davis, remarked that "Now and again, they'd write whole songs individually, but mostly one of them had half a song and the other one would finish it off."

Joining a Writers' Group

Having another writer provide feedback on your work is an important first step in putting that work in front of an audience. It also gives you access to the assistance and fellowship of another author. To expand your audience, as well as to learn from and enjoy the company of other wordsmiths, you may want to consider joining a writers' group. Many authors, from those whose books climb the bestseller lists to those just starting out, find the tips, constructive criticism, brainstorming possibilities, contacts, friendships, and encouragement available in writing groups to be essential to their writing process.

FACTS

Once you join a group, you may want to expand the program. Consider inviting outside authors to speak, having an expert such as a tax preparer or agent visit, or starting an online newsletter to keep in touch between meetings.

To make the experience enjoyable as well as valuable, look for a group that will meet your needs. If you write in a specific genre, hooking up with a group of similarly directed authors is probably best. If you're primarily interested in getting and giving feedback, you may want to join a group that spends all of its meeting time critiquing work. If you're also looking for a social element, or to learn about publishing or the business end of writing, a group that invites speakers or holds an after-meeting social time may be more to your liking. Think about what you want out of a group before you start interviewing.

That's Right—Interviewing

Unless you start your own group, which you certainly can do, any group you contact will most likely ask you to show them samples of your work and attend a meeting. This will benefit both parties. The writers in the club will be able to assess the level of your writing and also see the kind of criticism and experience you'd contribute. By interviewing, you'll have the opportunity to determine if you'll be comfortable in the group, and with the level of the members' writing and expertise. You'll also get a chance to see the kind of help they might offer. Aim to join a group whose writing is more advanced than your own. In that way you'll learn the most—and be inspired to reach a higher level.

When interviewing writers' groups, look for peers who are knowledgeable, kind, honest, and who love language. Be sure you'll enjoy spending time with the members and that they'll offer both support and useful information.

A Group of Critics

All writers' groups don't function in the same way. In some, every member brings something to read or discuss—a chapter, an outline, an idea, a completed article or story, a troublesome paragraph. In others, the group focuses on a different member's material or questions each time they meet. Some groups meet weekly, some monthly, some when a member needs help. But all groups meet to support members and to provide a critical ear that will help improve their work.

Just as you would ask one outside reader for specific comments, do the same with the group. Explain exactly what you want help with, or the information you need. Read your material aloud clearly; you may also want to hand out copies of the work for the members to follow. Listen carefully to all comments, and try not to be upset by negative feedback. Focus on the work.

When it's your turn to critique another member's writing, put yourself in his or her shoes. Criticize the work, not the writer. Give your full attention to the material. Make notes if that will help you convey your thoughts. And keep in mind that your role is to help improve the material. If you have something negative to say, begin with something positive. Relay the criticism as gently as you can while still making the point. Mention both strengths and weaknesses. And try to offer suggestions for improvement when you find flaws. "This section confused me" doesn't help the author. "This section confused me—I think I would understand it better if you add a flashback that reveals why Irene would act this way" offers useful information.

ALERT

If you continually leave meetings feeling beaten up and depressed, you're probably in the wrong group. Negative feedback can be helpful if it's presented carefully and constructively. But if members trash your work and don't offer helpful advice, look for a new group with a more positive approach.

Finding a Group

If you think you might benefit from joining a compatible writing group, the next step is to locate one. There are a number of ways to go about this.

- Word of mouth is always the best. Friends who are writers, or who know other writers, may be able to tell you about groups to contact.
- Your local bookstore may post information on writing groups in the area or may sponsor its own group. Likewise, the local library may be home to a group of writers.
- Other organizations that sometimes host writing groups or can direct you in the right direction include YWCAs or YMCAs, city recreational departments, adult education centers, or civic groups.
- If your newspaper has a daily or weekly book section, you could contact the paper to see if they have information about groups.
- Writing conferences and workshops can be excellent sources of leads.
- The Internet can also connect writers in remote locations, or act as a help line, though meeting face-to-face is ideal.

Taking a Writing Class or Attending a Workshop

If the ongoing meetings of a writing group don't suit your schedule, you can still make contact with other writers by taking classes or going to the occasional workshop, seminar, conference, or retreat. Classes and workshops cost money, but if they're slanted to your genre and address your concerns, they'll most likely be worth every penny.

If you don't find a writing group that seems just right, consider starting your own by posting signs in the library or bookstore or placing an ad in the paper.

Writing classes can provide you with both the fellowship and the feedback of your classmates, plus access to the experience and insights of the instructor. Classes—on creative writing, writing mechanics, and the business of writing—are most likely available through your local high school or college. Many classes are also offered through adult education centers and writers' organizations. Retail stores, too, can be a resource for instruction. For example, a travel store in my area offers occasional travel-writing classes taught by experts. Travel agencies are another potential source: Classes and workshops are now given on cruise ships and in numerous ports of call as part of vacation/education packages. Classes are also given through cultural centers and sometimes through art centers such as museums and galleries. Another major source is the Internet, where numerous Web sites offer a huge variety of courses. (Check Appendix B for information on workshops, classes, and writing-related Web sites.)

The Writers Connection

One of the highlights of attending a writers' workshop or conference is the opportunity to meet and learn from successful authors. Not only will you be inspired, but you may have the opportunity to have your work critiqued by an expert. Some workshops offer one-on-one sessions with instructors or provide small-group coaching or feedback opportunities. Workshop follow-ups may also be possible, through online communication or a series of classes. Because workshops are usually just a day or a weekend long, you'll want to immerse yourself in the experience and make the most of every minute.

Another big plus of workshops is the chance to hang out with other authors. Often there are breaks between sessions that allow attendees to get together informally and share concerns and successes. "Talking shop" with other lovers of the language may turn you on to new techniques and resources and fire up your creativity. And the writers you meet may turn into lifelong friends.

FACTS

Writers' colonies offer longer-term writing experiences. The intention is to provide writers with quiet, comfortable surroundings while they work on a project, for a weekend or a month or longer.

Because so many different types of writing workshops are available, spend some time researching what's out there. Aim for a workshop that:

- Suits your focus and goal.
- Offers small classes.
- Features a respected, experienced author or instructor.
- Offers consultation with the keynote speaker or instructor.
- Provides an open, nonthreatening forum for learning.

To find out about upcoming conferences and workshops in your area, check notices in your local library or bookstore. Writing magazines such as *The Writer* and *Writer's Digest* (see Appendix B for publishing information) also notify readers of programs each month. When you learn about several that sound interesting, write or e-mail for additional information and registration materials.

CHAPTER 21
Getting Published

I f you would like your work to be published, it's time to gear up for the business of getting it into print. That's right—business. To make it happen, you will need to put in a huge amount of work—as well as have determination, patience, and, in some cases, luck.

Making It Happen

If you've never been published, you may believe that it's an easy step from completing your manuscript to the glamorous world of speaking tours and press interviews, perhaps lunching at chic restaurants with your agent or making an appearance on the *Today Show* to tout your book. Submission acceptances and publication contracts *do* happen, to first-timers as well as experienced writers, if you *make* them happen.

FACTS

"You may think a previously unpublished writer has a difficult time breaking into the field. As with any profession, experience is valued, but that doesn't mean publishers are closed to new writers . . . most are open to professional submissions and good ideas from any writer."

—from *Writer's Market*

If you choose to seek out an established publisher, rather than publish your work independently, you need to keep in mind that publishers are in business, too—not only to put beautifully crafted words into print but to make money doing it. Publishers seek out work that will sell well, whether it's a travel article or a short story or a romance novel.

But even if your work meets every publishing criterion—it's brilliantly written, it would appeal to a wide audience, it could be sold through a variety of outlets, you have solid credentials—it still may not be gobbled up. Often, the decision on what's published has much to do with timing. A magazine you submit to may have just published an article on the same topic—yours may be better written and more engaging, but the magazine won't cover the same area again for some time. Or the editor may have set the topics for the next several issues, and yours isn't one of them. Or he or she may just not be interested in the subject you wrote about. A book publisher may love your writing but be on the lookout only for books covering the latest hot topics. While top-notch writing is important, having your work accepted by a publisher also involves dealing with many issues you can't control.

Don't Get Discouraged

If being published is your goal, be encouraged by the fact that there are thousands of publishers throughout the world. Be encouraged by all the books and magazines you see on bookstore shelves, and by all the writing you find online, in newspapers, newsletters, journals, and business materials; in the theater, at the movies, and on TV and the radio. There are many roads to getting published, and many writers have successfully walked down them. You can, too.

"You write a book and it's like putting a message in a bottle and throwing it in the ocean. You don't know if it will ever reach any shores. And there, you see, sometimes it falls in the hands of the right person."

—Isabelle Allende, novelist

Protecting Your Work

Before you begin your quest for publication, you may want to register your work with the Copyright Office (as long as your work has been created in the United States). By registering your work you gain additional protection, particularly the ability to sue for damages in the case of infringement, and you can show legal proof of the date of your copyright.

Technically, once you complete a piece of writing—the moment it's in "fixed form"—the piece is copyrighted. Since 1989, no formal copyright notice has been necessary to protect work from illegal use by others.

Copyrighting your work makes it clear that you are the owner of the work and gives you all the rights and privileges of that ownership. It enables you to make and distribute copies of your work, to sell it or give it away. It prevents anyone else from publishing it and profiting from it without your permission. Protection covers any type of writing: book, article, short story, essay, song, poem, script, audiotape, videotape, even a recipe—all "original works of authorship." Copyright protection does not extend to titles, facts, or ideas.

To Copyright Your Work

If you want to play it safe and copyright your work, you'll need to fill out an application form and send it to the Copyright Office with a nonreturnable copy of your work and $30. Write to the Library of Congress, Copyright Office, Register of Copyrights, 101 Independence Ave., S.E., Washington, DC 20559-6000. You can also order copyright forms by phone at (202) 707-9100 or download them from *http://lcweb.loc.gov/copyright.* The Web site also offers additional copyright information, which you can also receive by calling (202) 707-3000.

For additional protection, screenwriters may want to send a copy of their work to the Writers Guild of America (see Appendix B for contact information). The guild will register your script, treatment, synopsis, or outline for five years, renewable for an additional five years.

Once your work is copyrighted, whether you register it or not, it's a good idea to include the copyright symbol (©), the year of copyright, and your name on any work you have published. In most cases, copyright protection extends for the lifetime of the author plus seventy years.

Other Copyright Issues

Here is what else you should know about copyright laws and practices.

- Work for Hire. If you write a piece under a "work for hire" arrangement— you're paid a one-time fee by a company and receive no royalties—the company, not you, owns the work. The company will hold the copyright.
- Serial Rights. When you sell a piece to a magazine, you retain the copyright. The magazine buys either the first or second serial rights. The first serial rights allow the magazine to be the first-time publisher

of the work; the second serial rights are sold when the piece has been published before.

Starting Small

If you have dreams of speaking tours and *Today Show* appearances, don't give them up. Nourish them—but be realistic. If you've had little experience being published, and haven't built up a big audience yet, most likely you're going to need to start much smaller. Some first-time writers do get contracts and their work does jump immediately to the bestseller lists, but that's quite rare.

Local outlets, especially for nonfiction writers, are often a great way to break into print. The pay may be minuscule or nonexistent, but having clips or reviews to send along with agent or publishing-house query letters can increase your chances of landing a contract (see the next section for information on how to find an agent). Reaching a local audience may also be the first step in becoming known statewide or nationwide.

One successful writer who started small is memoirist and National Public Radio essayist Marion Winik. Winik started out writing for her hometown alternative weekly paper, the *Austin Chronicle.* Her commentaries were read there by a National Public Radio correspondent—and, soon after, her pieces were airing regularly on the radio. Travel writer Louise Purwin Zobel began freelancing for several small magazines, including *Medical Economics.* She also taught writing at local colleges. As her audience grew, she was asked to speak at local writers' group meetings, which led to her publishing a travel article in *Writer's Digest,* which in turn led to her writing a book on travel writing. Both authors started small and worked their way up the writing and publishing ladder.

If you're writing nonfiction, think about nearby media outlets for your work. These might include:

- Newspapers—your weekly or daily town newspaper or a nearby city paper, the local business paper, nearby college papers, and local trade journals
- Company newsletters

- Local cable TV channels, radio stations, and theater companies
- Local bookstores, libraries, cafés, and social clubs
- Community gatherings, workshops, and adult education classes
- The Internet

Expanding Your Horizons

Once you've had some success locally, you can approach magazines and other publications with wider readership, but do your homework first. Target publications that feature the type of pieces you write. Study a variety of current magazines, newspapers, and books for similar work. Determine the publication's audience, approach, themes, and the length of the work they feature. Most publications have submission guidelines available. Search for them on the publication's Web site, or send the editor a self-addressed stamped envelope with a request.

Spend some time researching the various publishers and publications. As playwright George Bernard Shaw said, "Literature is like any other trade; you will never sell anything unless you go to the right shop."

You can also check such resources as *Books in Print* and *Writer's Market* to learn which subject areas different publishers focus on. Short-story writers can investigate "little" or "literary" magazines as well as the more competitive general-interest publications. "Little" magazines are often regional and sometimes published by educational or cultural organizations. Short-story writers' guides list a number of these lower-paying but well-respected publications.

Getting an Agent

Once you've become known as an author or developed an audience, you may want to seek out a literary agent to handle your nonfiction or fiction book idea or screenplay concept. While most poets, short-story writers, and nonfiction article writers don't need the services of an agent, publishing-minded book authors and screenwriters can benefit from working with one.

But just what do literary agents actually do? And is it worth the 15 percent or more commission they'll get from you for selling your proposal? Agents work for the authors they represent. They counsel and advise, give feedback, help with book or script development and the proposal, work to sell their authors' books or screenplays at the best terms possible, and then handle any author/publisher or screenwriter/producer problems that come up after the sale. Your agent can become a great partner and guide your work as well as look out for your best interests.

A Connection to the Publisher

One of the key things agents do is get your work seen by an editor, publisher, or producer who is likely to be interested in it. Agents generally spend a great deal of time developing relationships with editors and publishers and learning who handles what type of work. When they take on an author, they know who to approach with that author's material and have already opened a communication channel. Often publishers won't even look at work that isn't submitted by an agent because they believe unrepresented authors have probably been turned down by several agents, and that signals to them that the work is not what they're currently looking for. Agents act as screens for publishers as well as conduits for hot ideas and fresh faces—like yours!

How to Find a Great Agent

Often you'll hear about a good agent from another writer, and some represented authors may even set up a meeting for you with their agent if they believe your work is promising. Writers' workshops, conferences, and classes (see Chapter 20) are excellent places to learn about respected agents. You can also locate agents in several printed resources, including the *Writer's Market; The Everything® Get Published Book;* the *Literary Marketplace; The Writer's Guide to Book Editors, Publishers, and Literary Agents;* and the *Guide to Literary Agents.* Another possibility is to call the publisher of a writer you admire and ask for the name of his or her agent. Or you can contact professional writers' groups for recommendations. (See Appendix B for complete contact information.)

 **SSENTIALS**

Agents can't take on all the authors who approach them, so solicit them with an outstanding query letter. Craft a specific, well-worded, enthusiastic letter that says exactly why you want that agent to represent you. Include a summary of your book, why it will sell, and your credits or experience.

What Should You Look for in an Agent?

First of all, you want a representative who is excited by your work and shares your vision. When you look for an agent, double-check that the agent handles your type of material. Don't send a letter about your romance novel to an agent who handles only nonfiction. You also want someone who knows the publishing or screenwriting industry intimately and keeps up with changes in both "hot areas" and personnel.

Finding an agent with a good track record is also important; you can ask for a list of recent sales and the agent's client list. You also want someone whose personality meshes with your own—if you're going to be working together, perhaps for a long time, it's important that you get along and that you agree with the agent's way of doing business. Your agent may not hold your hand—agents are often kept very busy working with a good number of clients—but he or she should respond quickly to your questions and be accessible.

Finally, a good agent will not charge you a fee to read your manuscript. To check if anyone has made a complaint about an agent's operation, you can contact your local Better Business Bureau.

A Side Note

Editors at small presses are often open to reading work by writers not represented by an agent. The term *small press* refers to a publishing house that publishes only a few books each year, perhaps three or fewer. Small presses generally can't spend a lot on marketing, but they're often very committed to the books and the authors they take on. Listings of small presses can be found in the *Writer's Market* and other guides.

ALERT

Even if you work with an agent you respect and trust, if you're offered a publishing contract or the agent asks you to sign a contract with him or her, you may still want to hire a lawyer to see that your rights are protected.

Dealing with Rejection

It's a fact of a writer's life: At some point, something you write is going to be rejected. Just about every author, famous or not, has come up against this painful moment.

Horror-novel writer Stephen King saw seven of his novels rejected before *Carrie* was published. Dr. Seuss's *And to Think That I Saw It on Mulberry Street* was rejected forty-three times before a friend finally published it. Lawrence J. Peter and Raymond Hull endured having their business classic *The Peter Principle* turned down by thirty publishers before one gave them a contract. It can be incredibly depressing. And, yes, it hurts. And, yes, rejection letters can make you mad.

But it's simply impossible for every piece that every writer writes to be published. There aren't enough shelves in the world to hold all that writing. When you start looking for an agent or a publisher, prepare for the possibility that your work will be rejected. But read that last bit again—prepare for the possibility that your work will be rejected. *Your work. Not you.* This is terribly important to remember. If that form letter that you can barely stand to open tells you that your short story isn't being accepted for an anthology, remind yourself that it's the story, not you, that didn't make it in.

Remembering this might not make you any happier—it will probably still hurt that the piece you worked so hard on won't be in the book—but it should keep you from succumbing to that murderous self-doubt many writers have: I'm not good enough, I'll never be able to do this. You wrote something you're proud of, and it's very possible that a different publisher is out there looking for your very piece.

FACTS

> "Editors make mistakes. By actual count, 121 publishers said 'No thanks' to *Zen and the Art of Motorcycle Maintenance* . . . *Lolita* [was] turned down too . . . *The Clan of the Cave Bear, The Spy Who Came in from the Cold* . . . *To Kill a Mockingbird*—rejected, every one."
> —Judith Appelbaum, author of *How to Get Happily Published*

The Common Motives

Work can be rejected for so many reasons. Some are legitimate: You didn't send it to a publisher who handles the kind of material you write, your wording was tired or lacked clarity, the piece was too long or too difficult for the intended audience. But work is often rejected because the editor—one person—simply didn't like it, or because the topic was already covered, or because the editor had so many manuscripts to read that she didn't look past your cover letter or opening sentence. Whatever the reason, when a rejection notice drops into your mailbox, beat up your pillow, kick a pile of laundry, moan and groan, or let out a primal scream in your bathroom. Then put a copy of your work in a fresh, clean envelope, kiss it for luck, and send it to the next person (whom you of course researched thoroughly for suitability) on your list.

Many agents and editors don't have time for personal notes or conversations about rejections, so they will return your manuscript to you along with a form rejection slip. But sometimes you might receive a rejection letter, and this is actually a good letter to get. That's because it may give you some information that you can use to improve your chances of success the next time. If the letter gives some reasons why your piece wasn't accepted, read them carefully and decide if you want to rework the piece to suit them—for example, to refocus it so it would appeal to a wider audience. If someone has signed the letter, you can also try to contact him or her to see if you can get additional information, perhaps a reaction to your book proposal or specific suggestions for improvement.

Self-Publishing

Luckily, there are many, many resources available today to help the independent publisher. Word processing software and page design software are available at every computer store. Experienced freelance editors and proofreaders can be hired. Printers will print smaller quantities of copies, plus there's the new option of Print on Demand, or POD, which lets you print just the number of books you need at a time. You can also have your book published as an electronic book, which can be instantly downloaded as soon as the order is placed. E-books can also be distributed on CDs, disks, and DVDs. The Internet provides new marketing avenues, in addition to the traditional ones of bookstore and library readings, speaking engagements, press releases, mailers, and media spots. If you go with POD, there's no longer the problem of storing stacks of books; copies can be printed and shipped as the orders come in. You can also distribute your book through direct mail and retail stores, by advertising in magazines and newspapers, and by selling it yourself after speaking engagements or workshops.

SSENTIALS

Several books offer excellent, extensive self-publishing information: Robert Holt's *How to Promote and Sell Your Own Book*, Dan Poynter's *The Self-Publishing Manual*, Bill Henderson's *Publish-It-Yourself Handbook*, and Judith Appelbaum's *How to Get Happily Published.*

Even with all this help, it's an enormous amount of work. Self-publishing is not for everyone, and it's definitely not for you if you want writing to be your only business. But many independent publishers find the satisfaction of taking their work to the next step—placing their words on handsomely bound pages that will find their way into the hands of eager readers (and doing it their way)—a rewarding conclusion to the writing process.

Self-Publishing Tips

Here are some tips to guide you through self-publishing and promoting:

- Self-publishing a book can cost from hundreds to thousands of dollars. Spend as much as your budget allows to produce a quality book—an attractive, well-designed book will be much more appealing to potential readers than one thrown together with shoddy materials.
- Some authors handle every stage of self-publishing except the printing. But if your editing and proofreading skills aren't the best, consider hiring a professional; you don't want to end up with a great-looking book filled with typos and grammatical errors.
- Shop around for whatever parts of the process you hire out. Prices can differ widely among printers, editors, designers, and marketing professionals.
- Apply for an International Standard Book Number (ISBN) prefix for your book. You can apply at *www.bowker.com,* a publishing information site. Or you can visit *www.isbn.org* and follow the application process. You can also apply at this site for the barcode you'll need for bookstore sales.
- Contact the Library of Congress for a preassigned card number. The address is 101 Independence Ave., S.E., Washington, DC 20559-6000; the Web site is *www.loc.gov/copyright/forms.*

To promote your work:

- Send releases to newspapers, magazines, newsletters, and writing-related Web sites.
- Organize readings and book-signing parties.
- Ask to speak at community or club events.
- Prepare and distribute media kits that include your bio, a photo, a fact sheet about your book, clips of reviews, and copies of any articles you've written.
- Contact local TV and radio stations about doing an interview.

- Post notices in bookstores and on your Web site.
- Send notices to everyone you know.
- Send review copies to anyone who writes about books.
- Find a well-known authority to endorse the book.
- Make T-shirts, pens, or bumper stickers that keep the book's name n front of people.
- Do it all again, and again.

FACTS

For an all-encompassing source of independent publishing information, visit *www.published.com*. The site details all that's involved in self-publishing; lists sources of writing and promotional assistance; lists printing and publishing sources, including for e-books; and links you to sites that provide essential application forms.

One last point about self-publishing: It can be the route to a contract with an established publisher. Often publishers will become aware of a self-published book that's met with success, and negotiate to take it on. This happened with James Redfield, the author of the wildly popular *Celestine Prophecies*. Redfield self-published his book and sold it after speaking engagements. Eventually he drew an audience and ended up with a major contract from Warner Books.

Interview with Magazine Editor Mark Whiteley

Mark Whiteley is an editor, writer, videographer, and award-winning photographer. He is the editor of *Slap,* a ten-year-old skateboarding magazine that offers profiles, travel articles, pro interviews, industry news, how-tos, and product and music reviews for teen and older skateboard aficionados. Mark's work has been featured in *Slap* as well as in *Copper Press, Stance, The Kids' How to Do (Almost) Everything Guide, e-How,* and *Sunset* magazine.

CW: Mark, I imagine a lot of freelancers send articles and story ideas to you. How would you recommend that a writer new to a magazine approach the editor?

MW: Writers I haven't worked with before will usually call or e-mail to express an interest in writing for the magazine. I'll ask them to send me an example to read of something that would be suitable for the magazine. If the writing's decent, I'll get back in touch and ask if they have a story idea they want to work on. If they have something in mind, I'll ask them to write it, and if not, I'll ask them to write a short piece for one of the magazine's regular departments. A short or a report—I always start with something small. If they do a good job, I'll try to give them something longer the next time. Most of the writers who freelance regularly for the magazine started that way, and we've been working together for a couple of years now.

For music reviews, people generally send in a sample review they've had published in a newspaper or magazine, or online or in a college paper. Or sometimes writers say they have an interview lined up with a music group and, judging from the kinds of things the magazine covers, they thought it would interest me. They send the piece in, and if I like it, I'll try to use it. But if I can't use it right away, I'll try them out on a CD review.

• • •

CW: Do you ever get involved in developmental editing?

MW: On longer articles, I work with the person before and while they're writing to shape the piece. I don't try to redirect it, but I make suggestions to help them along with it; we do a lot of brainstorming. Then, when they send it in, I'll do some more editing, changing some of the wording and the structure if it's needed. Writers need to be open to the fact that some of their work is going to be changed.

• • •

CW: For features and interviews, do you ask writers to accompany their articles with photographs—is that necessary because *Slap* is a sports magazine, very visual?

MW: To get a foot in the door, it's always a good idea for writers to send in photos with a feature idea. At least in *Slap,* most of our feature articles include photographs, because for a lot of readers it's more important to see the photos than to read the words. So being able to shoot a basic photo or knowing a photographer who can help you out is a big plus. Once you've shown what you can do and editors start to look to you as a regular contributor, they'll start assigning a staff photographer to work with you, to get more in-depth coverage. But if you can present an entire idea for a story, including at least one photo, it's really helpful. It's good to have the whole package, even if it's a small one. Music reviews and interviews don't need to be accompanied by photos—usually the record label will provide artwork or we'll send a staff photographer on an interview.

 • • •

CW: How do you decide which feature articles to run? Does a writer always have to focus on a very current topic?

MW: I don't always look for a piece on the latest thing. What I look for is a writer with a deep knowledge of the field, who's been around or who's done a lot of homework. It's generally a good idea for a writer to propose a hot topic—especially with the teenage market, which sometimes needs the latest thing to hold their attention—but for me it's more important that the writer has an understanding of the finer points of the subject and an understanding of the culture. Readers look to writers to learn what's going on, for insight, and they don't like to be tricked or told something that's not true. As far as music reviews go, I look for someone who can describe the feeling you get from a piece of music, who can convey that. I don't want a report here—it shouldn't be an exercise in superlatives. Being able to talk about feelings and, again, having experience with the type of music are more important. Plus being able to write with flair.

 • • •

CW: Do you have other suggestions for writers who want to approach a new publication?

MW: When writers contact me, I assume they're getting in touch because they've studied and know my magazine and like it above other similar ones. You really need to study publications before you approach them to see the subtle differences between them and to learn what kinds of articles they publish. Then you're more likely to make a connection.

APPENDIX A
Writing Samples

SHORT-STORY EXCERPT

Impressionists in Winter

by Susan Fry

An hour and a half. I sighed again. Until several years ago, of course, painting outside during the winter at all would have been impossible. That's when paint was stored and carried in pigs' bladders, which froze and chipped in cold weather. Now that we had paints in little metal tubes, even cold couldn't prevent us from coaxing them out onto the palette in the most freezing storm. Of course, we still needed the little braziers nearby as a source of heat. I lit mine. Its flame was the brightest thing in the landscape. It barely warmed my hands.

The brush felt stiff and unwieldy through my fur-lined gloves. The paint was truculent, congealing from the cold as soon as I got it onto the canvas. I was tempted to paint exactly what I saw: straight lines, black, white, gray. But I knew that a painting like that wouldn't get me into Monet's exhibition. Even if it did, I'd probably be banned from the Academy for life. So instead I began to dab little spots of stiff paint onto the canvas, hoping they would resolve into something recognizable.

Time passed. My painting grew. The scene got more and more ugly. I felt shivers run up the backs of my legs and my spine, as if someone were watching us. My feet, even in their knee-length boots, had somehow gotten wet. I stomped each one to bring life back into my frozen toes. I pulled my hat lower over my forehead, and my scarf higher across my nose.

I wasn't going to be the first one to say that we should go back. René had called me a "lazy dog" the day before, and I wasn't going to give him the satisfaction of seeing me admit to being cold.

Finally, René said, with apparent regret, "The light's changing. We should come back tomorrow." He stood up, stretched, and looked over at me.

Some stubborn streak in my personality made me say, "You go ahead. I want to finish one last thing."

He grinned as if he knew exactly what I was doing, but he packed up and went back to the inn. I counted a hundred frozen puffs of breath before I finally allowed myself to pack up as well. By then the shadows had lengthened. The trees looked as if they had feet and could walk after me. And as I left, I felt more shivers up my back, as if something was indeed following me.

It's just an ordinary lane, I told myself, but I was relieved to get back to the warmth of the inn.

From "Impressionists in Winter," by Susan Fry, *The Museum of Horrors*. Edited by Dennis Etchison (Leisure Books, 2001). Reprinted with permission of the author.

SCREENPLAY EXCERPT

ANGEL AND BIG JOE
by Bert Salzman

Time is the present. The place is an agricultural area in southern New Jersey.

EXT. SMALL RURAL TWO-LANE HIGHWAY - DAY

ANGEL DIAZ, 14, walks along the highway carrying a paper shopping bag and a can of kerosene. It is cold. We hear the wind sounding through the trees. Angel's field jacket is turned up against the cold as he trudges down the road.

CUT TO:
EXT. SAME HIGHWAY FURTHER ALONG - DAY

A telephone company panel truck is parked on the shoulder, and a telephone lineman—BIG JOE, 45—is on a pole as Angel passes below. Angel stops to rest for a moment, and puts down the heavy can of kerosene. He looks up at Big Joe.

> ANGEL
>
> It's cold, huh?

> BIG JOE
>
> Cold? This ain't cold.

Angel picks up the can of kerosene and begins to walk off.

> ANGEL
> (muttering to himself)
> Well, for me it's cold.

CUT TO:
EXT. BARREN FIELD - DAY

Low-angle shot of Angel walking.

> ANGEL (V.O.)
> I'm what people call a migrant worker. That means me and my family travel all over the country picking crops. You know like beans and grapes and lettuce and things like that. Me and my mother and my brother Nikki were living out in the migrant shacks out by the tomato fields. The tomatoes had

already been picked, and the other migrant workers' families had left. My father was out in Arizona looking for work, and we were waiting for him to telephone us to tell us where to go. And so I was getting nervous because we were running out of money and I didn't know what to do.

Angel approaches a drab cement block migrant shack. He puts down the kerosene can and enters the building.

CUT TO:
INT. SHACK'S KITCHEN - DAY

Angel puts the paper bag down on the kitchen table and sits.

CUT TO:
INT. SHACK'S BEDROOM - DAY

Angel's MOTHER and five-year-old BROTHER NIKKI are sitting in bed with blankets over their legs. They are both dressed with heavy sweaters against the cold. The mother looks up when she hears Angel enter.

> MOTHER
>
> Angel? Angel?

She rises from the bed and heads toward the kitchen.

CUT TO:
INT. KITCHEN - DAY

Mother enters the kitchen and walks to the kitchen table and inspects the contents of the grocery bag. Angel sits reading a comic book. Mother begins to take cans from the bag.

> MOTHER
> That's all you bought?

> ANGEL
> We hardly got any more money.

> MOTHER
> What happened to the money Poppa left?

> ANGEL
> (impatiently)

We spent it.

> MOTHER
> How are we going to eat if we ain't got money?

> ANGEL
> I don't know. Why don't you ask Poppa how we gonna eat?

Angrily, Angel's Mother grabs him by the arm and pulls him upright.

> MOTHER
> Don't you talk to your mother that way.
> *¡Ten respeto!*

Mother sits at the table. She places her hands over her face and sobs softly. Angel puts down the comic book and looks at her guiltily. He rises and puts his arms around his mother.

> ANGEL
> (gently)
> I'm sorry, Mommy, okay? Don't cry. I'm going to call Aunt Marie in Texas. Maybe she knows where Poppa is. Okay.

Angel walks to the door. His mother watches with a sad look.

CUT TO:
EXT. SHACK - DAY

Angel walks to a pay phone hanging on the wall of the shack. He picks up the receiver and drops a coin into the phone. After several moments, when there is no dial tone, Angel clicks the receiver several times. When no coin returns, he begins to bang on the telephone.

Mother exits the shack and stands by the door.

> MOTHER
> Angel, what happened?

> ANGEL
> (frustrated)
> The phone don't work.

> MOTHER
> (very concerned)
> The phone don't work? How's Poppa going to call? Angel, you have to bring a man to fix the phone.

> ANGEL
> Don't worry, Momma, I'll get someone to fix it.
> (to himself)
> Always something going wrong.

He walks off.

CUT TO:
EXT. HIGHWAY - DAY

Angel walks up to the telephone panel truck that he had passed earlier. He stops a few feet from the telephone pole and looks up.

> ANGEL
> Hey, mister.

The lineman does not respond.

> ANGEL
> (louder)
> Hey, mister.

> BIG JOE
> What do you want?

> ANGEL
> I want you to come fix my phone. It's broken.

> BIG JOE
> You gotta call the telephone office.

> ANGEL
> How am I gonna call the telephone office if my phone's broken?

> BIG JOE
> Use somebody else's phone.

                    ANGEL
                (frustrated)
        Whose?

                    BIG JOE
        Whose. I don't know. Anybody else's. That's whose.

Big Joe returns to the work he was doing.

                    ANGEL
                (really annoyed)
        Hey, mister.

Big Joe doesn't respond.

                    ANGEL
                (shouting)
        Hey, mister.

Angel begins to pound on the truck.

                    BIG JOE
        Hey, beat it.

                    ANGEL
                (shouting)
        I ain't gonna beat it until you come and fix my phone . . .

Angel walks to the telephone pole. He pulls two climbing pegs from the pole.

                    ANGEL
        . . . and you ain't coming off that pole until you come and fix my phone.

Big Joe looks down with a bemused smile, a mixture of annoyance and admiration at Angel's determination.

                    BIG JOE
        Where do you live?

                    ANGEL
        In the houses behind the tomato fields.

Big Joe looks in the direction of the migrant shacks.

                    BIG JOE
I thought all you people moved out a couple months ago.

                    ANGEL
No. Some of us people are still here. And some of us people
even got broken telephones.

                    BIG JOE
Okay, I'll call my office and they'll send a man tomorrow.

                    ANGEL
No good!

                    BIG JOE
What do you mean "No good"?

                    ANGEL
It's gotta get fixed today.

                    BIG JOE
What's the hurry?

                    ANGEL
The hurry is my father's supposed to call from Arizona.

                    BIG JOE
So he'll call tomorrow.

                    ANGEL
Aw, come on, man. My mother's home crying and you're just
going to sit up there doing nothing.
                    (frustrated)
What is it with you?

                    BIG JOE
                    (sympathetic)
All right. I'll call the office and see if it's all right, OK?

CUT TO:
EXT. SHACK - DAY

Angel sits on a stool as Big Joe begins to repair the pay phone.

ANGEL

Pretty cold, eh?

BIG JOE

So go inside.

ANGEL

It's cold inside, too.

BIG JOE

No heat?

Angel shakes his head.

ANGEL

Not too much. Doesn't matter 'cause soon as my father calls we'll be leaving for Arizona.

Angel looks down at Big Joe's tool box and he sees the name "Big Joe" written on a piece of tape.

ANGEL
(amused, to himself)

Big Joe from Mexico. Hey, Big Joe, you got any jobs around your house? Paint your garage. Clean your attic. You know, that kind of stuff.

BIG JOE

No, no jobs, sorry.

Big Joe dials the phone and talks to his telephone office.

BIG JOE

Hello, this is Joe Zunza. Give me a check on 555-9728 and call me right back.

He hangs up and immediately we hear the phone ring. Joe picks up the receiver.

BIG JOE

Yeah, how's the line look? Okay, thanks, release the line.

> (to Angel)
> Okay, your phone's working.

Joe takes out a notebook.

> BIG JOE
> Okay, what's your name?

> ANGEL
> Angel.

> BIG JOE
> What?

> ANGEL
> Angel. You know, like in heaven?

He makes a halo over his head with his hands.

> BIG JOE
> Angel what?

> ANGEL
> Angel Diaz.

> BIG JOE
> How do you spell that?

> ANGEL
> D-I-A-Z.

> BIG JOE
> C?

> ANGEL
> No, D-I-A-Z.

Angel's mother approaches holding a jar of hot coffee and offers it to Big Joe.

> MOTHER
> Hot coffee, mister?

> BIG JOE
> No, no thank you, ma'am, I gotta go.
> (to Angel)
> Hope you get your call, Angel.

Big Joe walks to the panel truck and drives off.

CLOSE-UP of Angel, who watches the truck move away.

Reprinted with permission of the author.

LETTER TO THE EDITOR

by Shirley Ledgerwood

Editor,

I wonder how many of us in the plush economy of Silicon Valley are aware that the richest 1 percent of people own more than 35 percent of the nation's wealth, according to the *New York Times Magazine*. 14.5 million (or 20.5 percent) of children live in poverty. Also, a large number of families are losing access to food stamps under federal welfare repeal. Add to this the homeless, who are of course at the bottom of the barrel.

The ideology of "personal responsibility" and "welfare-to-work" forms a mainstream of discourse around poverty and homelessness instead of a good look at the regressive policies that cause poverty: lack of jobs, of housing, and of education.

In light of these sad facts, I wish to give a tribute to the humaneness of a group called Peninsula Interfaith Action that has met in Palo Alto to begin a crusade for a community multi-service day facility for the homeless. This alliance of sixteen churches plus civic organizations is spearheaded by the All Saints Episcopal Church and the First Presbyterian Church, both of Palo Alto. It is supported by representatives of the city councils of Palo Alto and Menlo Park, of Stanford, of the Chamber of Commerce, the Red Cross, and others.

I urge the readers of this paper to come to the second meeting of this group to be held June 16 at 7:30 at All Saints Episcopal Church on Hamilton and Waverley. Your support will help furnish a meal for the homeless, lockers, showers, and a place to do laundry, as well as counseling for rehabilitation and job-skills training.

Letter to the editor first printed in the Palo Alto Weekly, *June 10, 1998.*

TRAVEL PIECE

There's Family Fare on Berkeley's Fourth Street
by Carol Whiteley

If you've always thought of Berkeley as a destination only for multi-pierced teens and twenty-somethings, you may be in for a surprise—a day trip to the city's Fourth Street area should please just about everyone in your family.

Only minutes from the Bay (take the University exit off Route 80, turn left on Sixth and left again on Hearst), close enough to catch the cooling breezes, the long block of Fourth between Hearst and Virginia is the unassuming home to an inviting mix of shops and services. Once you park in the big public lot at Hearst and Fourth or in one of the flower-lined lots further along, you and your fellow day-trippers can begin enjoying a great break-from-the-beach summer outing.

Start your day by arriving early enough to grab a table or some counter space at **Bette's Oceanview Diner**—by nine a line usually begins to form, one that can last all day. Bette's opened its doors in 1982, and still serves up great diner-style fare: a big choice of breakfast dishes (the Maryland boasts poached eggs and corned beef hash, or you can have your scrambles accompanied by one of Bette's popular cream scones), and tasty and filling lunch plates, including New York franks, BLTs, and meatloaf. The jukebox at the front, and the smaller ones that sit on the counter and tables, feature a wild mix of rhythm-and-blues titles, plus songs in French and German—there's even a French song sung by the late actor Omar Sharif. The comfy surroundings (Formica tables, highchairs available), cheerful bustle, and abundance of good food make Bette's a great place to gear up for the day.

Once everyone's fed, you can start walking and exploring. One good way to approach the street might be to size up your group, then hit the spots that will be of most interest. Just be sure to stop every now and then to enjoy the sights and sounds—there are lots of benches and newspaper racks to entice those in need of a break to rest and people-watch; there's a row of beautifully cared-for Victorian houses to ooh and aah over at the end of the parking lot that runs between Fourth and Sixth; and there may even be an accordion-playing cowboy or a silly juggler to entertain the troops when you take a break for croissants, colas, or cones.

For fashion plates: If one or more of your group are into fashion, they'll be very glad they came along. The small but chic **Rabat** features out-of-the-ordinary shoes for men and women. Many of the lines are European, and many won't be found in local department stores. Robert Clergerie, Luc Berjen, and little-seen Stuart Weitzman models are just some of the footwear on display. The upscale but casual store also offers a small selection of sunglasses, watches, and purses.

Several women's-clothing shops offer department store alternatives. The artfully decorated **Molly's** is filled with loose, drapey linens and silks, plus many styles with a vintage or European feel. **Mishi's,** which is actually on Fifth Street across from the parking lot that crosses from mid-Fourth to Fifth, has a slightly younger appeal. The bright colors and natural fabrics are touted as "100% wearable," and there's a great choice of easy tops and skirts, plus jackets and tees to tempt you. (You can find the Mishi line in some department stores, but there's a much wider selection here.) **Bryn Walker** is another small shop where you can find dressier, flowing styles and handsome jewelry, particularly pins; **Margaret O'Leary** features lovely, very contemporary fashion firsts.

For readers: Cody's Bookstore is a big, inviting Berkeley favorite. Quiet and bright, with plenty of room to wander and browse (the family dog can even have a snooze between the aisles while you choose), the store has excellent travel, cooking, and business sections, as well as well-stocked nature, kids' books, and fiction areas. Several times a week the store holds readings and other events, and for those who live in the Berkeley area, book delivery is available by Pedal Express. Another great place to find just what you're looking for is **Builders Booksource,** whose shelves carry just about everything for the home owner or builder: books on urban planning, interior design, building codes, environmental issues, gardening, architecture, and house plans, to name just a few. (If you get hungry while you're browsing, they even sell chocolate tools.)

For kids: Younger kids, especially girls, will love the **Sweet Potatoes** clothing store. The store carries sizes newborn through 7, and a truly terrific range of styles. All of the lines, including Marimekko, Big Fish, and Little Arlene, are Sweet Potatoes' own brands, and while they do sell to department stores, you'll find a huge selection here. You'll also find the Goody Goody line of shoes—some are topped with adorable leather daisies—plus beachwear and cozy comforters.

Hearth Song is another great spot for kids. Here they can try out a kid-sized, ladybug-style tent, play a junior-sized guitar, fall in love with a huge Madeleine doll or stuffed gorilla, or choose from the wonderful animal posters, books, puzzles, and crafts. They also can find their own area in **Cody's Bookstore** (see above); the kids' section surrounds a real-life version of one of the paintings from the beloved children's book *Goodnight Moon,* and kids can hunker down there and read. Older kids might enjoy some of the unusual items in **Zosaku,** including sushi-shaped candles, or find just the magazine they've been looking for while they slurp down a fresh-fruit smoothie at **Juicy News.** They can also check out the latest sounds at the small **Hear Music** store.

For gardeners/home bodies: On the corner of Hearst and Fourth, **Summer House** offers lovely and unusual home accessories to those who like to decorate. The items on hand change every few weeks, but at the time of this writing the shop carried beautiful appliqued shower curtains, whimsical papier-mâché wall hangings by a European artist, tiny boxes that looked like elegant wedding cakes, a gorgeous library table, and thigh-high column candles, to name a few. For more substantial furnishings, there are lots of contemporary pieces at **Slater/Marinoff,** and older styles at **Traditions Antiques.** And for those who can never stock their kitchen well enough, there's **Sur la Table,** with a truly juicy choice of kitchen supplies.

For foodies: If all the shopping and savoring starts stomachs grumbling, there are a number of places to ease the pain. To add to your Bette's breakfast experience, you might want to take a mid-morning break at **Bette's To-Go and Deli.** There's a great choice of bakery items and coffee to be found, plus for those who need a bigger pick-me-up, sandwiches, tacos, and pizza. For lunch you'll have big decisions to make: oysters at the **Oyster Bar and Meat Market,** Asian fare at **Ginger Island,** East Meets West delicacies at **O Chame,** or takeout salads and sandwiches from the wonderful shops in **Market Plaza,** where you can sit outside and watch the world go by. Then, if you can't contemplate making dinner after your day out, you can stop back at the Plaza on the way home for all the fixings, from ready-to-cook roasted carrot and garlic ravioli to shepherd's pie to pad thai.

ESSAY EXCERPT

The Poetics of Security: Skateboarding, Urban Design, and the New Public Space

by Ocean Howell

Abstract

Skateboarding is a thorn in the side of landscape architects, planners, and building owners; so much so that there are now design workshops that teach a series of defensive architectural tactics for deterring the activity. The type of skateboarding that plagues these architects and the spaces they create, "street skating," has only existed for about fifteen years, and in fact was born out of the barren, defensive spaces created by redevelopment. Thus street skating is not only an impetus for defensive architecture, but also a symptom of defensive architecture. Recognizing that redevelopment spaces fostered pathologies, cities and corporations have begun to build more friendly spaces in the past fifteen years. But they have been careful to ensure that the spaces are only friendly to a select subset of the public, namely, office workers and consumers. It is not only skateboarding that is excluded, but also any activity not directly tied to either production or consumption, including, in many cases, simply lying down on a bench.

To create such spaces requires detailed knowledge of the minutest details of undesirable behaviors—a knowledge that can only be gleaned through surveillance. Because the resultant spaces appear open but exclude the vast majority of the citizenry, they are not public spaces at all, but rather sophisticated simulations of public space. Although this essay will argue that the destructive effects of skateboarding have been exaggerated, the purpose is not to argue that skateboarding should be permitted in public space. It is by virtue of its status as a misuse of these spaces—and because it is a symptom of defensive design—that skateboarding is exceptionally good at drawing attention to the quietly exclusionary nature of the new public space. Ultimately, skateboarding affords an observer glimpses of the larger processes of surveillance and simulation by which public space, both physical and cultural, is produced. . . . Through the example of skateboarding, this essay will argue that the determination of which activities are legitimately public and which activities are pathological is nearly indistinguishable from the determination of which activities generate profit and which activities threaten profit.

Michael Fotheringham, the architect who is presently giving San Francisco's Union Square a makeover, explains how good design should focus on the "needs and comforts" of the "prime client" (Hansen April 2001, 23). Where designers used to talk about "citizens," they now talk about "consumers." Public space is commercial space. Literature on cities is replete with the metaphor of public space as the site, the physical embodiment, of democracy. Its purpose is to facilitate interaction between all citizens, not just consumers; it exists to foster debate—even conflict—among the various competing interests that are represented in the citizenry. To these ends, a public space should be both "physically and psychologically accessible" (Loukaitou 1998, 301), as Kevin Lynch would put it, to the public, in all of its unmanageable diversity.

The work of William H. Whyte alone provides abundant evidence that when this is accomplished, a space will not need to be managed from the outside—it will regulate itself. . . . [M]any critics, like Rosalyn Deutsche, rightly argue that there has never been a space that unequivocally welcomes the public, that constructions of publicness have always entailed exclusions. Certainly Frederic Law Olmsted's Central Park, one of the most beneficent of all public works, represents a paternal and missionary philosophy of public space. The idea was to manufacture a bucolic idyll in the dense urban center in order to divert the potentially revolutionary passions of the workers away from the industrial system that subjugated them. Allowing the workers to mingle with the elites was to have the effect of civilizing the lower classes. Later, City Beautiful plans—which were always sponsored by corporations (Loukaitou 1998, 17)—sought to "inspire" good citizenship among the lower classes with grand neoclassical symmetries.

Even though these spaces fall short of the ideal democratic space, the fact is that the marginalized were still conceived of as a presence. While these spaces took it as their duty to gently coerce the dispossessed, thus acknowledging the presence if not the necessity of conflict, the new public spaces have taken up the task of denying the existence of competing viewpoints and the people who advance them. The new spaces take as their ideal not the public space as a site of debate, but the public space as a site of repose for consumers and clients. Anastasia Loukaitou-Sideris and Tridib Banerjee point out, in their book *Urban Design Downtown,* how the design metaphors that architects use to describe public spaces have shifted from the "plaza" and the "green" to the "room," "terrace," "court," "garden," and other soothing, private spaces (1998, 229).

Skateboarding is not terribly important in the grand scheme of things; it is a young counterculture that admirably seeks to challenge power relations and less admirably seeks to escape from them. But it does provide a unique perspective on the creeping privatization of public space. Homelessness, drug abuse, and prostitution have been around—in various forms and in varying degrees of severity—probably as long as cities have; and they are undoubtedly exacerbated by exclusionary design insofar as they are isolated and ghettoized. Skateboarding is clearly different from these urban pathologies in that it is a recreational activity, not a sustaining activity. But it is further different in that it is not only an impetus for exclusionary architecture, but also the direct product of exclusionary architecture. Like the Freudian symptom of "return of the repressed," skateboarding was born out of the defensive, barren plazas of redevelopment—on the sites where street life was forcibly subverted to property values.

Of course, no one defends redevelopment spaces anymore, and there has been a push for a resurgence of the public sphere in cities. The designers of public spaces in Giuliani's New York, for example, have taken certain of William H. Whyte's recommendations to heart, creating spaces that people want to inhabit. But they have been careful about selecting which people. The redevelopment spaces succeeded in excluding the marginalized people whose neighborhoods they supplanted, but their hostility also warded off the middle class whose safety the spaces sought to assure. Pleasant spaces have the opposite problem of welcoming everyone. To attract the upscale public while deterring the masses has been a primary urban design goal of the last ten years. This is a complicated task that this essay will argue has only been accomplished with extensive surveillance of undesirable behavior. This information is used to create exclusionary spaces that appear public to the selected users; it is used to simulate a public sphere. Through a discussion of how skateboarding has been appropriated by corporate marketers, this essay will also argue that the cultural space of advertising and public opinion is produced by the same processes of surveillance and simulation. . . .

Misused Transportation/Misused Space: A Brief History

Skateboarding was invented in the 1950s in Southern Californian beach towns when surfers tore the T-handlebars off their scooters and skated on the asphalt banks of the local schoolyards as though they were surfing waves. The sport quickly took on a life of its own, and throughout the '70s people could be found riding in the empty backyard swimming pools of vacant houses. The basic move was to ride up the transitioned wall of the pool, slide along the edge, and plunge back down the wall. Soon cities and private companies began building pools exclusively for skateboarders. The most commonly accepted story about the origin of street skating starts with a group of skaters being thrown out of the privately owned Skate City park in Whittier, California, in the early 1980s. Apparently they didn't have the money to pay the entrance fee, so they snuck in. After being escorted out, a professional skater named John Lucero led the group in a kind of sarcastic protest in the parking lot. In full view of the owners of the park and the skaters inside, they began to do tricks on the edges of the curbs, as though they were the edges of a pool. These undesirables came back and did this day after day and soon skaters from inside the park came out to try this new style.

In the early and mid-80s the style expanded out of the suburban parking lot and into the more varied terrain of redeveloped urban centers, primarily Los Angeles and San Francisco. This happened to coincide with America's explosion of personal liability suits and, although *Landscape Architecture* magazine reported in March 1998 that there has never been a successful skateboarding liability suit (Thompson, p. 82), nearly every one of the parks was bulldozed—to be replaced by family fun centers. By and large, the only people who could continue to practice the old style were those who could afford to build private ramps. Thus street skating quickly became the most urban and populist version of the sport: it didn't cost anything except the price of the board itself, and it could be done anywhere there was pavement. In 1999 there were an estimated 9.5 million skateboarders in the U.S. alone (Levine July 26, 1999; 70), and by all accounts, skateboarders are now a strong presence in nearly every modern city, from San Francisco to Osaka to São Paulo.

For length reasons, this essay cannot undertake a study of the socioeconomic characteristics of skateboarders. But it is important to note that American skaters are typically from lower-middle-class families: they are economically stable but don't usually continue their education past high school. And while many influential skaters have come from the upscale suburbs of Marin, Orange County, and the San Fernando Valley; at least as many have come from such neighborhoods as East Hollywood, Gardena, and [San Francisco's] Mission.

Skate and Destroy/Skate and Create

. . . . Skateboarding is not protest or activism, but is more like what Michel de Certeau described, in *The Practice of Everyday Life,* as a "spatial practice." Skateboarding is "a certain play within a system of defined places" (1984, 106). As the public space of the Central Business District (CBD) becomes more authoritarian, skateboarding "authorizes the production of an area of free play on a checkerboard that analyzes and classifies identities. It makes places habitable" (1984, 106). William H. Whyte provides a good example of a spatial practice, in his film *The Social Life of Small Urban Spaces,* when he affectionately shows how people can find a place to sit even where they are architecturally discouraged from doing so. In a demonstration of remarkable adaptability and quotidian creativity, people place small blankets over spikes that are meant to intimidate them, balance on intentionally narrow ledges overlooking fountains, and remain perched on canted planters that are designed to deposit them right back onto the sidewalk (1998b). Whyte laments the way that open spaces enhance a corporate image while alienating the public that they nominally serve. In one scene he shows an intentionally solitary bench, and announces that "this is a design object, the purpose of which is to punctuate architectural photos" (1988b). But because there are no obstructions (people), this is precisely the type of bench that skateboarders love to inhabit. In spite of the corporate space's disregard for the public, a small, resourceful portion of the public can still find a way to put the space to public use.

Bibliography

Acconci, Vito. Interview. (April 28, 2000). *www.temaceleste.com* (accessed April 15, 2001).

—. Interview. *Dialogues in Public Art.* T. Finkelpearl, ed. Cambridge, MA: MIT Press, 2000.

Adams, Gerald. "Bank of America plaza gets a warmer make-over." *San Francisco Examiner.* (December 3, 1997) *www.sfgate.com*

—. "Skateboarders banned for art's sake." *San Francisco Examiner.* (December 20, 1995) *www.sfgate.com*

Boddy, Trevor. "The Analogous City." *Variations on a Themepark.* M. Sorkin, ed. New York: Hill and Wang, 1992.

Carroll, Greg. "EMB RIP: Remembering Our Old Pal Justin Herman." *Slap* (June 1999).

de Certeau, Michel. *The Practice of Everyday Life.* Berkeley: University of California Press, 1984.

Costantinou, Marianne. "Urban Daredevils on Wheels." *San Francisco Examiner.* (Monday, June 14, 1999) *www.sfgate.com*

Deutsche, Rosalyn. *Evictions: Art and Spatial Politics.* Cambridge, MA: MIT Press, 1996.

Foucault, Michel. *Discipline and Punish.* New York: Vintage, 1995.

Frank, Thomas. "Brand You." *Harper's.* (July 1999)

Fuller, Blair. "Letter to the Editor." *The San Francisco Examiner.* (December 20, 1999) *www.sfgate.com*

General Services Administration. "Plaza Renovation." (1998) *http://hydra.gsa.gov* (accessed April 15, 2001)

Gillette, Jane Brown. "Walking the Line." *Landscape Architecture Magazine.* (April 1996)

Hansen, Brooke Leigh. "Union Square's Renovation." *San Francisco Downtown.* (April 2001)

Husted, Deniene. "Defying Laws (of Physics)." *The Los Angeles Times.* (December 4, 2000) *www.latimes.com*

Kay, Ken. "Design Workshop." *Downtown Idea Exchange.* (January 15, 1998)

Kayden, Jerold S. with New York City Department of City Planning and the Municipal Art Society of New York. *Privately Owned Public Space.* New York: John Wiley and Sons, 2000.

Kelling, George L. and Catherine M. Coles. *Fixing Broken Windows.* New York: The Free Press, 1996.

Layne, Ann. "Skateboard Wars: Do Parks Help?" *The San Francisco Examiner.* (January 19, 1997) *www.sfgate.com*

Leccese, Michael. "The Death and Life of American Plazas." *Urban Land.* (November 1998)

Levine, Mark. "The Birdman." *The New Yorker.* (July 26, 1999) Reprinted on Look-Look: *www.look-look.com.* (accessed April 15, 2001).

Loukaitou-Sideris, Anastasia and Tridib Banerjee. *Urban Design Downtown.* Berkeley: University of California Press, 1998.

Matier and Ross. "Plaza Gets Retrofit Before it Opens." *The San Francisco Chronicle.* (November 8, 1999) *www.sfgate.com*

Nyren, Ron. "Very First Federal." *Metropolis.* (February/March 1999) *www.metropolismag.com* (accessed April 15, 2001)

Owings, Nathaniel A. *The American Aesthetic.* New York: Harper & Row, 1969.

—. *The Spaces In Between.* Boston: Houghton Mifflin, 1973.

Saddler, Simon. *The Situationist City.* Cambridge, MA: MIT Press, 1998.

San Francisco Department of City Planning. *Urban Design Plan for San Francisco.* (1971)

Sappenfield, Mark. "Skateboard's Soaring Superstars." *The Christian Science Monitor.* (August 15, 1995)

Sennett, Richard. *The Uses of Disorder: Personal Identity and City Life.* New York: Norton, 1970.

Thompson, J. William. "A Good Thrashing." *Landscape Architecture Magazine.* (March 1998)

Whyte, William H. *City.* New York: Doubleday, 1988.

—. *The Social Life of Small Urban Spaces.* New York: The Municipal Art Society of New York. (1988) (film)

Reprinted with permission of the author. First printed in Urban Action, *2001.*

POEM

Reading Chaucer at Broadway Laundromat near Columbia University
by Louis Phillips

I too have longed to go on
pilgrimages,
Forget the daily grind, the Oval
Offices of Debt & Power outages,
But this is as far as I travel,
To 107th, the Broadway Laundromat
To seek the holy blissful martyrdom
Of immaculate underwear.
Amid the bleach of relics,
I contemplate the navel
Of a tanktopped coed, &
Watch my shirts & socks unravel.
At my elbow, with her red stockings,
Someone's Wife of Bath
Turns the pages of a lurid novel,
A bodice ripper, while the homeless
Wander in & out, seeking warmth;
A student from Columbia
Pushes a red shopping cart of books,
Jots copious notes
On the music of Ravel.
I counted 9 & 20 in all. No Kings,
Nor friars, nor monks, &
Certainly I am no parfit gentil knight.
I have twin sons, but not one Squire
To carve at table for me,
Tho lusty are & sing all night.

Tho separated by centuries,
Geoffrey and I utter the same prayer:
That Christ have mercy on us &

Forgive our sins in someone's
translation.
We unwashed kneel at Maytag driers,
Every machine numbered
Like squat football players.
A blonde with a voice of gravel
Speaks of love most transiently.
The change machine,
In its own dour voice,
Dispenses quarters all day long.
Can never have too many quarters.
A Pakistani in a black stockingcap,
Announces a snow event: "The snow
Will cover all the germs," he says.
"This city has too many germs, &
Everybody is sick with flu."
I start a letter to a friend:
"If you need someone to grovel
At your funeral, here's one cheap."
Wide of girth, with a head
Like a berry, a Jamaican lady
Stirs our juices with stamp & go,
Codfish cakes with hot red peppers.
Nothing in this universe
Sells anymore two for a penny.
As wind bears snow & sleet
Up & down the frozen street,
All my clothes are heaped
Upon the white communal table.
All these lives are in tumble, &
I make thirty in this company.

Originally published in the South Carolina Review *(Fall 2000). Reprinted with permission of the author.*

Appendix B
Writing Resources

BOOKS

ON BEING CREATIVE

Berg, Elizabeth. *Escaping into the Open.* New York: HarperPerennial, 2000.

Zany writing exercises, plus encouragement to take risks and eat chocolate-covered cherries.

Cameron, Julie. *The Artist's Way: A Spiritual Path to Higher Creativity.* Los Angeles: J. P. Tarcher, 1992.

Many readers have used this twelve-week program to foster creativity in different aspects of their lives. The book offers exercises and techniques for freeing up creativity by overcoming fear, jealousy, and other blocks. Also check Cameron's follow-up book on creativity, *The Vein of Gold.*

Rekulak, Jason. *The Writer's Block: 786 Ideas to Jump-Start Your Imagination.* Philadelphia: Running Press, 2001.

Ideas and exercises to get your creativity in gear; many have been used in creative writing classes and by well-known authors.

Sternberg, Robert J. *Handbook of Creativity.* London and New York: Cambridge University Press, 1999.

A comprehensive academic review of the entire field of creativity.

Ueland, Brenda. *If You Want to Write: A Book About Art, Independence and Spirit,* 10th ed. St. Paul: Graywolf Press, 1997.

Written in 1938 (the tenth edition was published in 1997), this gem not only focuses on the art of writing, but on how to live creatively. One of its best pieces of advice—think of telling a story, not writing it.

von Oech, Roger. *A Whack on the Side of the Head.* New York: Warner Books, 1998.

A modern classic that whacks you into thinking in new ways, with explanations, puzzles, artwork, and more.

You may also want to read von Oech's other highly regarded book on creativity, *A Kick in the Seat of the Pants.*

Winik, Marion. *Rules for the Unruly: Living an Unconventional Life.* New York: Touchstone Books, 2001.

A personal, witty remembrance that encourages readers to take risks and live creatively.

ON WRITING

Bernays, Anne, and Pamela Painter. *What If?* New York: HarperCollins, 1991.

More than seventy-five exercises to help you think and write like a writer.

Bickham, Jack M. *Writing the Short Story.* Cincinnati: Writer's Digest Books, 1998.

Advice on plotting, structure, and writing creatively using Bickham's notecard system.

Brande, Dorothea, and John Gardner. *Becoming a Writer.* Los Angeles: J. P. Tarcher, 1981.

A how-to on getting over yourself and starting to write; includes techniques and exercises.

Burroway, Janet. *Writing Fiction,* 5th ed. New York: Longman, 2000.

The fifth edition of this highly regarded work presents a practical yet personal guide to writing exciting fiction. The book covers characterization, style, atmosphere, imagery, and much more.

Dillard, Annie. *The Writing Life.* New York: Harper & Row, 1989.

The author of *An American Childhood* and *Pilgrim at Tinker Creek* provides illuminating insights into the risks and rewards of being a writer.

Dils, Tracey. *You Can Write Children's Books.* Cincinnati: Writer's Digest Books, 1998.

Guidelines for getting your children's book into print.

Field, Syd. *Screenplay: The Foundations of Screenwriting.* New York: Dell, 1994.

A step-by-step guide to writing a successful screenplay.

Ford, Richard. *Writers on Writing: Collected Essays from the New York Times.* New York: Henry Holt, 2001.

Insights that first appeared in a *New York Times* writing series dispatched by more than forty famous writers.

Frye, Northrop. *Anatomy of Criticism.* Princeton, NJ: Princeton University Press, 2000.

Four essays on historical, ethical, archetypal, and rhetorical criticism based on Frye's belief that literary criticism is a total history.

Gardner, John. *The Art of Fiction.* New York: Vintage, 1991.

A highly respected, essential handbook for writing fiction.

Griffith, Kelley. *Writing Essays About Literature.* San Diego: Harcourt Brace Jovanovich, 1990.

An in-depth guide to reading critically and writing a critical essay.

Gutkind, Lee. *The Art of Creative Nonfiction.* New York: John Wiley & Sons, 1997.

Award-winning professor and author Gutkind offers up techniques for choosing, researching, and structuring essays, articles, memoirs, and other nonfiction forms.

Hale, Constance. *Sin and Syntax: How to Write Wickedly Effective Prose.* New York: Random House, 1999.

The subtitle says it all. Also see Hale's *Wired Style,* a guide to online English usage.

Herman, Jeff, and Deborah Levine Herman. *Write the Perfect Book Proposal.* New York: John Wiley & Sons, 2001.

Directors of a top literary agency take you through ten book proposals that sold, pointing out strengths and weaknesses.

Kuchl, John. *Write & Rewrite.* New York: Meredith Press, 1967.

The "befores and afters" of chapters written by several well-known authors, including Eudora Welty, F. Scott Fitzgerald, and Philip Roth. Each draft/published version combination shows how the author dealt with a particular writing problem. Out of print, but check your library.

Lamott, Anne. *Bird by Bird.* New York: Pantheon Books, 1994.

Following her father's advice to her brother to take writing a report on birds "bird by bird," Lamott has written a number of outstanding novels that focus on modern relationships. In this "instruction guide," she shares her techniques for and feelings about creative writing.

Mayes, Frances. *The Discovery of Poetry.* Fort Worth: Harcourt Brace College Publishers, 1994.

Poet, nonfiction author, and chair of the Creative Writing Department at San Francisco State University, Frances Mayes discusses wording, poetry sources, images, rhyme, and repetition as well as invoking the muse.

Moyers, Bill. *Fooling with Words: A Celebration of Poets and Their Craft.* New York: William Morrow, 1999.

Moyers, a renowned television journalist, discusses form and the creative process with eleven poets with diverse approaches.

Plimpton, George, ed. *Writers at Work: The Paris Review Interviews.* New York: Viking Press, 1965.

The second volume of highly acclaimed interviews with such distinguished authors and poets as Robert Frost, Marianne Moore, Aldous Huxley, Ernest Hemingway, and Katherine Anne Porter. Though out of print, as are the first and third volumes of the series, your library may have this treasure available for readers. Also look for the in-print *Beat Writers at Work* and *Women Writers at Work.*

Rhodes, Richard. *How to Write.* New York: William Morrow, 1996.

Advice and reflections on the writing life from a Pulitzer Prize–winning author who believes that "if you want to write you can."

Saltzman, Joel. *If You Can Talk You Can Write.* New York: Warner Books, 1993.

Techniques and advice to get you to write and to keep you writing.

Vonnegut, Kurt, and Lee Stringer. *Like Shaking Hands with God: A Conversation About Writing.* New York: Washington Square Press, 1999.

One experienced and one new-to-it author speak candidly about the craft of writing and what it means to be a writer.

Winokur, Jon. *Advice to Writers.* New York: Vintage Books, 1999.

Pearls of wisdom and inspiring anecdotes from a wide range of literary luminaries. There are sections on secrets, style, tricks of the trade, publishing, even money and drink.

Zinsser, William. *Inventing the Truth: The Art and Craft of Memoir.* New York: Houghton Mifflin, 1998.

Insights on writing memoirs from those who do it well, including Jill Ker Conway, Henry Louis Gates Jr., and Frank McCourt. Zinsser has also written several other books on writing, including *On Writing Well: The Classic Guide to Writing Nonfiction.*

Zobel, Louise Purwin. *The Travel Writer's Handbook.* Chicago: Surrey Books, 1997.

A classic travel writer's handbook that covers finding a hook, doing research and marketing, writing a query letter, and how to write engaging travel pieces.

REFERENCES

Appelbaum, Judith. *How to Get Happily Published.* New York: HarperCollins, 1998.

A mini-course on editors, agents, self-publishing, and much more from an author who states that "it is largely in your power whether your work will get published."

Bartlett, John. *Bartlett's Familiar Quotations.* Boston: Little, Brown, 1992.

Passages, phrases, and proverbs from both ancient and modern literature.

Blake, Gary, and Robert W. Bly. *Elements of Copywriting.* New York: Longman, 1998.

A complete guidebook to writing effective ads, press releases, brochures, and other marketing materials.

Buchanan-Brown, John, ed. *Le Mot Juste: A Dictionary of Classical & Foreign Words & Phrases.* New York: Vintage, 1991.

The meanings of hundreds of Greek, French, Russian, Latin, Spanish, and other foreign phrases that have made their way into the English language.

Chapman, Robert L. *Roget's International Thesaurus.* New York: HarperCollins, 1992. The thesaurus—an invaluable guide to synonyms, antonyms, and related words.

The Chicago Manual of Style. Chicago: The University of Chicago Press, 1993.

An essential reference for everyone who works with words, this comprehensive guide, now in its fourteenth edition, covers bookmaking, style, and production and printing.

Corbeil, Jean Claude, and Ariane Archambault, eds. *The Macmillan Visual Dictionary.* St. Paul: Hungry Minds, Inc., 1992.

Thousands of illustrations increase vocabulary-learning pleasure.

Cudden, J. A. *The Penguin Dictionary of Literary Term and Literary Theory.* New York: Penguin, 2000.

Explains writing jargon as well as literary forms, genres, and theory.

Henderson, Bill. *Publish-It-Yourself Handbook.* New York: W. W. Norton, 1998.

Authors who have self-published share their stories about the experience.

Herman, Jeff. *Writer's Guide to Book Editors, Publishers, and Literary Agents.* Rocklin, CA: Prima Publishing, 2000.

Names and areas of interest for thousands of editors, publishers, and agents, plus advice and tips for writers.

Holm, Kirsten, ed. *Writer's Market.* Cincinnati: Writer's Digest Books, 2001.

The complete publishing guide: listings of publishers, agents, magazines, Web sites, screenwriting and playwrighting markets, contests, and so much more. Also see *Children's Writer's & Illustrator's Market, Poet's Market,* and *Novel and Short-Story Writer's Market.*

O'Connor, Patricia T. *Woe Is I.* New York: G. P. Putnam's Sons, 1996.

An easy-to-read, lighthearted, yet completely grounded guide to proper English usage. The chapter called "Comma Sutra" covers punctuation; "Death Sentence" asks the question, "Do clichés deserve to die?"

Random House Webster's College Dictionary. New York: Random House, 1999.

Over 207,000 definitions, plus tips and information for writers.

Ross-Larson, Bruce. *Edit Yourself: A Manual for Everyone Who Works with Words.* New York: W. W. Norton, 1996.

An easy-to-use and comprehensive editing guide.

Rubie, Peter. *The Everything® Get Published Book.* Avon, MA: Adams Media, 2000.

All the information you need to get your manuscript in print.

Strunk, William, and E. B. White. *The Elements of Style.* New York: Macmillan, 1979.

Many consider this to be *the* guide to writing well, whether you write novels, letters, term papers, or plays. Making "every word tell" is the focus of this small masterpiece.

Tedesco, Anthony, and Paul Tedesco. *Online Markets for Writers.* New York: Owl Books, 2000.

Contact information and the editorial needs of numerous Web sites, plus pointers from online editors and a sample Internet writing contract.

Walsh, Bill. *Lapsing into a Comma.* Lincolnwood, IL: NTC Publishing Group, 2000.

Walsh, the chief copy editor of the *Washington Post,* uses a humorous style to explain how to properly apply the rules of grammar and word usage.

Writer's Essential Desk Reference. Cincinnati: Writer's Digest Books, 1996.

Great information and advice for freelancers, from tips on agents to copyright law to promoting your book.

WEB SITES

www.aar-online.org—The site of the Association of Authors' Representatives, a not-for-profit organization of independent literary and dramatic agents. You can also contact the association at P. O. Box 237201, Ansonia Station, New York, NY 10013.

www.authorlink.com—An information service for writers, agents, and editors.

www.bookzone.com—An e-publication and Print on Demand (POD) service source, plus information on online promotion, industry news, and links to other publishing and writing-related sites.

www.coffeehouse4writers.com—An excellent site for writers that contains online courses, tips, contests, and other valuable resources.

www.favoritepoem.org—Former U.S. Poet Laureate Robert Pinsky's site for encouraging poetry in the classroom.

www.instantpublisher.com—Download their free POD software, then send a digital file to have them print twenty-five to 5,000 books.

www.isbn.org—An online source for applying for an International Standard Book Number prefix and a bar code. You can also write to ISBN–U.S. Agency, 121 Chanlon Rd., New Providence, NJ 07974, or call (877) 310-7333.

www.literaryagent.com—Listings of agents, plus a writer's corner, monthly columns, and announcements of forums and other events.

www.loc.gov/copyright—The homepage for the U.S. Copyright Office. You can also receive copyright information by writing to the Copyright Office at 101 Independence Ave., S.E., Washington, DC 20559-6000, or calling (202) 707-3000.

www.newyorker.com—The legendary literary magazine's online version.

www.published.com—The online resource for independent publishing.

www.rejectioncollection.com—Take heart from hearing how other authors—including many famous ones—have dealt with having work rejected, and gone on to success.

www.thesaurus.com and *www.dictionary.com*—Online sources of synonyms and definitions.

www.write4kids.com—Information on many aspects of writing and publishing books for children; from the *Children's Book Insider,* a newsletter for children's writers.

www.writeread.com—Contains courses, writing-related articles, an online zine on craft and marketing, job listings, and more.

www.writersdigest.com—The Web site for the world's largest writers' magazine; provides writers' guidelines, market updates, classes, conference lists, and more. You can also write for information to *Writer's Digest*, 1507 Dana Avenue, Cincinnati, OH 45207, or call (513) 531-2222.

www.writingdoctor.com—An online source of expert professional editing, proofreading, coaching, evaluation, and publishing services, plus tips, author-to-author contact, and other resources.

WRITING PROGRAMS

Associated Writing Programs—Funded in 1967 by fifteen writers, this organization now serves 20,000 writers through 320 college and university creative writing programs and sixty writers' conferences and centers in the United States, Canada, and the UK.

> Associated Writing Programs
> Tallwood House MSN 1E3
> George Mason University
> Fairfax, VA 22030
> (703) 993-4301
> *www.gmu.edu/departments/awp.*

Gotham Writers' Workshop—New York City's largest private creative writing school, which offers ten-week classes and workshops on the premises, in exotic locations, and online. Includes screenwriting and songwriting classes.

> Gotham Writers' Workshop
> 1841 Broadway, Suite 809
> New York, NY 10023
> (212) 974-8377 or (877) 974-8377
> *www.writingclasses.com* (online writing courses)

Writer's Digest School—The world's largest writers' magazine provides eight at-home courses and workshops for writers that focus on both fiction and nonfiction.

> Writer's Digest
> 1507 Dana Avenue
> Cincinnati, OH 45207
> (513) 531-2222
> *www.writersdigest.com/school*

WRITERS' WORKSHOPS AND COLONIES

For a complete listing of upcoming conferences and workshops, see current writers' magazines, the Associated Writing Programs' Directory of Conferences and Centers (see "Writing Programs," above), or the ShawGuides, which also provide information on writing colonies:

> ShawGuides, Inc.
> P. O. Box 231295
> New York, NY 10023
> (212) 799-6464
> *www.shawguides.com*

Following is a short list of well-known writers' colonies:

Byrdcliffe Arts Colony
34 Tinker Street
Woodstock, NY 12498
(914) 679-2079

Djerassi Resident Artists Program
2325 Bear Gulch Road
Woodside, CA 94062-4405
(650) 747-1250

Dorset Colony House for Writers
P. O. Box 519
Dorset, VT 05251
(802) 867-9390

Helene Wurlitzer Foundation of New Mexico
P. O. Box 545
Taos, NM 87571
(505) 758-2413

MacDowell Colony
100 High Street
Peterborough, NH 03458
(603) 924-3886

Ragdale Foundation
1260 North Green Bay Road
Lake Forest, IL 60045
(708) 234-1063

Ucross Foundation
2836 U.S. Highway 14–16 East
Clearmont, WY 82835
(307) 737-2291

Yaddo
P. O. Box 395
Saratoga Springs, NY 12866
(518) 584-0746

WRITING GUILDS

The Authors Guild—The largest U.S. society of published authors. Provides industry news, copyright information, and assistance to members.
> The Authors Guild
> 31 East 28th Street, 10th Floor
> New York, NY 10016
> (212) 563-5904
> *www.authorsguild.org*

Writers Guild of America—Represents published writers in motion pictures, broadcasting, cable, and new media. Provides an online mentoring service, script registration, lists of agents, industry news, and more.

Writers Guild of America, West (for writers living west of the Mississippi)
> 7000 W. Third Street
> Los Angeles, CA 90048
> (323) 951-4000 or (800) 548-4532
> *www.wga.org*

Writers Guild of America, East (for writers living east of the Mississippi)
> 555 West 57th Street, Suite 1230
> New York, NY 10019
> (212) 757-4360
> *www.wgae.org*

Index

THE EVERYTHING GET PUBLISHED BOOK

By Peter Rubie

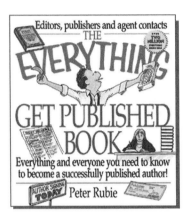

The Everything® Get Published Book gives step-by-step instructions on how to take control of the publishing process and turn your ideas into a printed book. Inside, you'll find invaluable lessons on how the book industry really works, and how you can fit into the system. This book includes information on which publishing houses to approach, writing proposals, contract negotiations, when to self-publish, and what electronic publishing can do for you. Most important, there are hundreds of names and addresses of potential book publishers, executives, and literary agents to contact.

Trade paperback, $12.95
1-58062-315-8, 336 pages

OTHER *EVERYTHING*® BOOKS BY ADAMS MEDIA CORPORATION

Everything® **After College Book**
$12.95, 1-55850-847-3

Everything® **American History Book**
$12.95, 1-58062-531-2

Everything® **Angels Book**
$12.95, 1-58062-398-0

Everything® **Anti-Aging Book**
$12.95, 1-58062-565-7

Everything® **Astrology Book**
$12.95, 1-58062-062-0

Everything® **Astronomy Book**
$14.95, 1-58062-723-4

Everything® **Baby Names Book**
$12.95, 1-55850-655-1

Everything® **Baby Shower Book**
$12.95, 1-58062-305-0

Everything® **Baby's First Food Book**
$12.95, 1-58062-512-6

Everything® **Baby's First Year Book**
$12.95, 1-58062-581-9

Everything® **Barbecue Cookbook**
$14.95, 1-58062-316-6

Everything® **Bartender's Book**
$9.95, 1-55850-536-9

Everything® **Bedtime Story Book**
$12.95, 1-58062-147-3

Everything® **Bible Stories Book**
$14.95, 1-58062-547-9

Everything® **Bicycle Book**
$12.00, 1-55850-706-X

Everything® **Breastfeeding Book**
$12.95, 1-58062-582-7

Everything® **Budgeting Book**
$14.95, 1-58062-786-2

Everything® **Build Your Own Home Page Book**
$12.95, 1-58062-339-5

Everything® **Business Planning Book**
$12.95, 1-58062-491-X

Everything® **Candlemaking Book**
$12.95, 1-58062-623-8

Everything® **Car Care Book**
$14.95, 1-58062-732-3

Everything® **Casino Gambling Book**
$12.95, 1-55850-762-0

Everything® **Cat Book**
$12.95, 1-55850-710-8

Everything® **Chocolate Cookbook**
$12.95, 1-58062-405-7

Everything® **Christmas Book**
$15.00, 1-55850-697-7

Everything® **Civil War Book**
$12.95, 1-58062-366-2

Everything® **Classical Mythology Book**
$12.95, 1-58062-653-X

Everything® **Coaching & Mentoring Book**
$14.95, 1-58062-730-7

Everything® **Collectibles Book**
$12.95, 1-58062-645-9

Everything® **College Survival Book**
$14.95, 1-55850-720-5

Everything® **Computer Book**
$12.95, 1-58062-401-4

Everything® **Cookbook**
$14.95, 1-58062-400-6

Everything® **Cover Letter Book**
$12.95, 1-58062-312-3

Everything® **Creative Writing Book**
$14.95, 1-58062-647-5

Everything® **Crossword and Puzzle Book**
$14.95, 1-55850-764-7

Everything® **Dating Book**
$12.95, 1-58062-185-6

Everything® **Pregnancy Organizer**
$15.00, 1-58062-336-0

Everything® **Project Management Book**
$12.95, 1-58062-583-5

Everything® **Puppy Book**
$12.95, 1-58062-576-2

Everything® **Quick Meals Cookbook**
$14.95, 1-58062-488-X

Everything® **Resume Book**
$12.95, 1-58062-311-5

Everything® **Romance Book**
$12.95, 1-58062-566-5

Everything® **Running Book**
$12.95, 1-58062-618-1

Everything® **Sailing Book, 2nd Ed.**
$12.95, 1-58062-671-8

Everything® **Saints Book**
$12.95, 1-58062-534-7

Everything® **Scrapbooking Book**
$14.95, 1-58062-729-3

Everything® **Selling Book**
$12.95, 1-58062-319-0

Everything® **Shakespeare Book**
$14.95, 1-58062-591-6

Everything® **Slow Cooker Cookbook**
$14.95, 1-58062-667-X

Everything® **Soup Cookbook**
$14.95, 1-58062-556-8

Everything® **Spells and Charms Book**
$12.95, 1-58062-532-0

Everything® **Start Your Own Business Book**
$14.95, 1-58062-650-5

Everything® **Stress Management Book**
$14.95, 1-58062-578-9

Everything® **Study Book**
$12.95, 1-55850-615-2

Everything® **T'ai Chi and QiGong Book**
$12.95, 1-58062-646-7

Everything® **Tall Tales, Legends, and Other Outrageous Lies Book**
$12.95, 1-58062-514-2

Everything® **Tarot Book**
$12.95, 1-58062-191-0

Everything® **Thai Cookbook**
$14.95, 1-58062-733-1

Everything® **Time Management Book**
$12.95, 1-58062-492-8

Everything® **Toasts Book**
$12.95, 1-58062-189-9

Everything® **Toddler Book**
$14.95, 1-58062-592-4

Everything® **Total Fitness Book**
$12.95, 1-58062-318-2

Everything® **Trivia Book**
$12.95, 1-58062-143-0

Everything® **Tropical Fish Book**
$12.95, 1-58062-343-3

Everything® **Vegetarian Cookbook**
$12.95, 1-58062-640-8

Everything® **Vitamins, Minerals, and Nutritional Supplements Book**
$12.95, 1-58062-496-0

Everything® **Weather Book**
$14.95, 1-58062-668-8

Everything® **Wedding Book, 2nd Ed.**
$14.95, 1-58062-190-2

Everything® **Wedding Checklist**
$7.95, 1-58062-456-1

Everything® **Wedding Etiquette Book**
$7.95, 1-58062-454-5

Everything® **Wedding Organizer**
$15.00, 1-55850-828-7

Everything® **Wedding Shower Book**
$7.95, 1-58062-188-0

Everything® **Wedding Vows Book**
$7.95, 1-58062-455-3

Everything® **Weddings on a Budget Book**
$9.95, 1-58062-782-X

Everything® **Weight Training Book**
$12.95, 1-58062-593-2

Everything® **Wicca and Witchcraft Book**
$14.95, 1-58062-725-0

Everything® **Wine Book**
$12.95, 1-55850-808-2

Everything® **World War II Book**
$14.95, 1-58062-572-X

Everything® **World's Religions Book**
$14.95, 1-58062-648-3

Everything® **Yoga Book**
$14.95, 1-58062-594-0

*Prices subject to change without notice.

EVERYTHING KIDS' SERIES!

Everything® **Kids' Baseball Book, 2nd Ed.**
$6.95, 1-58062-688-2

Everything® **Kids' Cookbook**
$6.95, 1-58062-658-0

Everything® **Kids' Joke Book**
$6.95, 1-58062-686-6

Everything® **Kids' Mazes Book**
$6.95, 1-58062-558-4

Everything® **Kids' Money Book**
$6.95, 1-58062-685-8

Everything® **Kids' Monsters Book**
$6.95, 1-58062-657-2

Everything® **Kids' Nature Book**
$6.95, 1-58062-684-X

Everything® **Kids' Puzzle Book**
$6.95, 1-58062-687-4

Everything® **Kids' Science Experiments Book**
$6.95, 1-58062-557-6

Everything® **Kids' Soccer Book**
$6.95, 1-58062-642-4

Everything® **Kids' Travel Activity Book**
$6.95, 1-58062-641-6

Available wherever books are sold!
To order, call 800-872-5627, or visit us at everything.com

Everything® is a registered trademark of Adams Media Corporation.